THE CONVERGENCE OF INTERNATIONAL AND DOMESTIC MARKETS

CONTRIBUTIONS TO ECONOMIC ANALYSIS

180

NORTH-HOLLAND
AMSTERDAM · NEW YORK · OXFORD · TOKYO

THE CONVERGENCE OF INTERNATIONAL AND DOMESTIC MARKETS

Edited by:

David B. AUDRETSCH

Wissenschaftszentrum Berlin für Sozialforschung
Berlin, Federal Republic of Germany

Leo SLEUWAEGEN

Catholic University of Leuven
Leuven, Belgium
and
Erasmus University
Rotterdam, The Netherlands

Hideki YAMAWAKI

Wissenschaftszentrum Berlin für Sozialforschung
Berlin, Federal Republic of Germany

1989

NORTH-HOLLAND
AMSTERDAM · NEW YORK · OXFORD · TOKYO

ISBN: 0 444 87346 5

Publishers:

ELSEVIER SCIENCE PUBLISHERS B.V.
P.O. Box 1991
1000 BZ Amsterdam
The Netherlands

Sole distributors for the U.S.A. and Canada:

ELSEVIER SCIENCE PUBLISHING COMPANY, INC.
655 Avenue of the Americas
New York, N.Y. 10010
U.S.A.

Library of Congress Cataloging-in-Publication Data

The Convergence of international and domestic markets / edited by David B.A. Aucretsch, Leo Sleuwaegen, Hideki Yamawaki.
p. cm. -- (Contributions to economic analysis ; 180)
"Edited version of scholarly papers presented at the Workshop on the Convergence of International and Domestic Markets and Policy Responses in Europe, Japan, and the U.S., which was held in Brussels on December 17-18, 1987"--Foreword.
Bibliography: p.
Includes index.
ISBN 0-444-87346-5 (U.S.)
1. Export marketing--Congresses. 2. International trade--Congresses. 3. Commercial policy--Congresses. 4. Competition, International--Congresses. I. Audretsch, David B. II. Sleuwaegen, Leo. III. Yamawaki, Hideki. IV. Workshop on the Convergence of International and Domestic Markets and Policy Responses in Europe, Japan, and the U.S. (1987 : Brussels, Belgium) V. Series.
HF1416.C66 1989
380.1--dc19 89-3046
CIP

PRINTED IN THE NETHERLANDS

Introduction to the series

This series consists of a number of hitherto unpublished studies, which are introduced by the editors in the belief that they represent fresh contributions to economic science.

The term 'economic analysis' as used in the title of the series has been adopted because it covers both the activities of the theoretical economist and the research worker.

Although the analytical methods used by the various contributors are not the same, they are nevertheless conditioned by the common origin of their studies, namely theoretical problems encountered in practical research. Since for this reason, business cycle research and national accounting, research work on behalf of economic policy, and problems of planning are the main sources of the subjects dealt with, they necessarily determine the manner of approach adopted by the authors. Their methods tend to be 'practical' in the sense of not being too far remote from application to actual economic conditions. In addition they are quantitative.

It is the hope of the editors that the publication of these studies will help to stimulate the exchange of scientific information and to reinforce international cooperation in the field of economics.

The Editors

FOREWORD

This volume contains an edited version of scholarly papers presented at the Workshop on the Convergence of International and Domestic Markets and Policy Responses in Europe, Japan and the U.S., which was held in Brussels on December 17-18, 1987. The conference was funded jointly by the European Institute for Advanced Studies in Management (EIASM), the Wissenschafstzentrum Berlin für Sozialforschung (WZB), along with additional assistance from the Catholic University of Leuven. The purpose of the Conference was to examine the increasing trend towards the integration of domestic with international markets. To address this issue, over forty experts on international trade and industrial organization from Asian, European, and North American countries were brought together to consider and discuss the findings from the eleven studies trying to shed light on this topic and which are presented in this volume.

This volume is motivated from a development in international markets that renders much of the literature perhaps less relevant. In this decade there has been a shift in markets away from the domestic sphere and towards a global sphere. Along with this globalization of markets has been a significant reallocation in comparative advantage in many industries away from the U.S. and towards Japan and Europe. As global competition has replaced domestic markets, countries from Europe as well as Japan have replaced the dominance of the U.S. Consequently, firm strategy has had to consider global counterparts as well as domestic rivals. The papers in this volume examine how firms and markets have responded to a globalized economy with several dominant countries instead of just one.

Therefore, the first two sections of this volume examine how market structure characteristics such as scale economies, concentration levels, advertising strategies, R&D strategies, entry, optimal plant size, and markets performance, such as productivity and profitability, have responded to market globalization. The third section of this volume attempts to address the following questions relating to the recent shift in the fundamental determinants of trade patterns among the most developed countries.

(1) How have the patterns of trade evolved among the EC, Japan, and the U.S. ?
(2) What accounts for the observed shifts in competitive advantage ?
(3) What is the appropriate role for government policy under this new regime of trade patterns ?

Finally, an emerging topic in the literature is the impact of R&D rivalry and innovative activity on the globalization of markets. Thus, the fourth section examines the relationship between innovation, market structure, and international trade.

The first section of the book examines the relationship between productivity, technology and international trade. Richard E. Caves and David R. Barton use a new data set to answer the questions of whether the static efficiency of an industry affects its ability to achieve productivity gains, and do changes in the intensity of international competition affect the productivity growth of a domestic industry. Dalia Marin also considers the relationship between productivity and trade performance. She examines if the increases in foreign market shares recently experienced by Japan and West Germany and the concomitant loss in the shares of foreign markets accounted for by the United States and the United Kingdom are attributable to the relative growth in productivity in each country, or if each country's productivity performance is the result of its success in international markets.

The relationship between market structure and foreign trade is the topic of the second section of the book. In "The Interaction between Domestic and Foreign Based Entrants", Paul A. Geroski attempts to determine the extent to which foreign entrants crowd out domestic entrants. He finds, in fact, that there is no evidence suggesting that foreign firms displace domestic counterparts. By contrast, William James Adams concludes that exposure to foreign trade has had a substantial effect on French firms. Richard E. Baldwin examines the link between the capital market and international trade, particularly with respect to the proposed unified capital market for the EC. He concludes that the integration of what are currently domestic capital markets will enable small firms and firms from countries in which the current domestic capital market is restricted to become competitive on an international scale.

In the third section of the book the determinants of the international trade advantage are examined in three empirical papers. In testing the hypothesis that international trade in manufacturing is determined by endowments of productive factors, trade frictions, industrial organization, and demand characteristics, Bruce Lyons concludes that transportation costs and scale economies are major forces in determining trade flows. In addition, he finds that the structure of trade has remained remarkably constant between 1968 and 1980 for both the world and the EC. Harry P. Bowen investigates the relationship between changes in the trade performance of the so-called less developed countries (LDC's) and changes in their endowments of resources between 1966 and 1980. Using a sample of forty-one countries, Bowen finds a high degree of similarity in the structure of trade across the LDC's. In particular, he identifies markets in which semiskilled labor and unskilled labor play a big role as being conductive to a strong LDC trade performance, whereas markets in which capital and skilled labor are the predominant imports tend to promote a trade advantage by the developed countries. Finally, in that last paper in this section a time series analysis of export competition between the EC, Japan, and the U.S. for the period 1965-1984 are examined by David B. Audretsch, Leo Sleuwaegen, and Hideki Yamawaki.

The relationship between innovation and international trade is considered in the last section of this book. Patrick J. van Cayseele applies club theory and finds that government policies such as royalty ceilings and price controls on new products may exert a negative influence on innovative activity. The various forms of cooperative research and development (R&D) agreements between countries are considered by Kirsty Hughes. Hughes predicts that future patterns of global competition are likely to be shaped by such cooperative agreements. Finally, Manfred Neumann finds the increase in market size as a result of trade liberalization, such as for the European Community, can be expected to enhance innovative activity in the domestic market.

Despite the importance of the emerging phenomenon of market globalization, the response to the growing convergence between international and domestic markets from the traditional disciplines within economics has been rather slow. Just as industrial organization economists have only barely begun to consider the impact of foreign competition on the traditional relationship between market structure and performance international economists have only recently included the structure of the industry in their analyses. In this volume these two groups come together, as an important example of how the industrial organization and international trade fields can be integrated to provide the basis for this new emerging field.

There are three new aspects that distinguish this Conference Volume from previous studies. First, there is an emphasis on empirical studies focusing on quantifiable relationships. Second, a number of the papers emphasize a dynamic rather than a static analysis. Third, instead of concentrating on the macro aspects of international trade and trade policy, the analysis is at the firm and the market level. Thus, the resulting conclusions have implications both for firms and for market level policy, rather than only for broad macro policies.

TABLE OF CONTENTS

IV. Innovation and Trade

ACKNOWLEDGEMENTS

We are grateful to the Wissenschaftszentrum Berlin für Sozialforschung (WZB), the European Institute for Advanced Studies in Management (EIASM) in Brussels and the Catholic University of Leuven for all their support in organizing the conference. Special thanks are due to Gerry Dirickx of EIASM and Manfred Fleischer of WZB for their generous assistance. The present volume would not have been possible without the capable technical editorial assistance of Kris De Rooms and Wim Dehandschutter in the final preparation of the manuscript. Our sincere thanks goes to them.

I

PRODUCTIVITY, TECHNOLOGY AND TRADE

The Convergence of International and Domestic Markets
D.B. Audretsch, L. Sleuwaegen, and H. Yamawaki (Editors)

1. EFFICIENCY, PRODUCTIVITY GROWTH, AND INTERNATIONAL TRADE*

Richard E. Caves and David R. Barton
Harvard University
Department of Economics

0. INTRODUCTION.

This paper addresses two questions that are important but not easily investigated with the data and theoretical groundwork that we have available. The first of these is the paper's primary focus, the second subsidiary :

1. Does the static efficiency of an industry affect its ability to achieve productivity gains?
2. Do changes in the intensity of international competition affect the productivity growth of a domestic industry?

The first section of the paper provides essential background by describing the study of technical efficiency in U.S. manufacturing industries that supplies the crucial measurement used in this study. The second considers the causal relations that might run between productivity growth and efficiency. The third summarizes our evidence on the effect of productivity growth on technical efficiency while the fourth advances some evidence on how productivity growth responds to technical efficiency and to changes in import competition.

---

* Professor Caves benefitted from research support by the Division of Research, Harvard Business School, and research assistance by Heng-fu Zou. The larger project from which this paper springs is supported by the U.S. Department of Commerce.

1. MEASURING TECHNICAL EFFICIENCY

This study hinges on the measurements of technical or productive efficiency developed in a project undertaken with the U.S. Department of Commerce. These measures were obtained for many of the manufacturing industries that are defined at the relatively fine four-digit level of aggregation of the U.S. Census of Manufactures (450 maximum). The method used to measure technical efficiency is summarized in some detail, because its properties affect the formulation of our hypotheses about how productivity growth and technical efficiency affect each other. Also, while conceptual discussion of technical efficiency has been a staple topic of industrial organization, the estimation method used here arose only in the past decade and has seen use mainly in specialized econometric studies.[1]

The systematic study of technical inefficiency began with Farrell's (1957) treatment of inefficient input combinations, which he disaggregated into the overuse of all inputs for the output actually obtained and the inappropriate combination of inputs given their relative input prices. The former component of technical inefficiency does not depend on the relative input prices actually prevailing, while the latter ("price inefficiency") does. Since Farrell's paper appeared, a number of methods have been proposed and investigated for measuring technical efficiency from available data; they were surveyed by FØrsund, Lovell, and Schmidt (1980).

The stochastic frontier production function proves the most attractive of these methods. Its central feature is to allow the residuals from the statistically estimated production function to consist of two components, a one-sided disturbance that represents the distribution of technical inefficiency levels and a conventional random disturbance to the output obtained from a given set of inputs. The stochastic production frontier may be written as

$$y = f(x)\exp(v - u),$$

where $\underline{y}$ represents output and $\underline{f(x)\exp(v)}$ is the deterministic core of the frontier production function multiplied by some symmetrical error $\underline{v}$. The one-sided error term, $\underline{u} > 0$, then captures technical inefficiency.

This formulation, introduced by Aigner, Lovell, and Schmidt (1977) and Meeusen and van den Broeck (1977), offers a number of compelling advantages over its competitors. As against a deterministic frontier, the technique is attractive in allowing for measurement errors and thus avoiding a high sensitivity to outlying observations that might contain them. It rests only on rather weak assumptions about the distributions of the $\underline{v}$ and $\underline{u}$ disturbance components. And it is easy to estimate. One can think of the computation process roughly as estimating a production function by conventional regression methods and correcting the intercept for the downward pull of the residual component that reflects technical inefficiency.

We have estimated stochastic frontier production functions for as many as possible of the four-digit manufacturing industries identified in the Standard Industrial Classification, using data for the Annual Survey of Manufactures panel of establishments in the year 1977. These functions were computed by the Bureau of the Census following intensive exploratory research on a small panel of industries, in which we experimented with various forms of the production function and with various editing rules for excluding unsatisfactory plant observations. Space does not permit us to report fully here on the results of these experiments and the decisions that were reached about how to estimate the main body of frontier production functions, so the principal choices are listed here without much explanation :

1. The composed-residuals model can be applied to any chosen form of the production function. Experimentation on our pilot panel of industries yielded a slight preference for the translogarithmic form over the Cobb-Douglas.

2. Either gross output or net output (value added) may serve as the dependent variable. Because materials inputs can be utilized inefficiently, just as much as inputs of the primary factors, our <u>a priori</u> preference was for gross output. However, when annual data are used, the high correlation across plants between gross output and materials inputs both violates the assumption of prior

choice of the inputs and renders the production functions' coefficients unstable and frequently unsatisfactory. Although we did in fact ascertain that functions using gross output as a dependent variable yield overall conclusions similar to those employing value added, only the latter are utilized in the research reported here.

3. Estimation of the composed-residuals model requires assumptions about the distributions of its two components. Although the central limit theorem warrants the normal distribution for $\underline{v}$, no such formal basis has so far emerged for selecting the distribution of $\underline{u}$. We followed the lead of most previous researchers in choosing the half-normal distribution for $\underline{u}$.[2]

4. Labor was measured alternatively as a "body count" and in production-worker-equivalent hours (on the assumption that a dollar's worth of production- and nonproduction-worker services produce equal value at the margin). Capital was taken as book value of plant, equipment, and inventories reported by the establishment plus the capitalized value of leased plant and equipment.

5. Because the composed-residuals model draws its inferences from the higher moments of the residuals from the OLS estimates of the production function, its conclusions are quite sensitive to extreme observations. This fact poses a delicate problem of how to devise editing rules to screen dubious observations: one does not wish to discard a plant that is either highly efficient or highly inefficient. The logarithmic estimation form required us to delete plants reporting zero values for output, labor, or capital, or negative value added. We excluded plants that had begun or ceased operation during the year, and those whose activities seemed to involve no manufacturing production (no production workers, or no machinery). And we excluded those that failed certain other checks on the consistency and plausibility of the data that they reported.

Stochastic frontier production functions could be estimated for approximately 410 industries (the remainder contained too few plants reporting satisfactory data). With value added serving as the dependent variable, we obtained "satisfactory" estimates for 347 industries, meaning that positive estimated values could be obtained for the variances of both the v and u components of the composed residuals. Estimates can be unsatisfactory because a negative value is implied for the variance of either the technical-inefficiency component or the random component. Such failures in practice almost invariably involve an implied negative variance for technical inefficiency, which means simply that the composite production-function residuals (before decomposition) are skewed in the wrong direction. A possible interpretation of such an errant case is that the industry involved suffers from no significant technical inefficiency,[3] a hypothesis that can be put into play when the interindustry determinants of technical inefficiency are examined.

The resulting estimate of technical inefficiency can be expressed and used in various forms. The one possessing the easiest direct interpretation is average technical inefficiency, which is the intercept shift required to "correct" the production function for the estimated incidence of technical inefficiency expressed as a fraction of output (the dependent variable). However, a more satisfactory theoretical rationale is enjoyed by the measure of expected technical efficiency proposed by Lee and Tyler (1978). Furthermore, we found that the Lee-Tyler measure gives slightly more robust and substantial results when we seek to explain industries' levels of technical efficiency in cross-section. The Lee-Tyler measure is the basis for the results reported below, and we refer to it hereafter simply as "technical efficiency."[4]

2. HYPOTHESES ABOUT TECHNICAL EFFICIENCY AND PRODUCTIVITY GROWTH

In seeking out hypotheses about technical inefficiency and productivity growth, we find ourselves in uncharted terrain. Because the constituents and sources of technical inefficiency have been subject to only limited research, we lack the guidance of either a strong theoretical framework or an established set of empirical regularities. The hypotheses developed here represent a judgment about what assumptions are most appropriate, and therefore what behavioral mechanisms are likely to assume the most importance. These judgments, however, might be proved wrong on further study.

2.1. Effect of Inefficiency on Productivity Growth

The hypothesis that inefficiency in the static sense is hostile to productivity growth has a plausible basis in organizational behavior. An organizational coalition that cannot manage its internal allocations so as to obtain the most output from its inputs is by definition failing to adopt superior arrangements that are known and in use in rival organizations. Whatever the source of its infirmity, we should not expect such an organization to reach out with alacrity for new production arrangements that are untried, or that it must discover itself. Although this line of reasoning is not a household staple in microeconomics, it does appear and claim some explanatory force in other contexts. Students of business administration frequently accept the notion that some business firms are excellently managed, and that their excellence is persistent if not eternal.[5] Economists who have tried to explain differences among industrial countries in long-run rates of output growth have urged that societies with widely prevalent rent-preserving contracts and institutions are prone to slow growth because growth inevitably involves redistributive changes (Olson, 1982). In short, to the extent that technical inefficiency turns out to result from suboptimization by organizational coalitions, it seems plausible that the failing should affect both their static and dynamic efficiency levels.

Acceptance of that hypothesis for individual units, however, still leaves us with only a weak link between technical inefficiency and productivity growth for the industry as a whole. The technical inefficiency that we measure stems from the apparent dispersion of efficiency levels among plants classified to an industry. The accuracy of the measurement depends, roughly speaking, on the presence of enough efficient units to define a production frontier from which the others' shortcomings can be detected. If all units in the U.S. industry are equally inefficient, none will be found out by the methodology we have employed. The productivity growth rate of an industry can be regarded as a (size-weighted) average of the productivity growth rates attained by all the units operating within it. All could be equally inefficient, and unprogressive, yet no association between technical inefficiency and productivity growth would be revealed.[6]

Even if we consider equal and substantial inefficiency of an industry's units to be an implausible special case, the hypothesis that low technical efficiency leads to slow productivity growth at the industry level faces another problem. Suppose that an industry, consisting of half "efficient" and half "inefficient" production units, gains access to a productivity raising innovation. In order to obtain the productivity gain, each unit must undertake a substantial investment. Each manager conjectures on the expected profitability of adopting the innovation. One datum entering into the calculus is the expected rate of adoption by competing units, because it influences the rate at which the industry's market price is expected to decline due to the expansion of output by successful innovators who obtain lower variable costs.[7] Inefficient units, on the general hypothesis advanced above, suffer infirmities for making profitable use of the innovation and are unlikely to adopt it quickly. But their very tardiness raises the payout to prompt adoption by the efficient units, because (assuming that efficient new units cannot quickly enter the industry) it limits the rate of intraindustry diffusion for the innovation and the speed with which total output expands and the market price declines. Because a technically inefficient industry necessarily contains both efficient and inefficient units, and because the delays of the inefficient raise the innovative rewards to the efficient, we have no assurance that the industry with more technical inefficiency will (ceteris paribus) show a slower rate of productivity growth overall.

Of course, this incentive structure implies that the extent of the industry's technical inefficiency itself cannot stay permanently unchanged when productivity is growing. Units inefficient at the outset become relatively more so when their efficient rivals adopt an innovation. It grows more likely that the ineffieient units cannot obtain revenues sufficient to keep their coalitions of inputs together, and their rates of business failure should increase. The presence of technically inefficient units need not necessarily delay industry-wide productivity gains, and furthermore the presence of productivity-raising investment opportunities may undermine and reduce technical inefficiency.

These considerations help us to identify the conditions that must hold if "persistent" technical inefficiency is to exert a negative influence on the growth of an industry's productivity. Static and dynamic inefficiency must be associated with one another within the firm, and structural conditions in the industry must limit the degree to which efficient units can expect to capitalize on the opportunities provided by their rivals' inefficiency.

2.2. Effect of Productivity Growth on Inefficiency

We also need to consider that causation might run from productivity growth to apparent technical inefficiency. Start an industry with its plants equally productive, and introduce an innovation that is capital-embodied and/or otherwise incapable of being retrofitted to installed productive capacity. New production units adopt the innovation, but older units continue to produce with the old technology as long as their variable costs are covered. Clearly the dispersion of apparent productivity levels in the industry can increase, so that the industry appears to display some technical inefficiency, even if scrappage and replacement decisions are being made optimally.[8] As long as the innovation's diffusion within the industry remains incomplete, the dispersion of efficiency levels is expanded, and the measured level of technical efficiency is reduced. Thus, productivity growth could reduce apparent technical efficiency (although with no normative implications).

This basis for a negative relation between productivity growth and technical efficiency is only a possibility, and it need not be evident in a broad range of manufacturing industries. If productivity growth is not embodied in equipment, or if an innovation can be retrofitted, the efficient survival of obsolete capacity will not appear to reduce technical efficiency, although it could still be depressed by other sources of delayed diffusion. Also, technical efficiency would not seem to decline when an innovation is so drastic that all producers adopt it promptly.

Nonetheless, some empirical evidence does seem to confirm the hypothesis that productivity growth appears to depress technical efficiency. Shen (1968) followed the positions of individual plants in the efficiency distribution over time. He found that a given plant tends to slip downward through the distribution until scrappage or a major re-equipment occurs. This intertemporal pattern is consistent with a negative relationship in cross-section between industries' productivity growth and technical efficiency, in that it confirms one precondition for a negative relation. The many studies that associate the diffusion of innovations with competition and certain organizational traits of industries confirm another: that a point-in-time snapshot of a progressive industry is likely to catch it with a stock of partly diffused innovations.

Thus, we can marshall at least limited theoretical support for the hypothesis that inefficiency reduces productivity growth, as well as establish some circumstances in which exogenous productivity growth would diminish apparent technical efficiency. Our empirical tests accordingly address both directions of causation.

3. PRODUCTIVITY GROWTH AND OTHER DETERMINANTS OF TECHNICAL EFFICIENCY

While the effect of efficiency on productivity growth commands more analytical and normative interest, our empirical resources are richer for addressing the effect of productivity growth on efficiency. The project described in Section 1 encompasses a cross-industry model of the determinants of technical efficiency that tests a number of hypotheses, and we list the main results for other hypotheses[9] in order to indicate what controls are in place when the effect of productivity growth is tested:

1. Technical efficiency measured via the stochastic frontier production function proves to decrease strongly with the number of plants observed in an industry. Various subsidiary tests have convinced us that the phenomenon of "order statistics" provides a sufficient explanation for this relation, and a behavioral

explanation is not needed. Nonetheless, its presence clouds any behavioral findings about the effects of competitive conditions.

2. Technical efficiency is not strongly related to indicators of competitive conditions in the industry. It does increase with the import competition faced by highly concentrated domestic industries, and it shows a weak tendency to diminish with the incidence of collusive price-fixing agreements.

3. Technical efficiency decreases with the incidence of corporate diversification, measured either as the extent to which firms based in a given industry operate plants in other industries or (even more strongly) the extent to which plants in this industry belong to firms based in other industries.

4. Technical efficiency increases with the utilization of part-time employees and shows a weak tendency to decrease with the unionization of the workforce in large-plant industries.

5. Product differentiation associated with information factors (advertising) increases apparent technical inefficiency, but not product differentiation associated with the intrinsic heterogeneity of products. Technical efficiency seems unrelated to heterogeneity in plants' unit costs or net revenues due to the localization of markets or to diverse-quality natural-resource inputs.

With these factors listed, we come to variables with direct relevance to the effect of productivity growth on apparent efficiency. Technical efficiency decreases with dispersion of the vintages of an industry's plant and equipment, confirming the findings of Shen (1968) and keeping open the possibility that productivity growth might decrease measured technical efficiency by increasing the dispersion of plants' capital vintages.[10] Technical efficiency also decreases with the importance of research and development expenditures (specifically, the industry's R&D/sales ratio). With these variables controlled, however, we find no relationship whatever of technical efficiency in 1977 to the industry's rate of growth of labor productivity, measured over either the decade 1968-77 or the two-decade period 1958-77.[11] That is, if productivity growth depresses our measure of technical efficiency, it either operates by expanding the capital-vintage dispersion or has its effect proxied by R&D spending (which may either scatter lumps of innovative rents unevenly through the industry or give rise to uncompleted diffusion processes).

4. EFFECTS OF EFFICIENCY AND FOREIGN COMPETITION ON PRODUCTIVITY GROWTH

That brings us to the more central question of whether an industry's productivity growth increases with its technical efficiency. We faced limitations for developing a cross-section test remotely as comprehensive as that just reported, for two reasons. The first lies in the paucity of statistical resources, the second in the lack of any strong operational model of the determinants of differences in industries' rates of productivity growth.

We consider the problem of data sources first. Total factor productivity growth is not available for manufacturing industries disaggregated to the level that we require, forcing resort to labor productivity. Two sources of labor-productivity growth rates are available, one emanating from the U.S. Bureau of Labor Statistics (BLS), the other from the U.S. International Trade Administation (ITA). We turned first to the BLS data (Bureau of Labor Statistics, 1979, 1986) on account of certain attractive properties, such as corrections for changes in finished-good inventories, use of current-weighted price indexes, and appropriate adjustments to employment data. However, the BLS data do not cover all manufacturing industries; matching them to the industries for which we possess measures of technical efficiency, we obtained only 88 observations. Furthermore, they are available only to 1984 (1983 for some industries), with the lost observations looking distinctly nonrandom. While we employed productivity-growth measures for 1977-84 taken from the BLS data, we shifted our attention to the ITA data, which are available through 1985 and cover almost all manufacturing industries. This data base is used to produce the publication U.S. Industrial Outlook ; it is based on four-digit SIC industries, it includes real output, employment, exports, and imports as well as other variables derived from the Annual Survey of Manufactures. Nearly quadrupling our number of industries seemed amply worth the lack of certain minor refinements in the ITA data, though we shall mention the fate of the BLS sample.

4.1. Controlling for Opportunities to Raise Productivity

In relating labor-productivity growth over 1977-85 to technical efficiency in 1977, we wanted to control as well as possible for the opportunities open to each industry to raise its productivity. The importance of suitable controls is underlined by the causal factors running from innovation to (measured) technical efficiency, discussed above, as well as the well-known importance of controls for "technological opportunity" for investigations of the effect of industry competition on innovative input or output (Scherer, 1965). Yet no economic model stands ready to identify the appropriate set of controls. We devised two control variables that can be justified by the substantial empirical evidence that links productivity growth to innovation and identifies the structural determinants for opportunities to raise productivity or generate innovations.

The first of these controls is the industry's ratio of company-financed research and development expenditures to sales, taken from the Federal Trade Commission Line of Business data and averaged over 1974-76. For industries not covered by the Line of Business data we employed similar data from the National Science Foundation (a source that reports data for coarser industry classifications than the FTC, but it does cover the whole manufacturing sector). The FTC data are available only for the mid-1970s, which precluded measuring the R&D variable over the whole period for which productivity growth is observed. Although an industry's productivity growth depends on innovative efforts made in other industries (for which we lack data), it also depends on its own R&D outlays.[12]

The other control used to indicate an industry's productivity-growth potential is its reliance on new capital equipment, which is one channel by which its productivity is influenced by R&D done by other industries. We therefore obtained for each industry the ratio of gross capital expenditure to employment for the years

1977-85 taken together. Besides controlling for the industry's access to and use of embodied new technology, this variable may help correct for the misspecification in using labor productivity rather than total factor productivity. Both the research intensity (R&D) and investment-intensity ($\Delta K/L$) variables should exert positive influences on productivity growth, as should technical efficiency (TE). Before we report the test of these relationships, however, we present another hypothesis concerning the effect on productivity growth of changes in the structure of international trade.

4.2 Import Competition and Productivity Growth

Because of the large effects of changing international competition on the structure of U.S. manufacturing industries and the evidence (reported above) of favorable effects of import competition on technical efficiency, we also investigated whether productivity growth has been affected by the incursion of foreign competitors on U.S. product markets. The relation of productivity growth to disturbances in international trade is a large subject associated with the whole question of changes in a nation's comparative-advantage structure. The neo-classical approach to that relation simply assumes that industries' relative productivity levels (like the nation's comparative-advantage structure) are determined by fundamental attributes of technology and factor supply, and by implication that changes in productivity stem from these same fundamentals. While the idea is now popular that comparative advantage may to some extent reflect will, desire, and public policy, that thought (and the strategic models to which it leads) has little support from systematic empirical evidence. The evidence to be offered here takes only the most casual, exploratory form, but it at least provides an occasion for launching the issue.

Suppose that productivity growth reflects the sum of intendedly rational decisions by managers and others in an industry to adopt new technologies, make best use of the changing stock of available inputs, and respond efficiently to changes in the structure of demand. When we observe productivity in a national industry facing import competition, changes in the import competition (think of it as changes in the home-delivered price of foreign supplies) shift the parameters governing resource use in ways that affect the industry's ratio of real output to real inputs. Consider these links:

1. Specific factors. Assume that industries are purely competitive and that each makes use of factors of production that are specialized or specific to the industry (at least in the short run). Then each industry operates on a rising supply curve. Any contraction in the face of lower prices of competing imports should raise labor productivity if labor is not the specific factor, as more intensive use is made of the specific factor.[13] Thus, import penetration and productivity growth could be positively related for reasons resting on a very spare characterization of industries' organization.

2. Product differentiation. The past decade's research on monopolistic competition and international trade (Helpman, 1981; Krugman, 1981) has established that production scales and thus industry average productivity levels may be affected by an industry's exposure to international trade. At a less abstract level, competitive processes in differentiated-product markets have been found both theoretically and empirically to make the mixture of "varieties" or "brands" offered by an industry depend on its international competitive position. The computable general equilibrium model of Harris (1984), for example, showed that Canada's protection of differentiated and imperfectly competitive manufacturing industries exacts a substantial cost in economic welfare that manifests itself as impaired real productivity in such industries. This model implies that tariff reduction (or, for that matter, other changes reducing the real delivered price of competing imports) will induce reallocations that raise productivity. An analysis of Canadian industries' adjustments to international disturbances in the 1970s found that tariff reductions led to increases in industries' capital expenditures, a necessary (but not sufficient) condition for rationalizing the product lines and brand scales offered by domestic producers (Caves, 1987). These rationalizing changes could account for a positive relation between import competition (import penetration, say) and productivity growth.

3. Productivity-raising investments. Policy-makers often urge industries pressed by import competition to invest in raising their productivity. However, apart from the product-line rationalization just noted, the expected returns from ordinary sorts of productivity-raising investments are unlikely to be rising at a time when import competition is growing more severe. The point is simply that expected values of quasi rents flowing from such investments are likely to be decreased by external changes that portend a lower product price and a smaller market to be served by domestic producers. Current increases in import competition have this withering effect if they represent secular shifts in comparative advantage (and not one-shot changes or temporary bursts associated with disturbances to the real exchange rate). This consideration could account for a negative relation observed in some period of time between import penetration of domestic markets and domestic industries' rates of productivity growth.

In conclusion, several distinct mechanisms with opposite-sign predictions stand ready to explain how changes in import competition and in productivity growth might be related. We include among the determinants of productivity growth the variable IM, which is the ratio of imports to the sum of imports and competing domestic product shipments for 1985, minus the corresponding ratio for 1977.

4.3. Statistical Results

To summarize the model developed in this section, we expect an industry's productivity growth over 1977-85 (PR, real output per employee) to increase with its technical efficiency in 1977 (TE), its level of R&D spending relative to sales (R&D), and its ratio of gross capital expenditures to employees over 1977-85 ($\Delta K/L$); it could either increase or decrease with the change in the ratio of imports to domestic supply (IM). When we test this model on the 228 industries for which all data are available (IM suffers from missing values), we obtain the following result:

$$PR = \underset{}{0.013} + \underset{(1.74)}{0.004\ TE} + \underset{(2.88)}{0.004\ R\&D} + \underset{(2.90)}{0.001\ \Delta K/L} + \underset{(2.22)}{0.050\ IM}$$

$$R^2 = 0.084.$$

The three variables with definite sign predictions take the expected signs, and their coefficients are significant at 5 percent or better in one-tail tests. IM takes a coefficient indicating that increasing import competition promotes productivity growth, significant at 5 percent (two-tail) test. It comes as no surprise that the explanatory power of the model is quite low, but its F-statistic (5.22) indicates that it is significant overall. Thus, the model supports behavioral roles for both technical efficiency and intensified international competition in raising productivity. Furthermore, the effects of these two variables are consistent with our underlying approach to the study of technical efficiency and productivity, which assumes that less than fully efficient production units can soldier on persistently unless more efficient competitors make it impossible for them to obtain enough revenue to keep their coalitions of resources together.

Several supplemental conclusions from the data help us to assess the validity of these results. First, recall that TE cannot be calculated from the stochastic frontier production estimated for every industry. The missing cases are typically those in which the residuals around the fitted production are skewed in the wrong direction. A possible interpretation is that these industries have no appreciable technical efficiency, and some although not all of the evidence from our larger project is consistent with this interpretation. If it holds for the relation just estimated, PR should be higher for those industries with TE missing than for those industries for which TE could be calculated. The mean value of PR for the former group is indeed 9 percent higher, but the difference is not statistically significant.

Several correlations in the data underlying the regression model are revealing. PR, estimated for 1977-85, is uncorrelated with its counterpart estimated for 1972-77 period; for the full set of (448) four-digit industries, the correlation is only 0.08. Hence, it is reasonable to expect PR to be sensitive to changes occurring within the same time period for which PR is measured, as the regression model indicates. The significant coefficient of IM was probed in several ways. First, IM is highly correlated with the level of the imports/supply ratio in earlier years (we used 1972), so the relation may represent partly the effect of persistent rather than intensified import competition. Because of the importance of intraindustry trade, we were concerned that IM might be correlated with the change in each industry's export intensity (exports/shipments ratio, EX), which in turn should be positively associated with productivity growth. The correlation between IM and EX is positive but not at all significant for 1977-85, although it is significant at the 2 percent level for the earlier period of 1972-77. A more bothersome correlation in the data is that between TE and IM, 0.23, significant at the 0.1 percent level; while this correlation is probably spurious,[14] it surely contributes to the significant positive influences of TE and IM on PR that we obtain in the regression model.

Correlations shed a little light on the mechanism by which both TE and IM affect PR. We obtained ratios of payroll to shipments and purchased materials to shipments for each industry in both 1977 and 1985. Technical efficiency in 1977 (TE) and the 1977-85 change in import competition (IM) were both negatively correlated with the change in payroll/shipments (-0.13 and -0.10, significant at 2 and 7 percent respectively), but uncorrelated with the change in materials/shipments. Thus, reductions in wages and/or labor-intensity were part of the adjustment process. The association is not due to imports' effect on the industry's growth, because real output growth and changes in payroll/shipments are negatively correlated (-0.22).

While these results based on the ITA data on labor-productivity growth hold considerable interest, we should recall the alternative data set utilizing BLS data on productivity growth for a truncated (and nonrandom) subsample of industries. In this study and in a previous exploration that involved a less satisfactory time-structure of its relationships (Caves, 1985), we found no significant relation between TE and PR based on BLS data. In the earlier study there was some suggestion of a truncation: no industries exhibited both high productivity growth and low technical efficiency, although the relation otherwise seemed random. With the current data base, no relationship whatsoever appears in the BLS sample between PR and TE, although the variable R&D, controlling for innovative opportunity, is again a significant influence on PR. Clearly the BLS sample is the inferior one, with many fewer observations and a suspect pattern of deleted industries, to be stacked against only minor improvements in the measurement of PR. Yet this divergence between the PR - TE relations in the two samples surely reduces the confidence with which the null hypothesis on TE is rejected for the ITA sample.

The BLS data did offer some small advantage, however, for extending our investigation of the relation between productivity growth and changes in international trade, because data on the smaller sample of industries could be extended back into the 1960s (the ITA data base goes back only to 1972). We gathered data on imports' shares of domestic supply (imports plus production) and also shares of domestic production exported for the 88 BLS industries in 1967, 1977, and 1982,[15] and obtained labor productivity growth rates for 1967-77 and 1977-84. The level of import penetration in 1967 was uncorrelated with subsequent productivity growth; the correlation is negative for 1967-77, positive for 1977-84, but significant in neither. Exports' shares in 1967 were negatively correlated with productivity growth throughout 1967-84 with values of -0.21 for 1967-77 (significant at 5 percent) and -0.13 for 1977-84. Because the evidence indicates that the U.S. comparative advantage has lain in the more innovative manufacturing industries, this result weakly suggests some erosion of the gains from trade.

Now consider the correlations between productivity growth and changes in trade exposure - the relationship found significantly positive in the regression model based on ITA data. The change in import penetration[16] is positively correlated with productivity growth after 1977 (0.15) in the BLS sample as well, but negatively correlated before 1977 (-0.22, significant at 5 percent), yielding no consistent picture. Changes in export activity were also erratically related to productivity growth, negatively correlated with productivity growth rates before 1977 (-0.15) but uncorrelated after. Before deciding what to make of this instability, we note one more relationship - the correlations between changes in trade shares and the change in productivity growth from 1967-77 to 1977-84. These are rather stronger than the correlations between trade-share changes and the productivity growth rates themselves. In the case of imports, a positive correlation (0.33) results that is significant at the 1 percent level. For exports the correlation is also positive but lower (0.16, just short of 10 percent significance).

Taking together these correlations observed in the BLS sample, we can tentatively conclude that the relation between PR and the change in import penetration (IM) found in the ITA data for 1977-85 does not extend back to the 1967-77 period. Nonetheless, the correlations just reported are consistent with a cumulative effect of import competition over the longer period of 1967-84.[17] Of course, we have no strong prior why a "bend" in productivity growth rates due to intensifying import competition should center on 1977 - that year was picked fortuitously as the year of our TE measures, and was not searched out inductively.

5. SUMMARY AND CONCLUSIONS

This paper has addressed two questions often heard in the street but seldom touched directly by economic analysis : Does static inefficiency drag down an industry's ability to seize new opportunities and thus its rate of productivity growth ? Does increased heat from international competition prompt an industry to "rationalize" and achieve additional productivity gains ? Each question should be avoided by those fearful of straying from safe and scientifically respectable paths of economic scholarship. Neither is backstopped by a solid body of theory, and neither can be given a thorough empirical investigation without a heavy investment in gathering and analyzing data.

This paper has sought to make some small headway from the vantage point of an extensive investigation of technical or productive efficiency - the size of the gap between average and best-practice productivity in an industry's plants. Although productivity growth might have a negative effect on technical efficiency as we measure it (because early and late adopters of changes increase the spread of the productivity distribution), we found no effect of past productivity growth on the technical efficiency of U.S. manufacturing industries in 1977. More precisely, we found no effect beyond that already captured by the negative influences on technical efficiency of the industry's R&D spending rate and the dispersion of its capital vintages.

A much less comprehensive investigation of the effect of technical efficiency in 1977 on productivity growth over 1977-85 rejected the null hypothesis in the superior one of two data sets - superior in number of observations and sample properties. The credibility of that conclusion was fortified by significant coefficients of two variables controlling for industries' opportunities to raise productivity - their R&D intensity and their gross additions to their capital stocks per employee. However, that credibility was undermined by the failure to replicate the relationship in a smaller sample based on a different source of data on productivity growth. The conclusion that technical inefficiency retards productivity growth thus gains only tenuous support.

As an adjunct to the analysis of technical efficiency and productivity growth, we noted some evidence on how productivity growth is affected by changing intensities of international competition. Even in a purely competitive industry, we might expect tougher international competition to increase productivity (for the same reason we expect productivity to move contracyclically in response to demand disturbances). Outside the realm of purely competitive industries, elements of both product differentiation and oligopoly supply additional reasons why stiffer import competition might prompt rationalizing investments and productivity gains, a prediction supported by some empirical work on small, open economies. We found limited evidence that increases in import competition during 1977-85 exerted a significant positive influence on the growth of industries' productivity. Furthermore, an analysis of correlations over a longer period in our smaller data set is consistent with a cumulative effect of intensifying import competition that became evident after 1977 but was not revealed by the data for 1967-77.

The study can be regarded as mainly supplying a guardedly optimistic estimate of the benefits and costs of a more intensive investigation. Such an inquiry would focus on the mechanisms by which international competition can promote productivity growth through changes in capital expenditure, workforce structure and utilization, and the distributions of product varieties and production scales in the competing domestic industry. It would also take a more sophisticated view than was done here of the temporal structures of the relationships.

"More research is needed" - it is so easy to say. But in this case it adverts to a fundamental choice of our research agenda in industrial economics. We have confined ourselves mostly to questions addressable via models of long-run market equilibrium, or at most short-run behavior that is capable of direct prediction from such models. At the same time, nonprofessional observers suspect that we turn our backs on questions of efficiency and productivity growth, although a lot of economic welfare may ride on them. And policy-makers call for industries pressed by import competition to stand up and fight, without anybody seriously weighing either the structure of private incentives or the social return to their doing so. The ultimate question is not whether we should do more research, but whether we take a chance on using our high-quality professional tools on these empirically important questions for which they were not specifically designed.

NOTES

1 The concept of technical or productive inefficiency is identical to what Leibenstein prefers to call "X-inefficiency", while that expression is well known, the former usage is well established in the field of industrial organization. For a recent controversy over the concept's analytical properties, see Leibenstein (1983) and de Alessi (1983); among the noteworthy empirical applications are Carlsson (1972), Shen (1973), and FØrsund and Hjalmarsson (1987).

2 The research by Corbo and de Melo (1983) on Chilean data suggests that the half-normal and its chief competitor, the exponential distribution, give quite similar results.

3 Other interpretations are also possible. The normal distribution is assumed for the random component of the composed residuals on the familiar logic of the central limit theorem. However, the particular forms of random outcome that predominate for certain industries could have nonnormal distributions.

4 We mention another summary measure of technical inefficiency that was used in exploratory work on this project, the ratio of the estimated standard deviation of the technical-inefficiency component to the estimated standard deviation of the random component of the composed residuals, usually designated as lambda : $\lambda = \sigma_u/\sigma_v$. The variable λ in fact is an attractive summary statistic, normalizing the variance imputed to technical inefficiency by that imputed to all other causes. It was used in an earlier version of this paper (Caves, 1985).

5 While the possibility that competing business units differ in their efficiency levels (and hence in profitability and market share) has been importantly debated in industrial organization, there is surprisingly little evidence on the longevity of inefficient units or the time for which efficient units can sustain their advantages (or preserve them from replication by competitors). The assumption that organizational coalitions and the contract structures that bind them are "sticky" and not quickly reorganized seems plausible but cannot be readily documented.

6 In this context, analyzing the production units classified to a given industry and located in a particular country appears somewhat arbitrary, if inevitable as a feasible research strategy. As part of the project underlying this report, parallel estimations of technical efficiency are being executed in several other countries. By comparing for a given industry in several countries levels of technical efficiency and of average productivity, we hope to shed some light on the accuracy of the implicit assumption that each national industry includes enough efficient units to define a production frontier.

7 This argument is related to the model originated by Scherer (1967) of the timing of innovation, which assumes diminishing returns to speeding the innovation process.

8 The argument assumes that net book values of capital stocks reflect depreciation associated with wear and tear but not obsolescence, so long as plant and equipment remain in use.

9 A few refinements to the statistical procedures remain, and so the findings that follow are tentative and subject to revision.

10 Technical efficiency also decreases with the variance of capital-labor ratios among plants classified to the industry. We are uncertain at this stage whether that variance itself is due to behavioral influences on efficiency, or whether it reflects some otherwise uncontrolled heterogeneity among the observed plants and their products.

11 The data represent growth rates of labor productivity and are taken from U.S. Bureau of Labor Statistics (1979). The industrial classification used in this source in some cases combines four-digit industries, so we were forced to assume that the reported productivity-growth rate for an aggregate applies to each of its constituents.

12 Scherer (1982) obtained results that differed from one sample of productivity-growth data to another, but generally suggested that both influences are significant.

13 The same conclusion obtains if we think of the fixed factor as comprising heterogeneous units, with the lowest-quality discarded as the industry contracts. Caves (1988) found some evidence that increased import competition tends to truncate the small-firm tails of U.S. manufacturing industries. If these contain the less-efficient firms in disproportionate numbers, the hypothesis is supported.

14 It may be partly due to high correlations between TE and the number of plants in an industry and between the number of plants and IM; import penetration made more headway in industries with large numbers of producers, no doubt reflecting the successes of the newly industrializing countries at the light end of the manufacturing spectrum.

15 The most recent year available for the published data source, U.S. Bureau of the Census (1970, 1986). The match between the international-trade and production classifications used in the United States is quite imperfect, as the former is based on commodities and the latter on the activities of production units. The majority of imperfections arise because the match pertains only to part of the commodities produced by the domestic industry (underinclusive) or to an aggregate of commodities larger than its output (overinclusive). These cases involve no necessary bias in the ratios of export or imports to domestic activity. A smaller number involve biases (thought to be small) because the trade flow embraces a wider or narrower range of commodities than the production measure. Because we did not wish to lose observations from the relatively small 88-industry sample yielded by the data on technical efficiency and productivity growth, we were somewhat aggressive in forging these matches.

16 Measured as the difference between ratios for 1967 and 1982.

17 This result suggested an experiment with the regresion model based on the ITA data base. To the version reported above, we added as a regressor the change in imports' share of domestic supply from 1972 to 1977. It took a positive coefficient; while its t-statistic was only 0.9, its magnitude was about the same as that for IM (the change from 1977 to 1985), broadly consistent with the results cited above.

REFERENCES

AIGNER, D.J., C.A.K. LOVELL and P. SCHMIDT (1977), "Formulation and Estimation of Stochastic Frontier Production Function Models", Journal of Econometrics, vol. 6, pp. 21-37.

CARLSSON, Bo (1972), "The Measurement of Efficiency in Production : An Application to Swedish Manufacturing Industries, 1968", Swedish Journal of Economics, vol. 74, pp. 468-85.

CAVES, Richard E. (1985), "Interindustry Differences in Productivity Growth and Technical Efficiency", Harvard Institute of Economic Research, Discussion Paper No. 1130.

CAVES, Richard E. (1987), "Market Structure, Seller Competition, and Adjustment to International Disturbances", Conference on New Issues in Industrial Economics, Case Western Reserve University, Cleveland.

CAVES, Richard E. (1988), "Trade Exposure and Changing Structures of U.S. Manufacturing Industries", in Spence, A.M. and H.A. Hazard (eds.), International Competitiveness, (Cambridge, MA: Ballinger, 1988), pp. 1-26.

CORBO, Vittorio, and Jaime DE MELO (1983), "Technical Efficiency in a Highly Protected Economy: Preliminary Results for the Chilean Manufacturing Sector: 1967", preliminary working paper, World Bank.

DE ALESSI, Louis (1983), "Property Rights, Transaction Costs, and X-Efficiency: An Essay in Economic Theory", American Economic Review, vol. 73, pp. 64-81.

FARRELL, M.J. (1957), "The Measurement of Productive Efficiency", Journal of the Royal Statistical Society, vol. 120 (Part 3), pp. 253-82.

FØRSUND, Finn R., and Lennart HJALMARSSON (1987), Analysis of Industrial Structure: A Putty-Clay Approach (Stockholm: Industrial Institute for Economic and Social Research).

FØRSUND, Finn R., C.A. KNOX LOVELL and Peter SCHMIDT (1980), "A Survey of Frontier Production Functions and of Their Relationship to Efficiency Measurement", Journal of Econometrics, vol. 13, pp. 5-25.

HARRIS, Richard (1984), "Applied General Equilibrium Analysis of Small Open Economies with Scale Economies and Imperfect Competition", American Economic Review, vol. 74, pp. 1016-32.

HELPMAN, Elhanan (1981), "International Trade in the Presence of Product Differentiation, Economies of Scale and Monopolistic Competition : A Chamberlin-Heckscher-Ohlin Approach", Journal of International Economics, vol. 11, pp. 305-40.

KRUGMAN, Paul R. (1981), "Intra-industry Specialization and the Gains from Trade", Journal of Political Economy, vol. 89, pp. 959-73.

LEE, Lung-Fei, and William G. TYLER (1978), "The Stochastic Frontier Production Function and Average Efficiency: An Empirical Analysis", Journal of Econometrics, vol. 7, pp. 285-9.

LEIBENSTEIN, Harvey (1983), "Property Rights and X-Efficiency; Comment", American Economic Review, vol. 73, pp. 831-42.

MEEUSEN, Wim, and Julien VAN DEN BROECK (1977), "Efficiency Estimation of Cobb Douglas Production Functions with Composed Error", International Economic Review, vol. 18, pp. 435-44.

OLSON, Mancur (1982), The Rise and Decline of Nations: Economic Growth, Stagflation, and Social Rigidities (New Haven: Yale University Press).

SCHERER, F. M. (1965), "Firm Size, Market Structure, Opportunity and the Output of Patented Inventions", American Economic Review, vol. 55, pp. 1097-1123.

SCHERER, F. M. (1967), "Research and Development Resource Allocation under Rivalry", Quarterly Journal of Economics, vol. 81, pp. 359-94.

SCHERER, F. M. (1982), "Interindustry Technology Flows and Productivity Growth", Review of Economics and Statistics, vol. 64, pp. 627-34.

SHEN, T.Y. (1968), "Competition, Technology and Market Shares", Review of Economics and Statistics, vol. 50, pp. 96-102.

SHEN, T.Y. (1973), "Technology Diffusion, Substitution, and X-Efficiency", Econometrica, vol. 41, pp. 263-84.

U.S. Bureau of Labor Statistics. Time Series Data for Input-Output Industries, Bulletin No. 2018 (Washington: Government Printing Office, 1979).

U.S. Bureau of Labor Statistics. Productivity Measures for Selected Industries, 1958-84, Bulletin No. 2256 (Washington: Government Printing Office, 1986).

U.S. Bureau of the Census. U.S. Commodity Exports and Imports as Related to Output, 1967 and 1966, Series E52, No. 10 (Washington: Government Printing Office, 1970).

U.S. Bureau of the Census. U.S. Commodity Exports and Imports and Related to Output, 1982 and 1981, Series E52-18 (Washington: Government Printing Office, 1986).

The Convergence of International and Domestic Markets
D.B. Audretsch, L. Sleuwaegen, and H. Yamawaki (Editors)

2. TRADE AND SCALE ECONOMIES

A Causality Test for the US, Japan, Germany and the UK

Dalia Marin
Institute for Advanced Studies*
Austria

0. INTRODUCTION

In the last twenty years the productivity and trade performance among the western industrialized countries have shown a nonuniform picture. Japan and West Germany have experienced above average productivity growth rates compared to those of other western industralized countries; and at the same time, they have achieved a favourable trade performance. In contrast, the US and the UK went through an unfavourable productivity as well as an inferior trade development. The experience of these four countries seems to suggest a direct link between trade and productivity. Countries which do well in their productivity performance seem also to do well in their trade performance and vice versa.

The observed positive association between trade and productivity seems to be consistent with recent trade theory incorporating economies of scale and imperfect competition. It considers trade to lead to extra welfare gains through its effect on static economies of scale on the one hand and sees economies of scale as the cause of trade between countries with similar factor endowments on the other. Though economies of scale greatly expand

---

* All econometric estimations and tests were done with the Institute for Advanced Studies' IAS-System Econometric Software package.

the gains from trade, they also give rise to incentives for interventionist unilateral trade policy. The direction of causality between trade and productivity on the one hand and between the terms of trade and productivity on the other might, therefore, have important implications for the way trade policy can influence industrial performance.

The paper attempts to answer the following two questions. First, have the increases in foreign market shares experienced by Japan and Germany and the loss in market shares of the US and the UK been caused by their productivity performance or has, on the contrary, export growth of these countries caused their productivity performance. Second, can one observe in these countries any causal influence of the terms of trade on productivity which might explain policy-induced divergences in productivity growth between these countries.

In order to answer the above questions vector autoregressive representations of trade, productivity, the terms of trade and world output for these four countries are shown and various causality tests are performed on the basis of Granger's concept of causality.

The paper is in three sections. Section 1 derives the causal implications for trade, productivity, the terms of trade and world output from models incorporating many of the features in the recent theoretical literature. Section 2 describes the methodology and data and looks at whether the data for the US, Japan, Great Britain and Germany are compatible with the causal implications derived in Section 1. Finally, Section 3 summarizes the results and suggests some policy conclusions.

1. CAUSAL IMPLICATIONS OF ALTERNATIVE MODELS

In recent trade models with economies of scale, imperfect competition and product differentiation (Helpman/Krugman (1985)) it is suggested that productivity increases through the exploitation of static economies of scale are the cause of trade between countries with similar factor endowments. Even if countries have no Heckscher-Ohlin type of comparative advantage vis-a-vis each other, they will engage in trade because of increasing returns to scale. Besides, economies of scale being the cause of intra-industry trade, trade is also assumed to effect economies of scale. Three potential gains from trade are considered. First, there may be gains from the exploitation of economies of scale as international trade enlarges the market served by individual firms. By expanding the total market, trade makes room for more efficient size in the domestic market thereby lowering average costs. Second, there might be a procompetitive effect as the monopoly power of domestic firms is reduced when foreign producers enter their markets. Thus, trade reduces the monopolistic distortion of imperfect domestic markets. Third, there might be a gain to consumers of differentiated products as trade widens the range of products available.

The purpose of this paper is to explore the first of these channels; whether trade leads to higher productivity through the realization of economies of scale. Though recent trade theory suggests that there are efficiency gains from trade, in an imperfeclty competitive environment with increasing returns to scale policy intervention in the form of trade restrictions and/or trade subsidies might lead to non trivial productivity gains as well.

In order to see the productivity consequences of trade policy, consider the model developed by Venables/Smith (1986) in which the welfare effects of trade and industrial policy on the UK refrigerator and footwear industry are studied. Since they use a partial equilibrium model focussing on one industry, intersectoral interactions are not taken into account which might alter the results (see Dixit and Grossman (1984))[1]. Despite this disadvantage of being a partial equilibrium model, the model captures many of the features in the theoretical literature so that it seems useful as a reference point for the following analysis. The model allows for study adjustment when the number of firms is fixed as well as when there is free entry. Furthermore, firms' market power is derived from oligopolistic interaction as well as from product differentiation.

Firms are assumed to make two choices, the number of brands they produce and the quantity of each brand of which x^d is sold on the home and x^f on the foreign market, respectively. The cost functions of the domestic firms have the form

$$(1) \qquad TC = m.c\,(x^d+x^f) + g(m)$$

where m denotes the number of brands, c marginal cost and TC is total cost. The production of a constant number of brands incurs fixed cost g(m) and output of a single one of the m brands are produced with constant marginal cost, c. There are increasing returns to scale, since average cost declines as output of each brand is increased. Adding an additional brand (at the same level of existing brands) raises the operating cost by $c(x^d + x^f)$ and the fixed cost by g'(m). The shape of g(m) captures returns to scale associated with an expansion of brands.

The revenue, R, of the firm is given by the sum of the sales revenue per brand in the home and foreign markets multiplied by the number of brands

$$(2) \qquad R = m[p^d\,(1-t^d)\,x^d + p^f\,(1-t^f)\,x^f]$$

where p^d and p^f denote price in the domestic and foreign markets, and t^d and t^f denote tax rates. By equating marginal revenue to marginal cost, each firm chooses sales of each brand in home and foreign markets which gives the conditions

$$(3) \qquad \begin{aligned} p^d\,(1-t^d)(1-1/\epsilon)&=c \\ p^f\,(1-t^f)(1-1/\epsilon)&=c \end{aligned}$$

where the elasticity ϵ is derived from a demand function for a separate brand of differentiated product which depends on its own price and on the industry price index. ϵ gives the resulting change in demand if the price of a single brand is changed, holding the industry price index constant. There exists also an aggregate industry demand function which depends on an associated price index. The aggregate demand function is assumed to have a constant elasticity η which describes the resulting changes in demand when all firms change their prices in the same proportion. Equations (3) describe mark-up pricing of differentiated products where quantities sold are determined from demand functions for each separate brand. Market power is derived solely from product differentiation as firms are assumed not to have an influence on the industry aggregate price or quantity.

In their choice of number of brands firms follow the following profit maximizing condition

$$(4)\qquad \begin{aligned} &x^d\{p^d(1-t^d)-c\}\,[1+(dx^d/dm).m/x^d] + \\ &x^f\{p^f(1-t^f)-c\}\,[1+(dx^f/dm).m/x^f]=g'(m) \end{aligned}$$

which states that firms will introduce new brands up to the point where the perceived gains from one new brand are equal to the cost of introducing it. The first term of equation (4) gives the increment to revenue of adding a brand taking into account that sales of existing m brands will be reduced by this expansion. $(dx^d/dm)(m/x^d)$ captures the conjecture that the firm makes about the effect of adding an extra brand on the industry aggregate sales and price in the domestic economy and thus on sales per brand in the domestic economy. In this case the aggregate industry demand function is relevant to obtain marginal revenue. The second term on the left hand side gives the same effect on export revenue while the right hand side gives the extra cost of introducing a new brand. In their choice of number of brands firm's market power comes from their influence on industry aggregates, and not from product differentiation thereby allowing for oligopolistic interaction.

Under free entry and exit the number of domestic firms will adjust so that in industry equilibrium profits are driven down to zero.

$$(5)\qquad R = TC$$

Foreign firms set prices in the same way as domestic firms, while the number of foreign firms and brands is assumed to be fixed. The supply price of foreign output of each brand is therefore constant and sales are demand determined.

There are three types of industry adjustment in response to a disturbance. First, output per brand is allowed to adjust in response to a policy change with the number of brands and firms constant allowing for monopolistic competition with differentiated products in which firms make positive profits as described by Krugman (1979). Second, the number of brands each firm produces is allowed to change, taking oligopolistic interaction into account, similar to Brander (1981) and Dixit (1984). Third, the number of firms is allowed to adjust resulting in a market structure which is monopolistically competitive in the sense that firms make zero profits (see Helpman and Krugman (1985).

In the model described so far, trade policy in the form of an import tariff will have the following effect on productivity. The tariff reduces imports and causes an increase in domestic production. The increase in sales per brand of domestic firms means that activities which are operating at an inefficiently small scale have been expanded thus increasing average productivity.

If firms can change their product range then an additional source for productivity gains is available. The tariff makes the introduction of additional brands profitable which allows firms to realize economies of scale through the fixed cost function g(m). Thus in the case of a fixed number of firms with endogenous number of brands there are two sources of efficiency gains. One is the productivity gain due to the tariff induced expansion of output of existing brands increasing the rate of capacity utilization. The second is the productivity gain resulting from the expansion of new brands produced with decreasing fixed cost as captured by the g(m) function. Whether there will be a net productivity gain compared to the case of a fixed product range, however, will depend on the relative magnitude of scale economies obtained through the expansion of output of existing brands as compared to that obtained through replicating brands, since the sales of new brands will lead to some contraction of existing brands. As newly introduced brands are sold on export markets as well, the import tariff induces additional exports, which is similar to the mechanism described by Krugman (1984) on import protection as export promotion. Protection of the home market from foreign rivals helps domestic firms not only in the protected market but in export markets as well.

If entry is endogenous, the tariff induced higher profitability of the home market induces entry until profits are reduced to zero. The increased number of firms means that existing firms output contract thereby lowering average productivity. Hence, the productivity effect of the tariff will depend on whether there is free entry to the market or not.[2]

The effect of an export subsidy on productivity is similar to that of the tariff. The subsidy increases exports, domestic production and the number of brands leading to an increase in productivity due to longer production runs as well as lower cost in the production of new brands. This productivity accelerating effect of higher exports might, however, again be reversed if new firms are allowed to enter the market.

In a general equilibrium two-sector model taking sectoral interactions through factor markets into account Flam and Helpman (1987) get similar results regarding the allocative consequences of trade policy. One sector is assumed to produce homogeneous products with constant returns to scale, while the other sector produces differentiated products with increasing returns to scale. Increasing returns to scale result from the existence of fixed costs for product development. The cost function of firms in the sector with differentiated goods looks similar to equation (1) and firms in this sector use mark-up pricing over marginal costs similar to equation (3), while homogeneous products are priced by marginal cost. Firms in the differentiated sector engage in monopolistic competition under free entry so that profits are driven down to zero. In contrast to the Venables/Smith model, however, each firm produces only one variety so that the number of varieties equals the number of firms with no oligopolistic interation between firms.

Whether an export subsidy or an import tariff will increase productivity will depend on the following factors. The tariff shifts home demand from foreign to domestic differentiated products which allows domestic firms to sell larger quantities at the initial price, making in turn an increase in prices and an expansion of production profitable. The increased profitability of the home production increases the returns to product development thereby inducing entry into the industry. The newly entered firms producing additional varieties will, however, reduce the demand of the incumbent firms thereby forcing them to contract output. Whether output per firm and thus productivity rises or declines will depend on whether or not the tariff induced demand increase will be taken away by new entrants producing additional varieties. The tariff will increase productivity, if the homogenous and differentiated sector use common input factors which are substitutable so that output expansion of existing varieties takes place by drawing on resources of the homogeneous sector, while product development for new varieties requires highly specific resources not available in the homogeneous sector. In this case, potential new entrants are resource constrained while incumbent firms are not, bringing about larger output per firm and hence higher productivity.[3]

The influence of an export subsidy on productivity depends on exactly the same factors as that of the import tariff. The export subsidy increases foreign demand for home varieties that makes domestic firms willing to expand output. Induced entry and additional varieties on the other hand, forces firms to reduce output, the net effect on productivity depending on which of the opposing forces dominate.

Although numerical simulations on the effects of trade policy on a high-technology industry (see Baldwin and Krugman 1986) and on the US car market (Dixit 1985) find productivity accelerating effects in response to tariff protection, Cox and Harris (1985) adopting a general equilibrium model with imperfect competition and economies of scale for the Canadian economy come to quite different results. A unilateral removal of domestic tariffs (unweighted average of 11 per cent) leads, according to their estimates, to a rationalization of industries with a lengthening of production runs and thus to increases in labour productivity of 20 per cent. The reason for this opposite result - not the imposition but the removal of the tariff increases productivity - is based on different assumptions about price behavior. In the market for imports domestic producers take as a collusive strategy the price of imported goods as given, while in export markets firms are assumed to choose mark-up pricing over unit cost. Domestic pricing behavior is, therefore, some combination of mark-up pricing and collusive pricing in which import prices inclusive of the domestic tariff are taken as a reference point. Thus, the pricing strategy of domestic firms is sufficiently collusive that a domestic tariff cut induces firms to cut prices so that they will make losses. In order to remain profitable, firms will increase output to lower average costs. Furthermore, lower profitability will induce some firms to exit from the market leaving a larger output for remaining firms. Productivity increases as a result of larger aggregate output as well as larger output per firm.

Moreover, in the Cox and Harris model it is not import protection but import liberalization which acts as export promotion. Protection of the home market allows for too many firms operating at an inefficiently small size indicating unexploited economies of scale which can be exhausted by the removal of the tariff. Trade liberalization leads to substantial rationalization with larger output per firm resulting in significant decreases in average costs which translates in lower export prices and thus higher exports. The magnitude of the export promoting effect of trade liberalization will depend on the ratio of fixed costs to variable costs (indicating the size of unexploited economies of scale) and on the size of the elasticity of export demand (indicating the increase in foreign market shares due to lower export prices).[4]

To sum up, according to the models described above one would expect the following causal relationships between exports, productivity and the terms of trade. Exports are supposed to have a positive causal impact on productivity the smaller the country is and the less entry occurs. In small countries it is more likely that minimum efficient scale is large relative to the home market size, indicating that the export induced own production effect will be large relative to the export induced prevention of the rationalization effect to work due to increased number of firms. Higher import tariffs as measured by a deterioration in the term of trade may have a positive or a negative causal impact on productivity depending on whether the tariff increases/decreases aggregate output and the number of firms. Productivity is supposed to have a negative causal influence on the terms of trade if average cost pricing prevails and the productivity increase is not offset by a proportional wage increase. A deterioration in the terms of trade (as proxy for an increase in price competitiveness) has a positive causal impact on exports, as has productivity indicating economies of scope of firms producing more than one variety. Thus, the theories predict a feedback (mutual causality) between exports and productivity on the one hand and between the terms of trade and productivity on the other, with only a one-way direction in causality between exports and the terms of trade.

The analysis which follows is meant to be a statistical test of the causal relationships just described. The results indicate whether the data contradict or are compatible with the causal hypotheses implied by the models of this section. While empirical studies available assume a specific causal structure without testing it, the present paper performs a statistical test on the causal structure without claiming to test the theories.

2. TIME SERIES REPRESENTATION OF EXPORTS, PRODUCTIVITY, THE TERMS OF TRADE AND WORLD OUTPUT FOR USA, JAPAN, WEST GERMANY AND UK

2.1. Test Procedure

In order to investigate whether the data for the US, Japan, UK and Germany are consistent with the models described in the previous section, an unconstrained vector autoregressive model for exports, productivity, the terms of trade and world output is estimated treating all variables as endogeneous in a first stage. Then the formal causality tests are performed based on Granger's (1969) concept of causality.[5] According to Granger's definition of causality x is said to cause y if the forecast for y is improved (has a smaller mean square error) by using additionally the history of x than by using just the history of y alone. This means that the hypothesis that x causes y can be examined by estimating (using lag operator notation $L^p y_t = y_{t-p}$)

$$(2.1) \qquad y_t = (\sum_{i=1}^{p} \theta_i L^i) y_t + (\sum_{j=1}^{z} \psi_j L^j) x_t + v_t$$

and testing whether the $(\sum_{j=1}^{z} \psi_j L^j)$ are jointly significantly different from zero based on a F-test of the OLS regression. The test requires that the disturbance term v_t is close to being white noise which involves a careful choice of suitable values of p and z. The value of p is particularly important since the omission of relevant lagged values of y could inflate the coefficients of the lagged x's generating spurious causality. I have used the Bayesian information criterion (BIC) to estimate the order of the univariate autoregressive process which is given by

$$\log \sigma_{pq}^2 + (p+q) \frac{\log T}{T} \tag{2.2}$$

σ_{pq}^2 is the estimated variance of the innovations in the ARMA process of order (p,q) and T is the sample size. The procedure searches over different values of p and q within a specified range until the above criterion function is minimized. The idea behind this criterion is that higher order models get penalized by the second term of equation (2.2) which is supposed to compensate for the reduction in variance of the innovations always brought about by an increase in the order of the model.

The value of z for each of the variables included in the regressions was set to four in accordance with the quarterly data. The four-lags model assume the causal linkages to work in between a year, so that longer-run influences are not detected by the model.[6] Besides the correct treatment of the lag structure the procedure relies on the assumption that the time series exhibit stationary features. Before estimating the vector autoregressive model all data were transformed into fourth logarithmic differences in order to eliminate the trend and seasonality from the time series. The detrended and deseasonalized series seemed not to incorporate non-stationary elements, since their autocorrelation functions quickly dropped to zero.

2.2. Data

Definitions and sources of the variables are as follows:

X = exports of manufacturing goods at constant prices
source: International Financial Statistics

TOT = terms of trade, export unit values divided by import unit values for manufacturing goods in local currency
source: International Financial Statistics

PR = labour productivity, manufacturing output per employee
source: OECD Main Economic Indicators

Q = OECD Output at constant prices
source: OECD Main Econmic Indicators

2.3. Vector Autoregression and Causal Ordering

In Tables 1 to 1C the four variable vector autoregressions fitten by least squares over the sample period indicated are reported for Germany, Japan, the US and the UK using the BIC criterion to determine the order of the univariate autoregressive representation for each of the variables and including four lags for all the other regressors.The percent reduction in variance in the univariate autoregressive representation of the four countries for exports, productivity and the terms of trade (not reported here) did not exceed 70 per cent in most cases indicating that the inclusion of additional information on past realizations of other variables is likely to improve the forecasting performance. All series were detrended and seasonally adjusted by fourth logarithmic differences. Tables 2 to 2C contain the more formal causality tests for exports (X), productivity (PR), the terms of trade (TOT), and world output (Q) for the four countries.[7]

Germany

In the vector autoregressive representation for Germany in Table 1 it can be seen that German exports and productivity follow an AR 4 process, respectively and the terms of trade an AR 3 process as obtained by the BIC criterion.

The first column of Table 1 shows that there is no indication of effects of lagged productivity and some indication of effects of the lagged terms of trade and lagged world output on German exports. Only the coefficient of the first quarter lagged terms of trade and the coefficient of the first quarter lagged world output are significant at the 5 per cent level. This result is also supported by the F-test for the null hypothesis that the coefficients of the four lagged values of each of the variables are jointly equal to zero given in Table 2. The F-ratios and prob-values to test whether German exports are jointly Granger-caused by productivity, the terms of trade (as proxy for price competitiveness) and world output indicate that price competitiveness and world output cause exports while the causal effect of productivity on exports is a great deal short of statistical significance.

In the second column of Table 1, current productivity is significantly influenced by exports at one and four quarter lags, respectively. The overall impact of exports on productivity as obtained by the sum of the coefficients, appears to be slightly positive suggesting that the scale effect of higher exports has dominated possible losses in productivity due to increased number of firms.[8] The evidence that the terms of trade influences German productivity is weak as only the terms of trade at one quarter lag is statistically significant. As the signs of the estimated coefficients of the lagged terms of trade show, an imposition of an import tariff (or an exchange rate devaluation) as reflected in a deterioration in the terms of trade seems to favour productivity. It seems, therefore, that the tariff induced capacity and scale effect has - similar to the effect of higher exports - outweighed the possible effect of the tariff induced prevention of the rationalization effect to work. However, the causal impact of the terms of trade on productivity is only significant at the 20 per cent level as the marginal significance level given by the prob-value in Table 2 indicates. Lagged world output seems also to have a significant influence on current productivity as is given by the significance of the first and second quarter lags. The F-statistic for the test of causality in Table 2 suggest a strong causal link of exports and world ouput on productivity, while causality of the terms of trade on productivity is not significant at conventional levels.

TABLE 1 : Vector autoregressive representation of exports (X), productivity (PR), the terms of trade (TOT), and world output (Q), Germany

Regressors	Dependent variables (t-values in parenthesis) X	PR	TOT
X-1	.35	-.14	.04
	(3.0)	(2.28)	(.49)
X-2	.27	.06	-.07
	(2.0)	(.87)	(.75)
X-3	.19	-.08	.15
	(1.44)	(1.26)	(1.62)
X-4	-.32	.19	-.001
	(2.62)	(2.97)	(.09)
PR-1	-.001	.48	.09
	(.01)	(4.04)	(.56)
PR-2	.41	.16	-.14
	(1.57)	(1.21)	(.74)
PR-3	.07	.14	.12
	(.25)	(1.04)	(.64)
PR-4	.02	-.40	-.06
	(.08)	(3.48)	(.36)
TOT-1	-.54	-.21	1.13
	(3.41)	(2.52)	(9.97)
TOT-2	.14	.14	-.28
	(.64)	(1.22)	(1.72)
TOT-3	.27	.03	-.03
	(1.20)	(.30)	(.23)
TOT-4	-.16	-.02	
	(.92)	(.24)	
Q-1	1.19	.79	-.42
	(2.56)	(3.32)	(1.27)
Q-2	-.64	-.78	.68
	(.90)	(2.14)	(1.34)
Q-3	-.34	.35	-.21
	(.48)	(.98)	(.44)
Q-4	.35	-.15	-.12
	(.85)	(.71)	(.42)
R^2	.739	.727	.781
SE	.04050	.0201	.02886

Note: All regressions cover 1962.2-1987.2. The series were detrended and seasonally adjusted by fourth logarithmic differences. The number of lagged values of the dependent variable included in the regression equals that obtained by the BIC criterion. X and PR follow an AR4 and TOT follows an AR3 process, respectively.

TABLE 2 : Causality tests for exports, productivity, and the terms of trade, Germany

Test for Causality of	by	Test (1) Statistic	Prob (2) Value
X	PR	.97	43.02
	TOT	4.31	.32
	Q	2.62	4.08
PR	X	3.25	1.58
	TOT	1.72	15.35
	Q	3.09	2.02
TOT	PR	.22	92.6
	X	.91	46.13
	Q	.64	63.49

(1) The Causality Test Statistic is an F-ratio for the null hypothesis that the coefficients of four lagged values of each of the variables in the second column are jointly equal to zero.

(2) Probability of obtaining an F-ratio at least as large as the test statistic under the null hypothesis. A prob value smaller than 5 indicates rejection of the null hypothesis at the 5 per cent significance level.

The third column of Table 1 provides estimates of the coefficients of lagged export, productivity and world output in the regression for the terms of trade. Except for 'own' lags, none of the other lagged variables seem to have a significant influence on the terms of trade which is confirmed by the causality tests in Table 2. This means that the terms of trade can be considered to be a truly exogenous variable to the system. The reason for this might be that average cost pricing is not a dominant price behavior in German manufacturing and/or increases in labour productivity are offset by wage increases with no change in unit labour costs.

To sum up, the causal orderings of the time series suggest that the German data are compatible only with some of the features in the theoretical literature. Exports have a significant positive impact on productivity, while the evidence that the terms of trade causes productivity is weak. Furthermore, the test that productivity Granger-cause exports finds no statistical support (see also Fig. 1).

Table 1A : Vector autoregressive representation of exports, productivity, the terms of trade, and world output, Japan

Regressors	Dependent Variables (t-values in parenthesis)		
	X	PR	TOT
X-1	.99 (9.32)	-.08 (1.86)	-.03 (.33)
X-2	-.40 (3.72)	.007 (.12)	-.03 (.22)
X-3		.08 (1.22)	.02 (.17)
X-4		.002 (.04)	.009 (.10)
PR-1	-.60 (2.01)	1.18 (9.99)	-.09 (.34)
PR-2	1.03 (2.22)	-.23 (1.27)	-.13 (.31)
PR-3	-.62 (1.34)	-.22 (1.82)	.31 (.77)
PR-4	.34 (1.12)		-.22 (.85)
TOT-1	-.55 (4.04)	-.06 (1.09)	1.50 (12.88)
TOT-2	.47 (2.01)	.007 (.07)	-.74 (3.83)
TOT-3	-.21 (.88)	.08 (.77)	.03 (.21)
TOT-4	-.001 (.08)	-.03 (.46)	
Q-1	1.35 (2.74)	.57 (2.94)	-.06 (.15)
Q-2	-.88 (1.09)	-.66 (2.07)	.08 (.11)
Q-3	-.35 (.43)	.35 (1.16)	.31 (.45)
Q-4	.41 (.86)	-.08 (.43)	-.24 (.57)
R^2	.869	.910	.895
SE	.05382	.02098	.04594

Note : See Note of Table 1. X follows an AR2 and PR, TOT an AR3 process, respectively.

Japan

Table 1A gives the estimated vector autoregressive representation of exports, productivity, the terms of trade, and world output for Japan. Table 2A summarizes the causal relationships between the series. In the export equation two coefficients of lagged productivity and two coefficients of the lagged terms of trade as well as one coefficient of lagged world output are significant at the 5 percent level. The causality tests reported in Table 2A also provide strong evidence that productivity (at the 10 per cent significance level), price competitiveness, and world output cause Japanese exports. In the productivity equation lagged exports and lagged world output have significant coefficients which is again confirmed by the causality tests given in Table 2A. Japan's productivity is Granger-caused by exports, and world output, while the statistic for the test of causality from the terms of trade to productivity is not significant at conventional levels. In the terms of trade equation there are no significant coefficients except that for own lags with a similar result obtained by the causality tests.

TABLE 2A : Causality tests for exports, productivity, and the terms of trade, Japan

Test for Causality of	by	Test (1) Statistic	Prob (1) Value
X	PR	2.24	7.11
	TOT	5.76	0.04
	Q	2.50	4.85
PR	X	2.54	4.56
	TOT	.94	44.64
	Q	2.53	4.62
TOT	PR	.29	88.29
	X	.15	96.37
	Q	.19	94.17

(1) See Note of Table 2.

Summing up, the causal structure of the Japanese time series look very similar to that of Germany. The only exception is the feedback found between exports and productivity. Both variables seem to have reinforced each other which is in accordance with the

TABLE 1B : Vector autoregressive representation of exports, productivity, terms of trade, and world output, U.S.A.

Regressors	Dependent Variables (t-values in parentheses)		
	X	PR	TOT
X-1	.46	-.005	-.02
	(4.24)	(.26)	(.50)
X-2	.36	-.05	-.07
	(3.08)	(2.09)	(1.76)
X-3	.19	-.03	.01
	(1.63)	(1.55)	(.38)
X-4	-.42	.01	-.07
	(3.73)	(.60)	(1.91)
PR-1	.32	1.03	-.26
	(.45)	(7.98)	(1.15)
PR-2	-.02	-.29	-.02
	(.02)	(2.28)	(.07)
PR-3	-1.18		.35
	(1.24)		(1.20)
PR-4	.75		-.29
	(1.23)		(1.52)
TOT-1	-.41	-.15	1.25
	(1.19)	(2.20)	(14.63)
TOT-2	-.02	.09	-.69
	(.03)	(.95)	(7.50)
TOT-3	.46	.02	
	(.91)	(.19)	
TOT-4	-.72	-.08	
	(1.97)	(1.14)	
Q-1	1.07	-.008	-.10
	(1.52)	(.06)	(.46)
Q-2	-.83	-.05	.28
	(.73)	(.22)	(.78)
Q-3	.82	.03	-.28
	(.74)	(.15)	(.80)
Q-4	-.59	-.02	.07
	(.93)	(.21)	(.36)
R^2	.726	.836	.845
SE	.06793	.01313	.02187

Note : See Note of Table 1. X follows an AR4 and PR, TOT an AR2 process, respectively.

causal implications of the models discussed in section 1. Japan's export market growth has been backed by its productivity growth and its export market growth has contributed to its productivity performance. Japan's productivity seems, however, not to have been policy induced (in the form of import tariffs) as no causal impact from the terms of trade on productivity could be found.[9]

United States

Tables 1B and 2B give the results for the US. The dominant feature of the findings is that US exports are exogeneous to the system neither caused by productivity, price competitiveness nor by world output. Furthermore, the test reported in Table 2B indicates that the null hypothesis of no causality from exports to productivity is easily rejected. It is interesting to observe that the overall impact of exports on productivity appears to be negative suggesting that export induced entry of firms seems to have outweighted possible scale effects of higher exports. As minimum efficient scale is more likely to be small relative to the home market size in the United States this result seems not to be particularly surprising. In contrast to the other countries, the causality tests provide strong evidence that exports cause the terms of trade while as for Germany and Japan there is no evidence that the terms of trade causes productivity.

United Kingdom

In Tables 1C and 2C the estimates for the United Kingdom are provided. It appears from the Tables that the causal relationship between the British time series look quite similar to those of the United States (for a summary of the causal orderings for all four countries see Fig. 1). Causality from productivity and world output to exports is rejected while lagged price competitiveness significantly influences current exports. The most interesting result is obtained for the productivity equation. The test statistic for joint causality from exports, the terms of trade, and world output to productivity is highly singificant. As in the United States the overall impact of exports on productivity appears to be negative which is not a result a priori expected for

TABLE 2B : Causality tests for exports, productivity, and the terms of trade, U.S.A.

Test for Causality of	by	Test (1) Statistic	Prob (1) Value
X	PR	0.63	64.51
	TOT	1.34	26.16
	Q	1.37	25.09
PR	X	3.48	1.11
	TOT	1.48	21.44
	Q	.18	94.76
TOT	PR	.96	43.68
	X	4.59	.21
	Q	.22	92.68

(1) See Note of Table 2.

a small open economy.[10] Moreover, an inspection of the coefficient estimates of the lagged terms of trade on productivity in column 2 of Table 1C shows that a deterioration in the terms of trade (due to an imposition of an import tariff and/or exchange rate devaluations) seems to have accelerated productivity. This ambiguous result, that higher exports did not exhibit productivity encouraging effects, while lower imports due to higher import prices did favour productivity might be explained by structural differences between the export and import competing sector in Britain. Higher exports might have shifted resources to low productivity areas thereby compensating any export induced scale effect, a reallocation which did not take place in response to higher demand in the import competing sector.[11]

4. SUMMARY AND CONCLUSIONS

This paper has investigated the relationship between exports, productivity, the terms of trade and world output for the US, Japan, Germany and the UK on the basis of VAR models and Granger's concept of causality. The findings of the econometric analysis can

TABLE 1C : Vector autoregressive representation of exports, productivity, terms of trade, and world output, UK

Regressors	X	PR	TOT
	Dependent variables (t- values in parentheses)		
X-1	.32	-.11	.04
	(2.62)	(3.48)	(1.23)
X-2	.28	-.02	.02
	(2.08)	(.58)	(.56)
X-3	.19	-.002	-.07
	(1.41)	(.06)	(1.73
X-4	-.17	.03	.00
	(1.27)	(1.01)	(.00)
PR-1	-.20	.56	.04
	(.41)	(4.59)	(.34)
PR-2	.09	.20	-.37
	(.16)	(1.47)	(2.52)
PR-3	.23	.13	.17
	(.43)	(.95)	(1.11)
PR-4	-.30	-.29	-.01
	(.64)	(2.46)	(.06)
TOT-1	-.69	-.15	1.19
	(1.46)	(1.24)	(8.57)
TOT-2	-.18	.40	-.27
	(.22)	(1.95)	(1.17)
TOT-3	.55	-.49	-.15
	(.65)	(2.27)	(1.03)
TOT-4	-.36	.09	
	(.63)	(.64)	
Q-1	.50	.34	-.09
	(.66)	(1.75)	(.42)
Q-2	-.30	-.13	.12
	(.24)	(.38)	(.31)
Q-3	.12	-.22	-.002
	(.10)	(.70)	(.01)
Q-4	-.56	-.04	.02
	(.78)	(.22)	(.10)
R^2	.571	.781	.855
SE	.07242	.01841	.02123

Note : All regressions cover 1962.1-1983.2. X and PR follow an AR4 and TOT an AR3 process, respectively.

be summarized as follows. Exports are Granger-caused by productivity only in Japan (at the 10 per cent level), while in the other countries no causal link from productivity to exports has been found. This would not be particularly surprising if

TABLE 2C : Causality tests for exports, productivity, and the terms of trade, UK

Test for Causality of	by	Test (1) Statistic	Prob (1) Value
X	PR	0.13	96.99
	TOT	2.66	3.99
	Q	.91	46.61
PR	X	4.82	.17
	TOT	3.01	2.39
	Q	3.22	1.76
TOT	PR	2.17	8.15
	X	1.02	40.25
	Q	.20	93.77

(1) See Note of Table 2.

FIGURE 1 : Causal Ordering of Exports (X), Productivity (PR), the Terms of Trade (TOT) and World Output (Q)

GERMANY

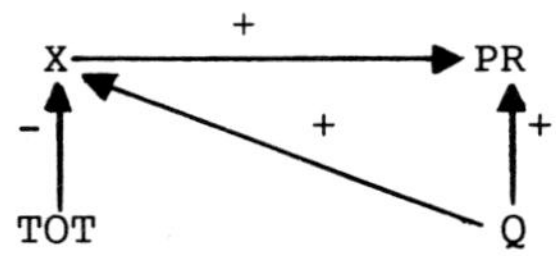

5 percent significance level

JAPAN

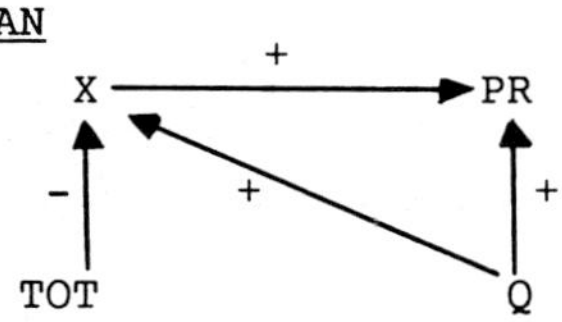

5 percent significance level

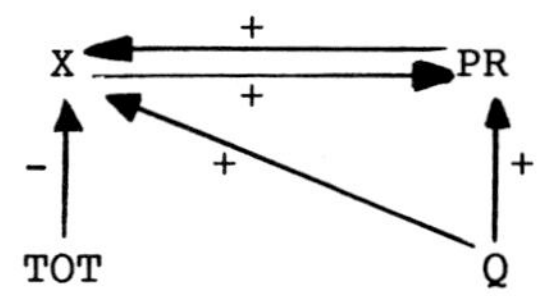

10 percent significance level

FIGURE 1 (cont.) : Causal Ordering of Exports (X), Productivity (PR), the Terms of Trade (TOT) and World Output (Q).

USA

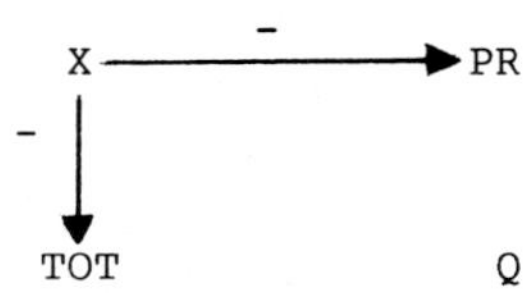

5 percent significance level

UK

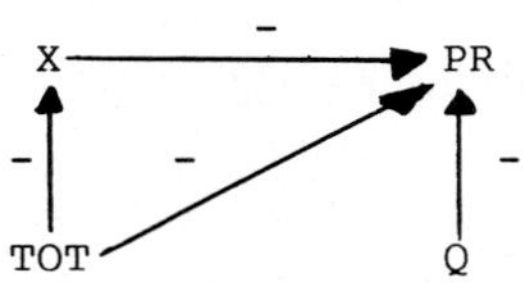

5 percent significance level

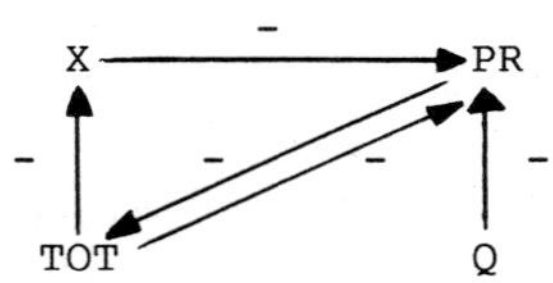

10 percent significance level

Note : An arrow running for example, from X to PR is used to denote that "X causes PR" where "+" or "-" indicates the sign of the causal link as obtained by the sum of the coefficients.

productivity changes were reflected in the terms of trade which, however, was only the case for the British data.

In all countries labour productivity has been Granger-caused by exports. While exports resulted in productivity gains in Germany and Japan, they led to a productivity decline in the US and the UK. Causality from the terms of trade to productivity - a link much stressed by the recent theoretical literature - has only been identified for the British data, while for the other countries causality from the terms of trade to productivity is not statistically significant at conventional levels. An inspection of the coefficient estimates indicates, however, that a deterioration of the terms of trade (due to a tariff increase and/or an exchange rate devaluation) favours productivity in all countries. The link is statistically least supported for Japan (Prob value:44.7) and strongest supported for Britain (Prob Value:2.4).

With the exception of the US, in all other countries - besides the causal link from world output via exports on productivity - a direct causal link from world output to productivity has been found. While in the UK increases in world output led to a productivity decline, in Japan and Germany world output resulted in productivity gains. Causality from world output to productivity might be an indication of internationally increasing returns to scale due to horizontal and vertical specialization in the presence of multinational corporations - productivity depending on the size of the international market rather than national output (see Ethier (1979)).

It seems, therefore, that the present causality analysis is only consistent with some aspects of recent trade theory. While the estimated causality from exports to productivity is in accordance with the causal hypotheses of the theories of intra-industry trade the estimated absence of any causal link from the terms of trade on productivity (with the exception of Britain), seems to suggest that disturbances caused by a devaluation of the exchange rate and/or by an import tariff do not seem to be capable of changing productivity as is implied by recent trade literature.

A comparison of the causal structure between the four countries reveals (see Fig. 1 for a summary) that Japan and Germany on the one hand and the US and the UK on the other share common causal features. Productivity in Japan and Germany has been supported by export as well as world market growth, while the unfavourable productivity performance in the US and the UK can also be attributed to exports and for the UK to world output[12]. As exports were Granger-caused by productivity only in Japan, the divergent development in export market shares in the other countries cannot be attributed to differences in productivity performance and thus is still open for further research.

NOTES

1 The potential impact of intersectoral interactions will be taken up in the empirical part.

2 Note, however, that the welfare implications are not symmetric to those of productivity. Welfare will be highest under free entry, if there is sufficient monopolistic distortion on the domestic market.

3 If, however, there exists a further sector producing differentiated goods with increasing returns to scale which uses input factors substitutable for product development in the other differentiated sector,then the tariff might lead to a productivity decline if scale economics are more important in the former than in the latter. See Dixit/Grossman (1984) for the consequences of intersectoral interactions.

4 For a similar result for the Austrian manufacturing sector in response to exchange rate changes see Marin (1985, 1986).

5 The term "causality" is somewhat misleading, since the criterion for the test is whether one variable "precedes" another one. For a critique on the notion see Leamer (1985).

6 In an other study, based on a subset model approach, however, longer-run causal linkages were not found, see Kunst/Marin (1988).

7 The correlation matrices of innovations measuring instantaneous causality are not reported and are available on request.

8 The summation of coefficients is, however, only an approximate way to determine the sign of the influence since the feedback loops running between the endogenous variables are ignored. See Kunst/Marin (1988).

9 This finding seems to contradict the Baldwin/Krugman (1986) result which suggests that import protection played a major role in Japan's success in 16K RAM in the domestic and foreign markets. As Baldwin/Krugman mention, however, major protection of the chips market did not take the form of tariffs and quotas but more hidden forms which are not reflected in terms of trade changes so that this form of protection is not captured by our analysis. Moreover, the Baldwin/Krugman result obtained for one very specific sector need not necessarily hold for manufacturing as a whole.

10 For the results for an other small open economy, see Kunst/Marin (1988).

11 See Stout (1977) supporting this explanation.

12 This does, of course, not imply that exports resulted in a welfare loss in the US and the UK, since the unfavourable effect on productivity might have been outweighted by the procompetitive effect of higher exports.

REFERENCES

AKAIKE, H. (1974), A New Look at Statistical Model Identification, IEEE Transactions on Automatic Control, AC-19, pp. 716-723.

BALDWIN, R. and P.R.KRUGMAN (1986), Market Access and International Competition: A Simulation Study of 16K Random Access Memories, National Bureau of Economic Research, Working Paper No. 1936.

BRANDER, J.A. (1981), "Intra-Industry Trade in Identical Commodities", Journal of International Economics, vol. 11, pp. 1-14.

BRANDER, J.A. and B.J. SPENCER (1985), "Export subsidies and International Market Share Rivalry", Journal of International Economics, vol. 18, pp. 83-100.

CAVES, R.E. (1981), Intra-Industry Trade and Market Structure in the Industrial Countries, Oxford Economic Papers 33, pp. 208-233.

CAVES, R.E., M. PORTER and A. SPENCE (1980), Competition in the Open Economy: A Model Applied to Canada, Cambridge.

COX, D. and R. HARRIS (1985), "Trade Liberalization and Industrial Organization: Some Estimates for Canada", Journal of Political Economy, vol. 93, pp. 115-45.

DEARDORFF, A.V. (1984), "Testing Trade Theories and Predicting Trade Flows" in R.W. Jones/P.B. Kenen, (eds.), Handbook of International Economics, Vol. 1, Amsterdam-New York-Oxford, pp. 467-517.

DIXIT, A.K. (1984), "Internatinal Trade Policy for Oligopolistic Industries", Economic Journal, vol. 94, pp. 1-16.

DIXIT, A.K. (1987), "Tariffs and Subsidies under Oligopoly: The Case of the US Automobile Industry" in Kierzkowski,H. (ed.), Protection and Competition in International Trade, Oxford 1987, pp. 112-127.

DIXIT, A.K. and G.M. GROSSMAN (1984), Targeted Export Promotion with Several Oligopolistic Industries, Discussion Paper in Economics No. 71, Woodrow Wilson School, Princeton University.

ETHIER, W. (1979), "Internationally Decreasing Costs and World Trade", Journal of International Economics, vol. 9, pp. 1-24.

FLAM, H. and E. HELPMAN (1987), "Industrial Policy Under Monopolistic Competition", Journal of International Economics, vol. 22, pp. 79-102.

GEROSKI, P. and A. JACQUEMIN (1985), "Industrial Change, Barriers to Mobility, and European Industrial Policy", Economic Policy, vol. 1, pp. 170-205.

GLEJSER, H., A. JACQUEMIN and J. PETIT (1980), "Exports in an Imperfect Competition Framework: An Analysis of 1446 Exporters", Quarterly Journal of Economics, vol. 94.

GEWEKE, J., R, MEESE and W. DENT (1983), "Comparing Alternative Tests of Causality in Temporal Systems - Analytic Results and Experimental Evidence", Journal of Econometrics, vol. 21, pp. 161-194.

GRANGER, C.W.J. (1969), "Investigating Causal Relations by Econometric Models and Cross-spectral Methods", Econometrica, vol. 37, pp. 424-438.

HELPMAN, E. and P. KRUGMAN (1985), Market Structure and Foreign Trade, Cambridge.

JACQUEMIN, A. (1982), Imperfect Market Structure and International Trade - Some Recent Research, Kyklos, vol. 35, pp. 75-93.

JACQUEMIN, A., E. DE GHELLINCK and C. HUVENEERS (1980), "Concentration and Profitability in a Small Open Economy", Journal of Industrial Economics, vol. 28.

KRUGMAN, P.R. (1979), "Increasing Returns, Monopolistic Competition and International Trade", Journal of International Economics, vol. 9, pp. 469-479.

KRUGMAN, P. (1984), "Import Protection as Export Promotion" in Kierzkowski, H. (ed.), Monopolistic Competition and International Trade, Oxford, pp. 180-193.

KUNST, R. and D. MARIN (1988), "On Exports and Productivity: A Causal Analysis", Review of Economics and Statistics, (forthcoming).

LEAMER, E. (1984), Sources of International Comparative Advantage: Theories and Evidence, Cambridge.

LEAMER, E. (1985), Vector Autoregressions for Causal Inference?, Carnegie Rochester Conference Series on Public Policy 22, pp. 255-304.

MARIN, D. (1985), Structural Change through Exchange Rate Policy, Weltwirtschaftliches Archiv 3, pp. 471-491.

MARIN, D. (1986), "Exchange Rate and Industrial Profits", Applied Economics, vol. 6, pp. 675-689.

PIERCE, D.A. and L.D. HAUGH (1977), "Causality in Temporal Systems", Journal of Econometrics, vol. 5, pp. 265-293.

SIMS, Ch.A. (1972), "Money, Income and Causality", American Economic Review, vol. 62, pp. 540-552.

STOUT, D. (1977), International Price Competitiveness, Non-Price Factors and Export Performance. National Economic Development Office, London.

VENABLES, A.J. and A. SMITH (1986), "Trade and Industrial Policy Under Imperfect Competition", Economic Policy, vol. 3, pp. 622-660.

YAMAWAKI, H. and D.B. AUDRETSCH (1987), Import Share under Internatinal Oligopoly with Differentiated Products: Japanese Imports in U.S. Manufacturing, Science Center Berlin.

II

MARKET STRUCTURE AND FOREIGN TRADE

The Convergence of International and Domestic Markets
D.B. Audretsch, L. Sleuwaegen, and H. Yamawaki (Editors)

3. THE INTERACTION BETWEEN DOMESTIC AND FOREIGN BASED ENTRANTS*

Paul A. Geroski
London Business School

0. INTRODUCTION

It is widely recognised that there exist many different types of entrant, and that some will succeed and prosper in circumstances where others will not. De novo entry, entry through acquisition by diversified firms, foreign based entry through imports, and so on are all the consequence of strategic choices made by firms who possess different skills and ambitions. These underlying differences in basic "competitive ability" make themselves felt in the speeds with which different types of entrants respond to the existence of excess profits, in the ease with which they surmount various barriers to entry, and in the challenge that they present to incumbents when they finally establish themselves in their host markets. It seems reasonable to think that if these differences are marked, then one may observe the presence of certain favoured types of entrant

* I am obliged to Saadet Toker for excellent research assistance, but wish to absolve her for any and all sins contained herein. John Cubbin and Richard Pomroy provided useful comments on a first draft; discussions with Charles Baden Fuller also proved helpful in clarifying some of the ideas presented here. Some of the data was obtained from a special tabulation made by the Business Statistics Office in Newport; this tabulation and the subsequent research using the data was financed by the ESRC and the Centre for Business Strategy at the LBS. I am grateful to numerous individuals in the BSO and the ESRC for their assistance in assembling the data, and to Jim Fairburn for integrating it with other data and mounting the whole thing on to the computer. Notwithstanding all these debts, the usual disclaimer applies.

"crowding out" other types of entrant less favoured in a particular market.

Consider, for example, the comparison between domestic based entry of all types and foreign entry through imports. The comparative advantages of these two broad types of entrant are well known, and need not be examined at length. Foreign entrants are, in general, not constrained by the need to achieve minimum efficient scale in small or restricted domestic markets. Domestic entrants, on the other hand, do not suffer from absolute cost disadvantages arising from tariff or non-tariff barriers to trade, and enjoy the advantages that familiarity and easy access to local, domestic markets convey. Clear as these different competitive advantages are, what is not clear is how strong they are on balance. In general, two types of possible outcome might emerge from the interaction between domestic and foreign entrants. On the one hand, it is possible to imagine that domestic entry might crowd out foreign entry whenever tariffs are high, or whenever knowledge of local circumstances is critical for success. Similarly, foreign entry might crowd out domestic based entry whenever scale economies are of importance, or whenever foreign firms have some comparative cost or demand advantage. On the other hand, it is also possible that one might observe the two types of entrant entering most markets hand in hand if these different types of competitive advantage are small, if they largely net out across the range of barriers present in each market, or if domestic and foreign based entrants compete in different segments of the same market.

These speculations suggest that it might be worth trying to determine the extent to which domestic and foreign entrants interact, and to ascertain whether one crowds the other out or not. The major problem to solve in conducting an exercise like this is the difficulty of accurately measuring the competitive ability of each type of entrant. For one type of entrant to crowd out another, it must be quicker to respond to profitable opportunities, and its response must foreclose entry possibilities for the other. What is relevant, then, is not so much the height of entry barriers considered as insurmountable obstacles, as the speed with which entrants can enter and compete in the market.[1]

However, in much the same way that "intelligence" is an unobservable which colours an individual's ability to progress through schooling and amass high earnings in good jobs, so the basic "competitive ability" of different firms to surmount difficulties thrown up by their environment is also unobservable. This observation does not, of course, preclude one from building a model to make inferences about unobservables, and that is what we shall try to do here. However, the observation does suggest that such exercises may often be hampered by a lack of information on variables of interest and, pursuant to this, we shall work with a very simple model which does not require us to measure latent variables like "competitive ability". The virtue of such a strategy is that one's inferences do not rely on possibly noisy and error ridden observations of a subset of the relevant variables of interest; the corresponding drawback is that ones inferences do depend on the structure of the underlying model that one imposes on the data. The model that we shall use is set out in Section 1 , the results from applying it to panel data on entry into 87 three digit UK industries, 1974-1979, are discussed in Section 2, and some final reflections appear in Section 3.

1. THE MODEL

The basic channel through which foreign and domestic entrants affect each other is via the effect that both have on post-entry profits. It is natural to suppose that entrants form expectations pre-entry about market outcomes likely to prevail after entry, and these can be expected to depend, inter alia, on the number and types of entrant that eventually materialise. If, say, domestic entrants suffer a competitive disadvantage vis-a-vis foreign entrants, then domestic entrants will find the possibility of entry by foreign based firms inhibiting, and one will observe the latter to crowd out the former. If neither type of entrant enjoys a competitive advantage relative to the other, then both will find the total volume of entry inhibiting, but neither will be particularly concerned with the composition of the total as between domestic and foreign firms. Finally, if the two types of entrant are basically non-competing, then neither will be concerned with total entry, or, more accurately, with that component of it associated with the other. Thus, to explore how domestic and foreign based entrants interact, one needs a model that describes the behaviour of each and the consequences that each type of entrant has on market outcomes, and thus on the other.

The basic theory of entry suggests that entrants, domestic and foreign, are likely to attempt entry whenever expected post-entry profits are positive. The profits they expect to enjoy depend on the same sorts of factors that the profits of incumbents do, factors such as market growth, post-entry market rivalry and so on. However, they also depend on the short run costs of adjustment that must be incurred in the initial years of operation in the market, costs which incumbents do not incur and may try to inflate through various types of strategic activity. Let the elements of expected post-entry profitability which are common to both types of entrant and to incumbents be denoted π_t, and suppose that the total expected profits of each type of entrant is equal to π_t plus some idiosyncratic factor, α_t, which may be less than zero and is specific to each type of entrant. For concreteness, one might imagine that π_t describes the expected post-entry price-cost margin of incumbents, and that each type of entrant will enjoy margins which differ from π_t by some amount α_t which depends on various types of absolute cost disadvantage suffered by the entrant. Under this interpretation, α_t is the sum of any differences in unit costs between entrant and incumbent incurred per unit of price (at least in homogeneous goods industries). We assume that the entrant forms expectations during the pre-entry period, t-1, about likely market outcomes in the post-entry period, t. It then sets in operation a market penetration plan which results in a market share, e_t, realised upon entry which, we assume, is proportional to expected profits,[2]

$$(1) \qquad e_t = \gamma\{\pi_t - \alpha_t\} .$$

Both the speed of response, γ, and the idiosyncratic component of profits, α_t, are taken to be entrant specific; γ is taken to be constant over time and across industries, while α_t is potentially both time and industry specific. This set of assumptions is not, in fact, very strong, since time or industry specific variations in the speed of response, γ, to a given π_t are difficult to distinguish from any disadvantages, α_t, suffered by entrants relative to incumbents. That is, barriers to entry may equally well be thought of as a reduction in profits relative to incumbents or as a slower response to some given level of profits however defined. Whenever it is necessary to do so, we shall distinguish domestic from foreign entrants using superscripts d and f respectively; industries are indexed by i (i=1,...,N) and time by t (t=1,...,T). Thus, our two entry equations are[3]

$$(2) \qquad \begin{aligned} e^d_{it} &= \gamma^d \{\pi^d_{it} - \alpha^d_{it}\} \\ e^f_{it} &= \gamma^f \{\pi^f_{it} - \alpha^f_{it}\} . \end{aligned}$$

The consequences of entry are assumed to be captured in movements in π_t, expected post-entry profits. We suppose that, in the absence of entry, profits at t would be μ_t. Entry, however, can be expected to reduce profits, and, indeed, one might suppose that entrants in any period t might have effects not only in t, but also in t+1, t+2, and so on. Thus, we assume that

$$(3) \qquad \pi_{it} = \mu_{it} - \beta(L)e^d_{it} - \psi(L)e^f_{it},$$

where $\beta(L)$ and $\psi(L)$ are polynomials in the distributed lag operator, L, and are assumed to be common over time and across industries. This assumption mirrors that made above regarding γ. Time and industry specific variations in the effect of current or recent entry are often difficult to distinguish from idiosyncratic shifts in profitability as captured by μ_{it}, and (3), like (1), makes no attempt to do so.

The three equation system, (2)-(3), captures the interaction between domestic and foreign entry identified at the beginning of this section. To see this interaction at work more clearly, consider the following simplification of (3),

$$(4) \qquad \pi_t = \mu_t - \beta_o e^d_t - \beta_1 e^d_{t-1} - \psi_o e^f_t - \psi_1 e^f_{t-1} ,$$

where we have suppressed the industry subscripts. At time t, e^d_{t-1} and e^f_{t-1} are fixed, μ_t is exogenous to the entry decision, but e^d_t and e^f_t are endogenous. Using (2) to eliminate these two endogenous variables, (4) becomes

$$(5) \qquad \pi_t = \mu_t - \beta_o\gamma^d\{\pi_t - \alpha^d_t\} - \beta_1 e^d_{t-1} - \psi_o\gamma^f\{\pi_t - \alpha^f_t\} - \psi_1 e^f_{t-1},$$

or, collecting terms,

$$(6) \qquad \pi_t = \Omega\{\mu_t + \beta_o\gamma^d\alpha^d_t + \psi_o\gamma^f\alpha^f_t - \beta_1 e^d_{t-1} - \psi_1 e^f_{t-1}\},$$

where $\Omega \equiv (1 + \beta_o\gamma^d + \psi_o\gamma^f)^{-1} > 0$. (6) shows that, for a given e^d_{t-1} and e^f_{t-1}, an increase in, say, α^f_t lowers the flow of foreign entry into the market, raising π_t ceteris paribus, and so raising the flow of domestic entry. Similarly, lowering γ^f raises π_t whenever $\pi_t > \alpha^f_t$, and lowers the flow of foreign entry relative to domestic entry; lowering ψ_o and ψ_1 have much the same effect.[4] All of these parametric changes describe an attrition in the competitive ability of foreign entrants: that is, a reduction in their unit cost advantages relative to incumbents (α^f_t), in their speed of response to profitable opportunities (γ^f), and in their impact on the market (ψ_o, ψ_1). Given the limited room available in the market for entry, these changes enable domestic entrants to crowd foreign entrants out to some extent. The consequence is likely to be a much enhanced flow of domestic relative to foreign entry, given the total volume of entry that the market can support.

As mentioned in the Introduction, the problem with using the model (2)-(3) in empirical work is that of measuring the competitive ability of entrants, of measuring the height of various barriers to entry that they face, their speed of response to profitable opportunities and their ability to foreclose entry possibilities for others. Inspection of (1) and (3) indicates that to do this, one must be able to observe α_t and μ_t without systematic error. Although this is not an impossible task, it is worth exploring how far one can go without the need for data on α_t and μ_t. Taking entry by domestic and foreign firms to be the only observables in the system means that it is impossible to get direct measures of γ^d, γ^f, the elements of $\beta(L)$ and the elements of $\psi(L)$. However, to assess the degree of crowding out of one type of entrant by the other, it is only necessary to observe the causes and consequences of entry in combination. As (6) makes plain, it is the joint effect of β_o, γ^d and α_t on π_t, and thence on e_t^f via γ^f, that matters in examining whether domestic entry inhibits foreign entry, and the joint effect of ψ_o, γ^f and α_t^f on domestic entry via γ^d that matters in looking at the degree to which foreign entrants inhibit domestic ones. As it happens, these joint effects can be estimated if domestic and foreign entry are the only observables available, and this makes it possible to proceed without any need to observe α_t and μ_t.

More formally, treating π_t as latent variable and eliminating it from (2) using (3), one finds that

$$(7)\qquad \begin{aligned} e_{it}^{d} &= \gamma^{d}\{\mu_{it} - \beta(L)e_{it}^{d} - \psi(L)e_{it}^{f} - \alpha_{it}^{d}\} \\ e_{it}^{f} &= \gamma^{f}\{\mu_{it} - \beta(L)e_{it}^{d} - \psi(L)e_{it}^{f} - \alpha_{it}^{f}\} . \end{aligned}$$

Letting the elements of $\beta(L)$ be β_o, β_1 and so on, and those of $\psi(L)$ be ψ_o, ψ_1 and so on, then each equation in (7) can be rearranged and the two can be simultaneously solved to yield a pair of equations in which e_{it}^d and e_{it}^f depend linearly on $x_{it}^d \equiv (\mu_{it} - \alpha_{it}^d)$, $x_{it}^f \equiv (\mu_{it} - \alpha_{it}^f)$, and on lagged values of e_{it}^d and e_{it}^f, say

$$(8)\qquad \begin{aligned} e_{it}^{d} &= \lambda_o x_{it}^{d} + \lambda_1 x_{it}^{f} + \lambda_2 e_{it-1}^{d} + \lambda_3 e_{it-1}^{f} + \ldots \\ e_{it}^{f} &= \eta_o x_{it}^{d} + \eta_1 x_{it}^{f} + \eta_2 e_{it-1}^{d} + \eta_3 e_{it-1}^{f} + \ldots . \end{aligned}$$

The unknown parameters in (8), the λ_j and η_j, $j\geq0$, are non-linear functions of those in (7) (ie, of γ^d, γ^f, the $\beta(L)$ and the $\psi(L)$), and contain all the information necessary to evaluate the effects of past entry of either type on current entry.[5]

To interpret (8), consider the following simple analogue to (2)-(3),

$$(9) \qquad e_t = \gamma\{\pi_t - \alpha\}$$

and

$$(10) \qquad \pi_t = \mu - \beta \sum_{k=1}^{\infty} e_{t-k}.$$

(9) simplifies (2) by focusing on one entrant with a constant disadvantage α relative to incumbents, while (10) assumes that entry has a permanent effect on profits which only materialises after a one period lag, and that, in the absence of entry, profits are constant at a level μ. The analogue of (8) can be obtained by substituting (10) into (9) to yield

$$(11) \qquad e_t = \lambda_o x + \lambda_1 \sum_{k=1}^{\infty} e_{t-k} ,$$

where $\lambda_o \equiv \gamma>0$, $\lambda_1 \equiv -\gamma\beta<0$ and $x \equiv \mu-\alpha$. Starting from an initial level of μ at time $t=0$, profits are eroded by entry over time until they reach a level given by α, at which point entry ceases. The volume of entry at any time t is proportional to the difference between π_t and α_t, and so is highest in period $t=0$ when $\pi_t = \mu$; ie $e_o = \gamma x = \gamma(\mu - \alpha)$. Thereafter, entry is positive, but is smaller and smaller in each period. The sense in which entry forecloses entry is the sense in which entry at t-1 removes the need for entry at time t, and this depends on how fast entry responds to profits in excess of α, and on how fast entrants bid profits away; ie on the combined effects of γ and β, as summarised by λ_1. (8) extends this model principally by allowing for two types of entrants, and, as a consequence, crowding out can be discussed by type of entrant. Thus, if the coefficient on e^d_{it-1} and higher lags in e^d_{it} exceed those on e^f_{it-1} and higher lags in e^f_{it} in <u>both</u> equations (8), then domestic entry has an impact on profits much larger than that associated with foreign entry, and thus crowds the latter out. Conversely, if the effect of e^f_{it-1}, e^f_{it-2}, and so on exceeds that of e^d_{it-1}, e^d_{it-2}, and so on in <u>both</u> equations (8), then the impact of foreign entry is so strong as to crowd out domestic entry. That is, domestic entry crowds out foreign entry if $\lambda_2 > \lambda_3$ <u>and</u> $\eta_2 > \eta_3$ and similarly for higher order lags, while foreign entry crowds out domestic entry if $\lambda_3 > \lambda_2$ <u>and</u> $\eta_3 > \eta_2$, and similarly for higher order lags.[6]

The two alternatives in which domestic entry crowds out foreign entry or in which foreign entry crowds out domestic entry do not exhaust all the possible types of interaction between domestic and foreign entrants. Two further possibilities remain. First, it is possible that the effects of e^d_{it-1}, e^d_{it-2} and so on are the same as those of e^f_{it-1}, e^f_{it-2} and so on in <u>each</u> equation. That is, past values of e^d_{it} and e^f_{it} may have an identical effect on current values of e^d_{it}, and both may have an identical effect on e^f_{it} (which, however, may not be the same as their common effect on e^d_{it}). This case corresponds to a situation in which the product of the speed of response and the size of effect on profits are broadly similar between types of entrant, and, therefore, to a state of affairs in which neither crowds the other out. Thus, while the total volume of entry crowds both types of entrant out, its composition between types does not affect either type of entrant, a situation is reflected in the parameter restrictions: $\lambda_2 = \lambda_3$ <u>and</u> $\eta_2 = \eta_3$ and similarly for the higher order lags in (8). If, in addition, $\lambda_2 = \lambda_3 = \lambda_2 = \lambda_3$ and similarly for the higher order lags, then the implication is that the two types of entrant are virtually identical.

The second possible form of interaction between the two types of entrant arises if the effect of e^d_{it-1}, e^d_{it-2}, etc on e^d_{it} dominates that of e^f_{it-1}, e^f_{it-2}, etc on e^d_{it}, <u>but</u> the effect of e^f_{it-1}, e^f_{it-2}, etc on e^f_{it} dominates that of e^d_{it-1}, e^d_{it-2}, etc on e^f_{it}; that is, if $\lambda_2 > \lambda_3$ <u>but</u> $\eta_3 > \eta_2$ and similarly for higher order lags. If $\lambda_3 = \eta_2 = 0$, the situation corresponds to one where domestic and foreign entrants are not competing at all in the same market, and hence where entry by one does not preclude entry by the other. If λ_3 and η_3 are non-zero, but if $\lambda_2 > \lambda_3$ and $\eta_3 > \eta_2$, the situation is one in which there is room for both of the two types of entrant in the market, either because the presence of one enhances opportunities for the other, or because the two enter relatively distinct, non-competing market segments. In this case, the expected profits, π^d_t, which attract domestic entrants are relatively unaffected by current and lagged foreign entry, while the expected profits, π^f_{it}, which attract foreign entrants are relatively unaffected by domestic entry; ie to the two equations (2), there correspond two versions of (3), one for each entrant.

To summarise, using the system (8), four possible parameter configurations exist which correspond to four possible interactions between domestic and foreign entry:

(i) domestic entry crowds foreign entry: $\lambda_2 > \lambda_3$ and $\eta_2 > \eta_3$, and similarly for higher order lags;

(ii) foreign entry crowds out domestic entry: $\lambda_3 > \lambda_2$ and $\eta_3 > \eta_2$, and similarly for higher order lags;

(iii) domestic and foreign entry are neutral vis-a-vis each other: $\lambda_2 = \lambda_3$ and $\eta_2 = \eta_3$, and similarly for higher order lags;

(iv) domestic and foreign entry are non-competing: $\lambda_2 > \lambda_3$ but $\eta_3 > \eta_2$.

These are the hypotheses that we propose to test.

2. RESULTS

We shall explore the hypotheses just discussed using data for 87 three digit UK industries, 1974-79. Foreign entry is defined as the annual change in import share, and this means that the corresponding domestic entry variable must be net entry penetration; ie the gross market share penetration of all new firms (calculated by comparing adjacent Censuses) less the market share attributable to those firms who exited during the same period (also calculated by comparing adjacent Censuses). Market share is defined relative to a market size calculated by adding domestic production to imports and then subtracting exports; ie market size is measured by domestic sales.

Table 1 provides some descriptive statistics on entry by both types of entrant over the period 1974-1979. On the whole, these six years were characterised by positive net foreign entry (on average, an increase in share per year of about 1%) and negative net domestic entry (on average, a loss of share of about ½% per year), leaving a total net entry flow of about ½% per year on average. This extremely modest net entry penetration seems to have occurred largely at the expense of firms outside the top five, since the share of the total market accounted for by the domestic production of the leading five firms rose in every year save 1975 and 1977, and, on average, rose by about ½% per year over the period. What the calculated means in the first column of Table 1 hide is an extraordinary variation across industries in their entry experience, particularly with respect to foreign entry. Those industries most subject to foreign entry might find a net market share penetration by foreign entrants on the order of

TABLE 1 : Descriptive Statistics Relating to Entry Penetration into 87.

Three Digit UK industries, 1974-79

Foreign entry

	mean	standard deviation	minimum	maximum
1979	.0151	.0520	-.0918	.3479
1978	.0087	.0458	-.1706	.2338
1977	.0090	.0321	-.0875	.1564
1976	.0150	.0446	-.1619	.1711
1975	-.0012	.0501	-.1333	.1914
1974	.0144	.0397	-.1223	.1520

Domestic Entry

	mean	standard deviation	minimum	maximum
1979	-.0053	.0211	-.0765	.0520
1978	-.0098	.0284	-.1295	.0889
1977	-.0120	.0248	-.0959	.0472
1976	.0022	.0208	-.0764	.0588
1975	-.0108	.0488	-.4219	.0478
1974	.0103	.0431	-.2409	.1008

15-20%, and, in exceptional periods, as high as 35%. At the same time, other industries might find foreign firms losing market share, perhaps by as much as 10-12%, and, in exceptional times, by as much as 16 or 17%. Domestic net entry, while also highly variable across industries, is nowhere near as variable as this. Maximum gains and losses after 1975 are of the order of 5-10%, while losses before 1975 were, for some reason, enormously large in one or two industries.

A broad glance at Table 1 suggests that there may be evidence in the data consistent with the view that foreign entry crowded domestic entry out during the period. To explore this apparent insight in more depth, we turn to the model developed in Section 1, and, in particular, to equation (8) and the four associated stylized patterns of interaction between domestic and foreign firms. To estimate equation (8), two decisions need to be made. These concern measuring x^d_{it} and x^f_{it}, and determining the length and perhaps the shape of the lag distribution in e^f_{it} and e^d_{it} to be used in both equations. Let us consider each in turn.

Recall that $x^d_{it} \equiv (\mu_{it} - \alpha^d_{it})$ and $x^f_{it} \equiv (\mu_{it} - \alpha^f_{it})$, the difference between the profitability of market i at t absent entry and the size of the entry barriers facing domestic/foreign entrants into i at t. At a long run equilibrium, profits will be determined by the height of entry barriers plus or minus some purely transitory effect. Thus, if the data are at or near a long run equilibrium, then it is likely that x^d_{it} and x^f_{it} can be modelled as a zero mean random variable whose variations reflect unsystematic and therefore unpredictable variations in market outcomes around equilibrium. A slightly more general specification might also allow some permanent, industry specific effects to be present. Both of these maintained hypotheses are captured by modelling x^d_{it} and x^f_{it} in terms of industry specific fixed effects, $\bar{x}^d_i$ and $\bar{x}^f_i$, and purely stochastic effects, v^d_{it} and v^f_{it}, assumed to have zero means and variances independent of i and t

$$x^d_{it} = \bar{x}^d_i + v^d_{it}$$

(12)

$$x^f_{it} = \bar{x}^f_i + v^f_{it} .$$

The second specification decision to be made concerns the lag distributions that appear in (8). Here two questions arise: What ought to be the shape of those distributions?, and How much information on the history of past entry is needed to measure it accurately? Although there seems to be little reason to suspect any particular lag distribution to emerge from the data, there are two shapes that the distribution might take which are of interest to explore. If entry has a purely temporary effect on market performance, then past entry will have no effect on current performance and thus on current entry, while if entry has a permanent effect on market performance, then past entry will have the same effect on current performance and thus on current entry whatever its vintage. When entry has a temporary effect, then, in (8), $\lambda_2 = \lambda_3 = \ldots = 0$ and, in (9), $\eta_2 = \eta_3 = \ldots = 0$, and no crowding out of any kind occurs. When entry has a permanent effect, then the co-efficient on e^d_{it-1} equals that on e^d_{it-2}, on e^d_{it-3}, and so on, while that on e^f_{it-1} equals that on e^f_{it-2}, on e^f_{it-3} and so on in both equations (8). The appropriate estimation strategy would appear to be to estimate an unconstrained set of lag co-efficients in the first instance, and then to check whether either of these two patterns emerge clearly. Since we are using annual data, we have allowed for three years lags in each equation.[7]

These two decisions convert (8) into

$$e^d_{it} = \lambda_i + \lambda_2 e^d_{it-1} + \lambda_3 e^f_{it-1} + \lambda_4 e^d_{it-2} + \lambda_5 e^f_{it-2} + \lambda_6 e^d_{it-3} + \lambda_7 e^f_{it-3} + \xi^d_{it}$$

(13)

$$e^f_{it} = \eta_i + \eta_2 e^f_{it-1} + \eta_3 e^d_{it-1} + \eta_4 e^f_{it-2} + \eta_5 e^d_{it-2} + \eta_6 e^f_{it-3} + \eta_7 e^d_{it-3} + \xi^f_{it}$$

where the N values of λ_i and of η_i are parameters to be estimated, and measure the fixed components of x^d_{it} and x^f_{it} ; ξ^d_{it} and ξ^f_{it} are purely stochastic terms which depend on v^d_{it} and v^f_t . Since both of the latter enter both equations (8), then ξ^d_{it} and ξ^f_{it} can be expected to be correlated and jointly estimating both equations (13) may improve efficiency. To estimate the λ_i and η_i one needs to be able to observe individual industries over time, and we have pooled the data into three cross-section panels which, taking account of the three year lags, exhaust the six panels available to us. There are, therefore, 261 observations on e^d_{it} to use to estimate the 85 λ_i plus λ_2-λ_7 and the variance of ξ^d_{it}, and similarly for e^f_{it}. The estimates of the e^d_{it} equation are shown on Table 2, while those for e^f_{it} are shown on Table 3.

It is simplest to start by recording the outcomes of several tests of restrictions on the coefficients of the various lagged values of e^d_{it} and e^f_{it}. Equation (i) on Table 2 is the most general model considered, (ii) is a simplification of (i) in which the constraints $\lambda_2 = \lambda_3$, $\lambda_4 = \lambda_5$, and $\lambda_6 = \lambda_7$ have been imposed, and (iii) is a simplification of (i) in which the constraints $\lambda_3 = \lambda_5 = \lambda_7 = 0$ have been imposed. Using a Likelihood Ratio test, the calculated $\chi^2(3) = 45.79$ for the simplification $\lambda_2 = \lambda_3, \lambda_4 = \lambda_5$, and $\lambda_6 = \lambda_7$, roughly four times larger than the 1% critical level; for the simplification $\lambda_3 = \lambda_5 = \lambda_7 = 0$, the calculated $\chi^2(3) = 4.114$, which is roughly half the size of the 5% critical level. Thus, (iii) is an acceptable simplification of (i) but (ii) is not. It is also not acceptable to simplify (i) either by setting the $\lambda_i = \bar{\lambda}$ (ie suppressing the fixed effects), or by setting $\lambda_2 = \lambda_3 = \ldots = \lambda_7 = 0$ (ie eliminating all the lagged entry terms). Very much the same set of observations applies to Table 3. The calculated $\chi^2(3) = 47.156$ for the simplification $\eta_2 = \eta_3$, $\eta_4 = \eta_5$ and $\eta_6 = \eta_7$ which converts (i) into (ii), and this statistic is roughly six times its 1% critical level. The simplification that transforms (i) to (iii) on Table 3, $\eta_3 = \eta_5 = \eta_7 = 0$, produces a calculated $\chi^2(3) = 4.336$, just over half the size of the 5% critical level. Again, the simplification to (iii) is data acceptable while that to (ii) is not, nor is that which sets $\eta_i = \bar{\eta}$ or that which sets $\eta_2 = \eta_3 = \ldots = \eta_7 = 0$. Surprisingly, estimating equations (i), (ii) and (iii) on Tables 2 and 3 jointly (to take account of the possible co-variance between ξ^d_{it} and ξ^f_{it}) had almost no effect on the estimates, and none whatsoever on these tests.

These results carry a straightforward if slightly surprising interpretation. What appears to stand out clearly from Tables 2 and 3 is that entry by either domestic or foreign firms does not have a merely transitory effect on market outcomes. Indeed, the effect appears to last at least three years with only a slight

TABLE 2 : Estimates of (13) for Domestic Entrants

	(i)	(ii)	(iii)
e^d_{it-1}	-.4153 (5.22)		-.4183 (5.23)
		-.1566 (3.89)	
e^f_{it-1}	-.0264 (.748)		- -
e^d_{it-2}	-.3074 (5.11)		-.2961 (4.83)
		-.1691 (5.71)	
e^f_{it-2}	-.0382 (.947)		- -
e^d_{it-3}	-.1516 (4.33)		-.1399 (4.23)
		-.0635 (2.82)	
e^f_{it-3}	.0311 (1.21)		- -
L.l'hood	684.418	661.523	682.361
$\bar{R}^2$	.234	.104	.234
SSR	.08063	.09609	.08191

The dependent variable is net domestic entry, e^d_{it}, and all equations include a full set of fixed effects; t-statistics in absolute value are given in brackets below the estimated coefficients. The data were not transformed to eliminate fixed effects.

TABLE 3 : Estimates of (13) for Foreign Entrants

	(i)	(ii)	(iii)
e^{f}_{it-1}	-.6580 (4.88)		-.6732 (5.06)
		-.4130 (3.80)	
e^{d}_{it-1}	.1024 (.960)		- -
e^{f}_{it-2}	-.3215 (2.73)		-.2978 (2.43)
		-.1054 (1.17)	
e^{d}_{it-2}	.0969 (1.16)		- -
e^{f}_{it-3}	-.3145 (2.63)		-.3036 (2.53)
		-.1787 (2.14)	
e^{d}_{it-3}	-.0585 (.794)		- -
L.l'hood	533.562	509.984	531.394
$\bar{R}^2$	.214	.074	.214
SSR	.2561	.3069	.2605

The dependent variable is net foreign entry, e^{f}_{it}, and all equations include a full set of fixed effects; t-statistics in absolute value are given in brackets below the estimated coefficients. The data were not transformed to eliminate fixed effects.

diminution over time, and one hazards the guess that it is more or less permanent. The estimates of the distributed lag coefficients are, of course, conditional on the ξ^d_{it} and ξ^f_{it} being serially uncorrelated, and so should be treated with some caution in view of the crude modelling of x^d_{it} and x^f_{it}.[8] However , extending (12) to allow for time varying effects (by introducing year specific dummies) had little effect on the results, and inspecting the residuals across industries i over t suggested no obvious systematic pattern in ξ^d_{it} or ξ^f_{it} . Thus, while one must be cautious, it nevertheless seems difficult to avoid the conclusion that there exists a noticeable degree of crowding out of later entrants by early entrants. Any change in market circumstances which makes space for new entry only does so for only a finite flow, and, if early entrants have a permanent effect on market performance, then their arrival preempts later entrants. The results presented in Tables 2 and 3 show clear evidence that such preemption lasts for at least three years, and probably for rather longer.

That early entrants crowd out later entrants is only part of the story. The question that we wish to address is whether one type of entrant crowds out the other by arriving faster and having a larger impact on market performance. The tests simplifying regressions (i) to (iii) but not to (ii) described above point to a very clear pattern of interaction between domestic and foreign firms. Inspection of (i) on Table 2 indicates that domestic entry lagged has an important negative effect on current domestic entry, a result consistent with expectations developed in Section 1. Foreign entry lagged, however, appears to play only a quantitatively small role, and one which is barely significant. Inspection of (i) on Table 3 shows the same pattern. Foreign entry lagged has a large negative effect on current foreign entry, but domestic entry seems to have very little effect at all. Both sets of conclusions are reinforced by the failure to simplify (i) to (ii) on Tables 2 and 3 : in both cases, this means that one cannot reasonably argue that it is only total entry and not it's composition which matters. That one can simplify (i) to (iii) on both tables means that only previous domestic entry affects current domestic entry and only previous foreign entry affects current foreign entry. In fact, Tables 2 and 3 suggest that the extent to which early foreign entry preempts later foreign entry exceeds the extent to which early domestic entry preempts later domestic entry, and there is some evidence that the foreign entry series oscillates about its long run equilibrium.[9] However, one way or the other, crowding out requires that either domestic or foreign entry matters in <u>both</u> equations, and this we clearly do not observe. It follows that the only one of the four alternative interactions between domestic and foreign entry listed at the end of Section 1 which seems to be consistent with the data is the last, namely that "<u>domestic and foreign entry are non-competing</u>".[10]

3. CONCLUSIONS

It has been widely recognised that there are many different types of entrant, and it seems more than reasonable to believe that they will differ in their underlying competitive abilities. The further possible implication of this, namely that one type of entrant might crowd out other types, has been the subject of this paper. In particular, we have used a very simple reduced form dynamic model which explains entry by domestic and by foreign firms into various three digit UK industries in the 1970s in terms of the recent history of entry into each industry by both types of entry. For both domestic and foreign based entry, evidence of crowding out exists in the sense that previous domestic entry preempts current domestic entry and previous foreign entry preempts current foreign entry. However, there is no tangible evidence to suggest that foreign entry crowds out domestic entry, or that domestic entry crowds out foreign entry.

The obvious inference to draw is that the two types of entrant are non-competing. This conclusion must, of course, be tempered both by reservations arising from the use of a simple reduced form model and by worries about model specification. However, it is not inconsistent with what is known much more widely about the effects of entry, and it is possible to identify two types of phenomena which may account for it. First, it is often accepted as a truism in business strategy discussions that foreign entrants tend to occupy the low price, highly standardised mass market, while domestic firms occupy more up market, custom niches. The Knitwear and Cutlery industries in the UK broadly conform to this pattern, and point to an evolutionary process in which foreign firms chase domestic firms up the quality ladder in markets. This segmentation of the market and allocation of different types of firm to different parts of it is likely to result in an outcome where different types of firms form non-competing groups even where domestic UK firms occupy the "low ground" and foreign entrants the "high" ground (eg Kitchen Manufacturers). Second, the two types of firm may form non-competing groups even in markets for homogeneous goods. For example, one might hazard the supposition that domestic entrants, being rather small firms by and large, have effects only on local markets, effects which do not spread widely in the national markets our data describe. By contrast, it is often the case that imports are controlled by large firms, and have no real competitive effects on markets in the large or the small. The combination of local (and perhaps very small) effects on the one hand and no systematic competitive effects on the other may produce a pattern of interaction similar to that which we have observed.

Thus, whether it is due to segmentation of markets by quality, local effects or to the control over imports exercised by large firms, the bottom line appears to be one which raises the possibility that foreign and domestic firms are largely non-competing in many markets. The implications that a conclusion like this has for future research are as clear as the need for corroborating evidence is compelling.

APPENDIX I: The Reduced Form of (2) and (4)

Equation (2) is

$$(14)\qquad \begin{aligned} e_t^d &= \gamma^d\{\pi_t - \alpha_t^d\} \\ e_t^f &= \gamma^f\{\pi_t - \alpha_t^f\}\ , \end{aligned}$$

while (4) is

$$(15)\qquad \pi_t = \mu_t - \beta_o e_t^d - \beta_1 e_{t-1}^d - \psi_o e_t^f - \psi_1 e_{t-1}^f .$$

Substituting (15) into (14) yields (6) in the text; ie

$$(17)\qquad \pi_t = \Omega\{\mu_t + \beta_o \gamma^d \alpha_t^d + \psi_o \gamma^f \alpha_t^f - \beta_1 e_{t-1}^d - \psi_1 e_{t-1}^f\},$$

where $\Omega \equiv (1 + \beta_o\gamma^d + \psi_o\gamma^f)^{-1} > 0$. Substituting (17) into (14) yields

$$(18)\qquad \begin{aligned} e_t^d &= \gamma^d\{\Omega[\mu_t + \beta_o \gamma^d \alpha_t^d + \psi_o \gamma^f \alpha_t^f - \beta_1 e_{t-1}^d \\ &\qquad - \psi_1 e_{t-1}^f] - \alpha_t^d\}\ , \\ e_t^f &= \gamma^f\{\Omega[\mu_t + \beta_o \gamma^d \alpha_t^d + \psi_o \gamma^f \alpha_t^f - \beta_1 e_{t-1}^d \\ &\qquad - \psi_1 e_{t-1}^f] - \alpha_t^f\}\ . \end{aligned}$$

It follows that

$$(19)\qquad \frac{\partial e_t^d}{\partial \alpha_t^f} = \gamma^d \ \Omega \ \frac{\partial \pi^t}{\partial \alpha_t^f} > 0$$

and

$$(20) \qquad \frac{\partial e_t^f}{\partial \alpha_t^f} = \gamma^f \Omega \left(\frac{\partial \pi_t}{\partial \alpha_t^f} - 1 \right) = \gamma^f \Omega \, (\psi_o \gamma^f - 1) < 0$$

if $\psi_o \gamma^f < 1$, as would be required to insure that the entry-profitability feedback system was stable. Similarly,

$$(21) \qquad \frac{\partial e_t^d}{\partial \gamma^f} = \gamma^d \left[\frac{\partial \Omega}{\partial \gamma^f} (\pi_t - \alpha_t^d) + \Omega \, (\psi_o \alpha_t^f) \right]$$

and

$$(22) \qquad \frac{\partial e_t^f}{\partial \gamma^f} = \Omega \, (\pi_t - \alpha_t^f) + \gamma^f \left[\frac{\partial \Omega}{\partial \gamma^f} (\pi_t - \alpha_t^f) + \Omega \, (\psi_o \alpha_t^f) \right]$$

which almost certainly exceeds $\partial e_t^d / \partial \gamma^f$ if $\pi_t > \alpha_t^f$, thus lowering (raising) e_t^d by more (less) than e_t^f .

APPENDIX II: The Relationship Between the Parameters of (7) and (8)

Writing (7) out in full and assuming the existence of only one lag,

$$(23) \qquad \begin{aligned} e_t^d &= \gamma^d (x_t^d - \beta_o e_t^d - \beta_1 e_{t-1}^d - \psi_o e_t^f - \psi_1 e_{t-1}^f) \\ e_t^f &= \gamma^f (x_t^f - \beta_o e_t^d - \beta_1 e_{t-1}^d - \psi_o e_t^f - \psi_1 e_{t-1}^f) \,. \end{aligned}$$

For simplicity, focus only on the reduced form equation for e_t^d . Putting (23b) into (23a) and solving for e_t^d yields

$$(24) \qquad \begin{aligned} e_t^d = \; & \Gamma[(1 + \gamma^d \beta_o)\{\gamma^d (x_t^d - \beta_1 e_{t-1}^d - \psi_1 e_{t-1}^f\} \\ & - (\gamma_o \psi_o)\{\gamma^f (x_t^f - \beta_1 e_{t-1}^d - \psi_1 e_{t-1}^f\}] \,, \end{aligned}$$

where $\Gamma \equiv (1 + \gamma^d \beta_o)(1 + \psi_o \gamma^f)$. Thus, the parameters of (8a) in the text are:

$$\lambda_o \equiv \Gamma(1 + \gamma^d \beta_o)\gamma^d , \tag{25}$$

$$\lambda_1 \equiv - \Gamma(\psi_o \gamma^d)\gamma^f , \tag{26}$$

$$\lambda_2 \equiv - \Gamma[(1 + \gamma^d \beta_o)\beta_1 + (\gamma^d \psi_o)\beta_1] , \tag{27}$$

$$\lambda_3 \equiv - \Gamma[(1 + \gamma^d \beta_o)\psi_1 + (\gamma^d \psi_o)\psi_1] . \tag{28}$$

Similar calculations apply to η_o, ..., η_3, as well as to higher order lags in both equations.

NOTES

1 Previous empirical work on the relative competitive abilities of different types of entrant have largely focused on identifying the different types of entry barriers that different entrants face; see, for example, Gorecki (1975), (1976).

2 The formal basis of this model is discussed in Fairburn and Geroski (1988); considered as a regression, it is very similar to that popularized by Orr (1974), Masson and Shaanan (1982) and others. For a survey of the results obtained using this type of model, see Geroski and Masson (1987).

3 Equations (2) implicitly assume that e^d_{it} and e^f_{it} interact only through the effect that each has on the other via π_t. One could imagine a second channel conveying a more direct effect by rewriting (2) as,

$$(2') \quad \begin{aligned} e^d_{it} &= \gamma^d \{\pi_{it} - \alpha^d_{it}\} + \theta^{df} e_{it}, \\ e^f_{it} &= \gamma^f \{\pi_{it} - \alpha^f_{it}\} + \theta^{fd} e_{it}. \end{aligned}$$

The system (2)-(3) has the same reduced form as (2')-(3) and so is observationally equivalent from our point of view. For expositional simplicity in what follows, we shall work with (2)-(3) rather than (2')-(3); readers outraged by this are invited to use (2') rather than (2) in interpreting the results. Masson and Shaanan (1987) have used a model like (2') to look at the effect of foreign competition on domestic entry in Canada as reflected in θ^d.

4 The full reduced form of the system (1) and (4) is given in Appendix I, together with a demonstration of the comparative static properties asserted in the text.

5 The relationship between the reduced form parameters, λ_j and η_j, and the structural parameters, γ^d, γ^f, the $\beta(L)$ and the $\psi(L)$ is set out in Appendix II.

6 As shown in Appendix II, $\lambda_2 > \lambda_3$ if $\beta_1 > \psi_1$; that is if the effect of e^d_{it-1} on π_{it} exceeds that of e^f_{it-1}. If this is the case, then an increase in domestic entry of any given magnitude leads to a larger reduction in profits, and so to a larger reduction in subsequent total entry, than does an equivalent increase in foreign entry. As β_1 rises relative to ψ_1, the ratio of domestic to foreign entry rises at any given time, and this is the sense in which one means that domestic entry crowds out foreign entry.

7 This decision was based on experience with modelling profit margins dynamics with this data in which three annual lags

seemed more than adequate to capture the systematic movements observed in the data; see Geroski (1988).

8 One might also reasonably ask whether γ, the $\beta(L)$ and the $\psi(L)$ vary across industries, perhaps modelling them as linear functions of various observables. Pursuant to our decision to stick to very simple models which make very limited demands in terms of observables, we have not pursued this course here. However, results reported by Geroski (1988) suggest that γ does not vary (see also Fairburn and Geroski (1988)), but that β may do so to some degree.

9 One must be alert to the possibility of truncation bias arising from an omission of terms in the lagged values of e^d_{it} and e^f_{it} on Tables 2 and 3 (eg see Griliches and Pakes (1984) for a discussion). This may be a possible explanation of the rather large size of the co-efficient on e^f_{it-3} on Table 3, although, in principle it may apply to all the co-efficients on both tables since both e^d_{it} and e^f_{it} are third order (at least) processes.

10 The results on dynamics reported here are broadly consistent with the pattern of dynamics suggested by estimates of the structural models (1)-(3) and (2)-(3) reported in Geroski (1988) and Fairburn and Geroski (1988). Both find very modest effects of entry - domestic and foreign - on margins, and a much stronger effect of margins on domestic rather than foreign entry.

REFERENCES

FAIRBURN, J. and P. GEROSKI (1988), "Domestic and Foreign Entry in the UK: 1983-84", mimeo, London Business School.

GEROSKI, P. and R. MASSON (1987), "Dynamic Market Models in Industrial Organization", International Journal of Industrial Organization, vol. 5, pp. 1-14.

GEROSKI, P. (1988), "The Effect of Entry on Margins in the Short and Long Run", mimeo, London Business School.

GORECKI, P. (1976), "The Determinants of Entry by Domestic and Foreign Enterprises in Canadian Manufacturing Industries", Review of Economics and Statistics, vol. 58, pp. 495-498.

GORECKI, P. (1975), "The Determinants of Entry by New and Diversifying Enterprises in the UK Manufacturing Sector, 1958-63", Applied Economics, vol. 7, pp. 139-147.

GRILICHES, Z. and A. PAKES (1984), "Estimating Distributed Lags in Short Panels, with an Application to the Specification of Depreciation Patterns and Capital Stock Contracts", Review of Economic Studies, vol. 51, pp. 243-62.

MASSON, R. and J. SHAANAN (1982), "Stochastic Dynamic Limit Pricing: Am Empirical Test", Review of Economics and Statistics, vol. 64, pp. 413-22.

MASSON, R. and J. SHAANAN (1987), "Optimal Oligopoly Pricing and the Threat of Entry: Canadian Evidence", International Journal of Industrial Organization, vol. 5, pp. 323-40.

ORR, D. (1974), "The Determinants of Entry: A Study of the Canadian Manufacturing Industries", Review of Economics and Statistics, vol. 61, pp. 58-66.

The Convergence of International and Domestic Markets
D.B. Audretsch, L. Sleuwaegen, and H. Yamawaki (Editors)

4. EXPOSURE OF FRENCH MANUFACTURING TO INTERNATIONAL COMPETITION : 1959 - 1980*

William James Adams
The University of Michigan

0. INTRODUCTION

Since World War II, the international environment of French business has been transformed profoundly. Creation of the European Communities led to elimination of most governmentally imposed barriers to merchandise trade within Europe. Implementation of the Kennedy and Tokyo rounds of GATT agreements extended some of that liberalization to relations with other rich market economies. Deregulation of transactions in foreign exchange and credit facilitated international investment as well as international trade. Involuntary withdrawal from Indochina and Algeria eliminated quasi-colonial privileges in those parts of the former empire that had been of greatest economic importance to France.

In this paper, I wish to explore the extent to which increased exposure to foreign business served to increase competitive pressures on French enterprises. I begin by exploring the impact of institutional change on the exposure of French business to foreign trade.[1] The evidence demonstrates clearly that international trade now impinges forcefully on most of French manufacturing. I then consider the impact of international

---

* This paper is a modified exerpt from William James Adams, Restructuring the French Economy: Government and the Rise of Market Competition Since World War II (The Brookings Institution, 1989). I wish to thank Richard Caves and Alexis Jacquemin for their contributions to the present effort.

exposure on the state of competition. After pointing out that rising exposure to foreigners does not imply rising exposure to competition, I present evidence to the effect that international trade has placed many French enterprises in substantially competitive environments.

1. EXPOSURE TO FOREIGN TRADE

Abandonment of tariffs and quotas does not guarantee increased trade. Not only do governments possess more subtle means of hindering international movements of goods and services, but private parties, bent on preserving national cartels, might themselves attempt to sterilize the effects of altered institutional arrangements. On both accounts, it has been argued, the European Communities have failed to create a genuine common market.[2]

This section documents the evolution of French exposure to international trade. As we shall see, goods produced abroad now account for considerable fractions of domestic consumption; and considerable fractions of domestic output are now sold abroad. These changes constitute the most important alteration of French market structure since World War II.

1.1. Exposure to Imports

In 1959, few French industries were exposed heavily to imports. In manufacturing, imports accounted on average for 8% of domestic consumption (table 1). Half of all manufacturing industries exhibited exposures below 5% (table 2). Fewer than 1 in 11 exhibited exposures of 20% or more. All four industries where imports accounted for at least one-fifth of domestic consumption were close to the raw materials ends of their vertical streams of production.[3]

Outside manufacturing, the mean exposure to imports (13%) exceeded its manufacturing counterpart (table 1); but the median exposure was only 2%. Thus, in a few nonmanufacturing industries, import-exposure attained very high levels;[4] in most, however, imports accounted for small fractions of domestic consumption: In 20 of the 32, exposure was under 5% (table 3); in 13 of the 20, imports were nil. Together, these 20 industries accounted for 71% of nonmanufacturing consumption.

Between 1959 and 1980, import-exposure changed fundamentally. Mean exposure increased by 17 percentage points in manufacturing (table 4) and by 7 percentage points in nonmanufacturing (table 5).

TABLE 1 : Mean Exposure to Imports, 1959-1980. Percent.

Year	Manaufacturing	Nonmanufacturing
1959	8	13
1960	9	13
1961	9	13
1962	10	13
1963	11	14
1964	11	14
1965	12	14
1966	12	15
1967	13	15
1968	14	15
1969	16	15
1970	17	16
1971	17	17
1972	18	17
1973	19	18
1974	21	19
1975	20	18
1976	22	19
1977	23	19
1978	23	19
1979	25	19
1980	25	20

Notes : Mean values for manufacturing (N=46) and non-manufacturing (N=32) industries. Exposure to imports is (100) (M+T)/(Q+M+T-X), where M=imports cif, T=tariff collected, X=exports fob, and Q=domestic output (production distribuée). Industries are defined according to NAP-S79. Industry S56 (scrap products) is omitted from nonmanufacturing.

Source : INSEE, input-output tables in current prices, level S (unpublished).

TABLE 2 : Distribution of Manufacturing Industries by Exposure to Imports, 1959 and 1980.

Exposure to Imports	Number of Industries 1959	Number of Industries 1980	Share of Consumption 1959	Share of Consumption 1980
0 ≤ IM < 5	23	4	53	9
5 ≤ IM < 10	10	4	21	5
10 ≤ IM < 15	8	5	15	25
15 ≤ IM < 20	1	5	5	6
20 ≤ IM < 30	1	12	2	27
30 ≤ IM	3	16	3	27
All	46	46	100	100

Notes : Exposure to imports (IM) is (100) (M+T)/(Q+M+T-X), where M=imports cif, T=tariff collected, Q=domestic output (<u>production distribuée</u>), and X=exports fob. Consumption is apparent home consumption (Q+M+T-X) of manufactures. Industries are defined according to NAP-S79.

Source : INSEE, input-output tables in current prices, level S (unpublished).

TABLE 3 : Distribution on Nonmanufacturing Industries by Exposure to Imports, 1959 and 1980.

Exposure to Imports	Number of Industries 1959	Number of Industries 1980	Share of Consumption 1959	Share of Consumption 1980
0 ≤ IM < 5	20	18	71	74
5 ≤ IM < 10	1	1	4	7
10 ≤ IM < 15	4	2	19	10
15 ≤ IM < 20	1	2	1	3
20 ≤ IM < 30	2	1	3	0
30 ≤ IM	4	8	2	6
All	32	32	100	100

Notes : Exposure to imports (IM) is (100) (M+T)/(Q+M+T-X), where M=imports cif, T=tariff collected, Q=domestic output (<u>production distribuée</u>), and X=exports fob. Consumption is apparent home consumption (Q+M+T-X) of nonmanufactures. Industries are defined according to NAP-S79. Industry S56(scrap products) is omitted.

Source : INSEE, input-output tables in current prices, level S (unpublished).

TABLE 4 : Evolution of Exposure to Imports, Manufacturing Industries.

Variable name V1	V2	Variable mean V1	V2	(V1-V2)	Std.dev. (V1-V2)	t N=46
IM80	IM59	25.3	8.4	16.9***	13.2	8.7
IM69	IM59	15.8	8.4	7.4***	8.3	6.0
IM80	IM70	25.3	16.7	8.7***	6.9	8.6
IM66	IM59	12.4	8.4	3.9***	5.0	5.3
IM80	IM73	25.3	19.1	6.2***	5.9	7.2
(IM80-IM70)	(IM69-IM59)	8.7	7.4	1.3	6.9	1.3
(IM80-IM73)	(IM66-IM59)	6.2	3.9	2.3***	5.6	2.8

Notes : IM=(100) (M+T)/(Q+M+T-X), where M=imports cif, T=tariff collected, Q=domestic output (<u>production distribuée</u>), and X=exports fob. IM80 is IM in 1980. Industries are defined according to NAP-S79. The t-statistics in column 7 and the asterisks in column 5 relate to tests of the hypothesis that the mean difference between variable 1 and variable 2 is 0. One, two, and three asterisks denote statistical significance at the .05, .01, and .001 levels, respectively, in one-tail t-tests.

Source : INSEE, input-output tables in current prices, level S, (unpublished).

TABLE 5 : Evolution of Exposure to Imports, Nonmanufacturing Industries.

Variable name V1	V2	Variable mean V1	V2	(V1-V2)	Std.dev. (V1-V2)	t N=32
IM80	IM59	19.7	13.1	6.6*	17.7	2.1
IM69	IM59	15.4	13.1	2.4	7.4	1.8
IM80	IM70	19.7	16.4	3.4*	9.0	2.1
IM66	IM59	14.6	13.1	1.5	5.2	1.7
IM80	IM73	19.7	17.5	2.2	7.3	1.7
(IM80-IM70)	(IM69-IM59)	3.4	2.4	1.0	6.4	0.9
(IM80-IM73)	(IM66-IM59)	2.2	1.5	0.6	6.0	0.6

Notes : IM=(100) (M+T)/((Q+M+T-X), where M=imports cif, T=tariff collected, Q=domestic output (<u>production distribuée</u>), and X=exports fob. IM80 is IM in 1980. Industries are defined according to NAP-S79. Industry S56 (srap products) is omitted. The t-statistics in column 7 and the asterisks in column 5 relate to tests of the hypothesis that the mean differnece between variable 1 and variable 2 is 0. One, two, and three asterisks denote statistical significance at the .05, .01, and .001 levels, respectively, in one-tail t-tests.

Source : INSEE, input-output tables in current prices, level S (unpublished).

Outside manufacturing, the rise in exposure was confined to four industries.[5] Leaving aside these exceptional cases, the ratio of imports to domestic consumption failed to rise appreciably. In fact, 8 of 32 nonmanufacturing industries experienced declining exposure.[6] Another 11 of the 32 experienced no imports at any time between 1959 and 1980. Altogether, in 25 of the 32, import-exposure failed to rise by as much as 5 percentage points (table 6).

In manufacturing, import-exposure increased appreciably and pervasively. In 31 of 46 industries, exposure increased by more than 10 percentage points (table 7). In 5 of these 31, it increased by at least 30 percentage points.[7] At the other end of the spectrum, exposure to imports declined in only 1 manufacturing industry.[8]

Many of the industries experiencing large increases in import-exposure had received substantial tariff protection in 1959. In the textiles sector, for example, high rates of duty had applied to manmade fibers (19%), shoes (23%), and knitwear (30%).[9]

TABLE 6 : Distribution of Nonmanufacturing Industries by Change in Exposure to Imports, 1959-1980.

Change in Exposure to Imports	Number of Industries	Share of output 1959	Share of output 1980
0 = (IM80-IM59)	8	22	14
0 < (IM80-IM59) < 5	17	69	79
5 ≤ (IM80-IM59) < 10	3	6	6
10 ≤ (IM80-IM59) < 20	0	0	0
20 ≤ (IM80-IM59)	4	3	1
All	32	100	100

Notes : IM=(100) (M+T)/((Q+M+T-X), where M=imports cif, T=tariff collected, Q=domestic output (production distribuée), and X=exports fob. IM80 is IM in 1980. Industries are defined according to NAP-S79. Industry S56 (scrap products) is omitted. Output is domestic output of nonmanufactures.

Source : INSEE, input-output tables in current prices, level S (unpublished).

TABLE 7 : Distribution of Manufacturing Industries by Change in Exposure to Imports, 1959-1980.

Change in Exposure to Imports	Number of Industries	Share of output 1959	Share of output 1980
0 = (IM80-IM59)	1	1	0
0 < (IM80-IM59) < 5	8	23	26
5 ≤ (IM80-IM59) < 10	6	19	15
10 ≤ (IM80-IM59) < 20	14	35	33
20 ≤ (IM80-IM59)	17	22	26
All	46	100	100

Notes : IM=(100) (M+T)/((Q+M+T-X), where M=imports cif, T=tariff collected, Q=domestic output (production distribuée), and X=exports fob. IM80 is IM in 1980. Industries are defined according to NAP-S79. Output is domestic output of manufactures.

Source : INSEE, input-output tables in current prices, level S (unpublished).

Associated with the high tariffs were meager imports: In each of the three industries mentioned just above, imports accounted for less than five percent of domestic consumption in 1959. By 1980, the rate of duty had fallen below 5% in each case; and, as we saw in the last paragraph, import-exposure had increased by over 30 percentage points. More generally, among all manufacturing industries, tariff level in 1959 correlates positively with change in import-exposure between 1959 and 1980.[10]

Table 8 identifies the manufacturing industries where exposure failed to increase by at least ten percentage points between 1959 and 1980. The list includes perishables, difficult-to-transport products, and goods rarely produced abroad in substitutable form. In these cases, it is hardly surprising that domestic production satisfied most internal consumption even after the economy opened. In other cases, however, the failure of exposure to rise cannot be attributed to "natural" protection of domestic producers. For example, government buys a large share of output and/or regulates the sale of petroleum products, ships, railway vehicles, and drugs. Moreover, drugs and petroleum products are produced by companies known to have engaged in cartel activities at the international level.[11] In these cases at least, the failure of exposure to rise appreciably is plausibly unnatural.

TABLE 8 : Manufacturing Industries Where Exposure to Imports Did Not Increase Substantially, 1959-1980. Percent unless otherwise specified.

Activity Code	Name	Exposure to Imports 1959	1980	Change
402	Sugar	33.6	16.2	-17.3
38-9	Grain mill prods., etc.	1.9	3.5	1.5
36	Dairy products	3.2	4.8	1.6
19	Drugs	2.2	4.2	2.0
32	Ships	4.2	6.6	2.3
41	Beverages	5.5	8.0	2.5
20	Foundry products	1.5	4.3	2.8
053	Petroleum products	6.5	11.4	4.9
51	Printing, publishing	3.4	8.4	5.0
15	Building materials	5.9	11.6	5.7
312	Railway vehicles	3.0	9.9	6.9
35	Meat	4.2	12.5	8.3
26	Military products	2.6	11.0	8.4
52	Rubber products	11.9	20.8	8.9
21	Metallic products	3.8	12.9	9.1

Notes : This tables includes all manufacturing industries where exposure to imports increased by less than 10 percentage points between 1959 and 1980. Exposure to imports is (100) (M+T)/(Q+M+T-X), where M=imports cif, T=tariff collected, Q=domestic output (<u>production distribuée</u>), and X=exports fob. Industries are defined according to NAP-S79. Change in exposure to imports is measured in percentage points.

Source : INSEE, input-output tables in current prices, level S (unpublished).

Given the widespread belief that the EC has come untracked - that early efforts to deregulate trade have been halted and perhaps eroded by revived protectionism - it is interesting to examine the timing of these changes in import-exposure. Toward that end, I divided in half the 22 years under observation and then compared the changes in import-exposure during the first subperiod (1959-69) with those during the second (1970-80). I also compared changes in import-exposure during 1959-66 with those during 1973-80. The earlier of these subperiods covers the first two stages of transition toward full achievement of the EEC; the later subperiod covers the years of substantial macroeconomic shock; in effect, this second comparison juxtaposes the period when tariffs within the common market were declining most substantially with the period when member countries were allegedly restricting imports most energetically.

Outside manufacturing, import-exposure proceeded at a fairly steady pace. Import-exposure rose to the same degree during 1970-80 as during 1959-69; ditto for 1973-80 in comparison with 1959-66 (table 5). Inside manufacturing, import-exposure also failed to decline over time. Changes in exposure tended to the same levels during 1959-69 as during 1970-80; and changes in exposure during 1973-80 actually tended to exceed those during 1973-80 (table 4).

By 1980, the manufacturing sector was substantially exposed to imports. At the industry level, the mean value of exposure was 25% (table 1). In virtually all 46 industries, imports accounted for major fractions of domestic consumption. Only 4 industries in 1980 (compared to 23 in 1959) displayed exposures of less than 5%. At the other end of the spectrum, 28 industries in 1980 (compared with 4 in 1959) displayed exposures in excess of 20%. In 16 product categories, accounting for over one-quarter of French consumption of manufactures in 1980, exposure exceeded 30%. In such major industries as bulk organic chemicals, crude steel, nonferrous metals and products, mechanical equipment, automobiles, household electrical equipment, professional electronic and office equipment - each of which accounted for more than 50 billion francs of domestic consumption in 1980 - imports accounted for more than one-quarter of domestic sales.

One way to appreciate this transformation is to examine exposure in 1980 where imports had accounted for less than 5% of domestic consumption in 1959. Table 9 identifies both the products and the evolution of exposure. In 7 of 23 cases, exposure remained below 10% in 1980. In another 6 cases, imports came to account for between 10% and 20% of domestic consumption. In 10 of 23 cases, however, imports ultimately accounted for over 20% of domestic consumption. Half of the ten involved textiles.[12] The other five included two major industries: Automobiles, where exposure rose from 4% in 1959 to 27% in 1980; and electrical equipment, where it rose from 4% in 1959 to 21% in 1980.

TABLE 9 : Evolution of Exposure to Imports in Manufacturing Industries Insulated from Imports in 1959.

Percent unless otherwise specified

Activity Code	Name	Exposure to 1959	Imports 1980	Change
49	Furniture	1.2	17.8	16.6
42	Tobacco products	1.4	15.6	14.2
20	Foundry products	1.5	4.3	2.8
46	Shoes	1.6	31.6	30.1
38-9	Grain mill prods., etc.	1.9	3.5	1.5
47	Apparel	1.9	19.1	17.1
452	Leather products	2.0	25.2	23.1
19	Drugs	2.2	4.2	2.0
26	Military products	2.6	11.0	8.4
442	Knitwear	2.9	37.7	34.8
312	Railway vehicles	3.0	9.9	6.9
36	Dairy products	3.2	4.8	1.6
443	Woven textiles	3.3	39.3	35.9
16	Glass	3.3	24.4	21.1
51	Printing, publishing	3.4	8.4	5.0
53	Plastics products	3.5	21.0	17.5
21	Metallic products	3.8	12.9	9.1
311	Road vehicles	4.0	26.8	22.8
35	Meat	4.2	12.5	8.3
32	Ships	4.2	6.6	2.3
18	Chemical products nec	4.3	21.7	17.3
43	Manmade fibers	4.4	60.1	55.8
28	Electrical equipment	4.4	20.9	16.5

Notes : This table inclused all manufacturing industries where imports amounted to less than 5% of apparent home consumption in 1959. Exposure to imports is (100) (M+T)/(Q+M+T-X), where M=imports cif, T=tariff collected, Q=domestic output (production distribuée), and X=exports fob. Industries are defined according to NAP-S79. Change in exposure to imports is measured in percentage points.

Source : INSEE, input-output tables in current prices, level S (unpublished).

Outside manufacturing, mean exposure to imports was 20% in 1980. At the industry level, exposure varied greatly. In the case of some products,[13] over half of domestic consumption was satisfied by imports. In other cases, however, including 12 categories of services, imports were nil. In one important case, agriculture, imports accounted for 13% of domestic consumption, a share almost identical to that obtaining in 1959 (14%).

With few exceptions, then, French manufacturing industries became exposed to imports between 1959 and 1980.

TABLE 10 : Mean propensity to Export, 1959-1980.

Percent

Year	Manufacturing	Nonmanufacturing
1959	14	9
1960	14	9
1961	14	9
1962	13	9
1963	13	8
1964	14	8
1965	15	8
1966	14	8
1967	15	8
1968	15	8
1969	16	8
1970	19	8
1971	19	8
1972	20	8
1973	21	8
1974	23	9
1975	23	8
1976	24	8
1977	25	9
1978	26	9
1979	27	8
1980	27	8

Notes : Mean values for manufacturing (N=46) and non-manufacturing (N=32) industries. Propensity to export is (100) (X)/(Q), where X=exports fob, and Q=domestic output (production distribuée). Industries are defined according to NAP-S79. Industry S56 (scrap products) is omitted from nonmanufacturing.

Source : INSEE, input-output tables in current prices, level S (unpublished).

1.2. Propensity to Export

In 1959, manufacturing industries displayed a mean propensity to export of 14% (table 10). Most manufacturing industries exported small fractions of their output: One-half of manufacturing output was attributable to industries exporting less than 10% of production (table 11). Nearly two-thirds of manufacturing output was attributable to industries exporting less than 15% of production. Only semifinished steel and sugar displayed ratios of exports to output of 30% or more. No manufacturing industry exported a majority of its output.

TABLE 11 : Distribution of Manufacturing Industries by propensity to Export, 1959 and 1980.

Propensity to Export	Number of Industries 1959	1980	Share of Output 1959	1980
0 ≤ EX < 5	4	2	16	2
5 ≤ EX < 10	15	6	34	27
10 ≤ EX < 15	12	3	16	9
15 ≤ EX < 20	7	7	14	12
20 ≤ EX < 30	6	9	18	10
30 ≤ EX	2	19	2	40
All	46	46	100	100

Notes : EX=(100)(X)/(Q), where X=exports fob and Q=domestic output (production distribuée). Industries are defined according to NAP-S79. In the last two columns, output is output of manufactures.

Source : INSEE, input-output tables in current prices, level S (unpublished).

Outside manufacturing, the mean propensity to export in 1959 was 9%. The corresponding median, however, was less than 1%. Thirteen of the 32 industries exported nothing; another 11 displayed export-propensities between 0% and 5%. Together, these 24 industries accounted for 91% of nonmanufacturing output (table 12). Meanwhile, 5 industries exported at least 20% of production.[14]

Between 1959 and 1980, the mean propensity to export doubled, increasing by 13 percentage points (table 13). Increases in export-propensity occurred in virtually all manufacturing industries (table 14).[15] In 10 of the 46, export-propensity increased by over 20 percentage points.[16]

Outside manufacturing, the mean ratio of exports to output fell by half a percentage point between 1959 and 1980 (table 15). Statistically speaking, however, export-propensity tended not to

TABLE 12 : Distribution of Nonmanufacturing Industries by Propensity to Export, 1959 and 1980.

Propensity to Export	Number of Industries 1959	Number of Industries 1980	Share of Output 1959	Share of Output 1980
0 ≤ EX < 5	24	20	91	76
5 ≤ EX < 10	2	2	5	1
10 ≤ EX < 15	1	4	0	14
15 ≤ EX < 20	0	3	0	8
20 ≤ EX < 30	2	2	2	0
30 ≤ EX	3	1	2	1
All	32	32	100	100

Notes : EX=(100)(X)/(Q), where X=exports fob and Q=domestic output (<u>production distribuée</u>). Industries are defined according to NAP-S79. Industry S56 (scrap products) is omitted. In the last two columns, output is output of nonmanufactures.

Source : INSEE, input-output tables in current prices, level S (unpublished).

TABLE 13 : Evolution of Propensity to Export, Manufacturing Industries.

Variable name V1	Variable name V2	Variable mean V1	Variable mean V2	Variable mean (V1-V2)	Std.dev. (V1-V2)	t N=46
EX80	IM59	26.5	13.5	13.0***	10.5	8.4
EX69	IM59	16.2	13.5	2.7*	7.0	2.6
EX80	IM70	26.5	18.5	8.0***	7.1	7.6
EX66	IM59	14.1	13.5	0.6	4.9	0.8
EX80	IM73	26.5	21.2	5.3***	4.9	7.3
(EX80-EX70)	(EX69-EX59)	8.0	2.7	5.3***	9.8	3.6
(EX80-EX73)	(EX66-EX59)	5.3	0.6	4.7***	6.9	4.6

Notes : EX=(100)(X)/((Q), where X=exports fob, and Q=domestic output (<u>production distribuée</u>). EX80 is EX in 1980. Industries are defined according to NAP-S79. The t-statistics in column 7 and the asterisks in column 5 relate to tests of the hypothesis that the mean difference between variable 1 and variable 2 is 0. One, two and three asterisks denote statistical significance at the .05, .01, and .001 levels, respectively, in one-tail t-tests.

Source : INSEE, input-output tables in current prices, level S (unpublished).

TABLE 14 : Distribution of Manufacturing Industries by Change in Propensity to Export, 1959-1980.

Change in Propensity to Export	Number of Industries	Share of Output 1959	Share of Output 1980
(EX80-EX59) < 0	2	2	3
0 < (EX80-EX59) < 5	7	15	21
5 ≤ (EX80-EX59) < 10	11	34	25
10 ≤ (EX80-EX59) < 20	16	36	35
20 ≤ (EX80-EX59)	10	12	16
All	46	100	100

Notes : EX=(100)(X)/((Q), where X=exports fob, and Q=domestic output (production distribuée). EX80 is EX in 1980. Industries are defined according to NAP-S79. Output is domestic output of manufactures.

Source : INSEE, input-output tables in current prices, level S (unpublished).

change over this period. At the industry level, export-propensity declined in 10 of 32 industries - sometimes substantially.[17] In no nonmanufacturing industries did export-propensity rise by as much as 20 percentage points. In only three[18] did it increase by as much as 10 percentage points.[19]

Returning to manufacturing, export-propensities did not increase steadily between 1959 and 1980. The mean propensity to export did not begin to rise monotonically until 1967 (table 10).[20] Between 1959 and 1967, the ratio of exports to output did not tend to grow (table 13). In 1969, the mean propensity to export exceeded its 1959 counterpart by less than 3 percentage points (table 13). After 1970, however, export-intensity tended to increase markedly. The mean ratio of exports to output increased signifcantly between 1970 and 1980, as well as between 1973 and 1980. The surge of export-propensity during the second half of our period accords poorly with the suppositions of Europessimism: It lends credence to the belief that the common market has continued to provide companies with opportunities to compete in the markets of other member countries.[21]

TABLE 15 : Evolution of Propensity to Export, Nonmanufacturing Industries.

Variable name V1	V2	Variable mean V1	V2	(V1-V2)	Std.dev. (V1-V2)	t N=32
EX80	EX59	8.4	8.9	-0.5	7.7	-0.4
EX69	EX59	7.7	8.9	-1.2	5.6	-1.2
EX80	EX70	8.4	7.7	0.7	4.7	0.8
EX66	EX59	8.2	8.9	-0.7	3.3	-1.3
EX80	EX73	8.4	7.9	0.5	3.8	0.7
(EX80-EX70)	(EX69-EX59)	0.7	-1.2	1.9	6.8	1.5
(EX80-EX73)	(EX66-EX59)	0.5	-0.7	1.2	4.8	1.4

Notes : EX=(100)(X)/((Q), where X=exports fob, and Q=domestic (production distribuée). EX80 is EX in 1980. Industries are defined according to NAP-S79. Industry S56 (Scrap products) is omitted. The t-statistics in column 7 relate to tests of the hypothesis that the mean difference between variable 1 and variable 2 is 0. In no case can the hypothesis be rejected at the .05 level in a one-tail test.

Source : INSEE, input-output tables in current prices, level S (unpublished).

By 1980, on average, manufacturing industries sent one-quarter of their output abroad. Some 19 manufacturing industries, accounting for 40% of manufacturing output, exported at least 30% of their output.[22] Five industries[23] exported over half their output.[24] By 1980, only the exceptional French manufacturing industry could be said not to rely substantially (and, over the business cycle, fairly consistently) on foreign markets.

2. FOREIGN EXPOSURE AND THE STATE OF COMPETITION

Increased exposure to international trade is often and rightly presumed to generate increased exposure to competition. But exposure of the first variety does not imply exposure of the second : For a variety of reasons, trade is logically compatible with sustained imperfections in competition; under certain circumstances, it might even promote market power. Europessimists tend to emphasize the obstructions littering the path from foreign trade to competition.

The vigor of competition in a market can often be predicted from its structure. Therefore, a natural way to explore empirically the impact of international exposure on competition is to study the effects of such exposure on the major elements of market structure. In this section, we shall consider the a priori linkages between international exposure and two established features of market structure: Both involve seller-concentration - one at the enterprise level, the other at the level of strategic groups.[25] Since the positive effects of foreign exposure on competition are straightforward, I shall dwell here on the neutral and negative effects. Unfortunately, we shall also have to explain why lack of information precludes complete structural analysis of the foreign impact on competition.

2.1. Foreign Exposure and Seller-Concentration

Seller-concentration is the element of market structure deployed most frequently to predict company behavior. Let us begin, therefore, with the relationship between foreign exposure and seller-concentration.

2.1.1. Imports, Concentration, and Competition

Increases in import-exposure do not necessarily reduce domestic seller-concentration. Included in international trade are goods traveling from one part of a multinational enterprise to another. Intrafirm trade, resulting in captive imports, does not alter the number of sellers supplying a market.[26] Since the importance of foreign operations varies positively with firm size, intrafirm trade may well increase seller-concentration.

Even if imports nudge seller-concentration downward, the change might not suffice to invigorate competition. Competition does not vary linearly with concentration. If the pool of foreign suppliers is sufficiently small, oligopolistic behavior might be preserved. If the pool of foreign suppliers is large, but each foreign supplier is small in relation to domestic rivals, then foreigners might align their prices on those of a domestic oligopoly group. Such alignment is especially likely when foreigners believe that aggressive behavior on their part will provoke the home government to shelter its market from outside competition.

2.1.2. Exports, Concentration, and Competition

Not all exports need travel to competitive world markets. Some might find their way to markets dominated by a small number of suppliers. Some might even find their way to markets dominated by exactly the same enterprises as dominate the home market. Exports to such markets are unlikely to expose the home industry to increased competition.

Dependent export markets appear especially frequently in colonial or postcolonial countries. Such countries contain few, if any, indigenous suppliers; and producers in third countries are excluded artificially from the market. As a result, the colonial market tends to be no less concentrated than its domestic counterpart. Given the positive correlation between company size and propensity to export, seller-concentration might well be greater in the colonial than in the domestic market.

2.1.3. Shortcomings of Direct Evidence on Seller-Concentration

In France, as in many countries where French goods are sold, government publishes data on concentration of production at the industry level. Unfortunately, this information measures true seller-concentration rather poorly.

In the first place, it measures the concentration of domestic production rather than the concentration of domestic sales. In other words, it ignores imports and exports. The correspondence between producer- and seller-concentration cannot be achieved merely by substituting apparent home consumption for domestic production in the denominator of the concentration ratio.[27] Where international trade impinges heavily on the domestic industry, and especially where international trade occurs between companies belonging to the same enterprise, producer-concentration not only fails to measure seller-concentration accurately but also fails to provide an upper or lower bound on the meaningful ratio.

The second major problem with French (and most other European) concentration data is the manner in which enterprise boundaries are established. Seller-concentration should measure the extent to which a few independent decisionmaking entities control most sales in a particular market. To the extent that decisions in some companies are ultimately made by executives in other companies - as, for example, when one company is a subsidiary of another - companies under common control should be grouped together and considered a single enterprise. The French data, however, treat each legally distinct company as a separate decisionmaking entity.[28] As a result, companies like Peugeot, Citroën, and Talbot are considered 3 distinct sellers of automobiles even though the last two are controlled by the first. Given the propensity of European enterprises to be structured in terms of subsidiaires (as opposed to operating divisions of a single company), this is an important problem in the French context.

2.2. Foreign Exposure and Strategic Groups

Given the level of seller-concentration, sellers are more likely to behave competitively the greater their heterogeneity. Sellers who produce the same mix of products in the same locations with the same mix of factors, and who sell in the same markets using the same distribution channels, can agree relatively easily on how best to extract profit from particular market situations: They are likely to constitute a strategic group. The smaller the number of such groups operating in a market, the greater the likelihood of oligopolistic behavior.

Nationality is likely to be an important determinant of strategic group affiliation. Foreign and domestic producers can be expected to differ regarding the geographic distribution of sales. They might also differ regarding methods of production and version of the product. The several foreign firms can be expected to differ among themselves on the same basis for the same reasons. Finally, if domestic firms differ with respect to their geographic patterns of sales, then they, too, might disagree about how to exploit the domestic market.

2.2.1. Absence of Direct Evidence on Strategic Groups

No government reports systematic information on strategic groups. Although such information would not be difficult to assemble for a small number of industries, systematic measurement of heterogeneity for the full population of domestic markets would require substantial effort indeed.

2.3. Implications

In the absence of direct information on the relationship between foreign exposure on the one hand and seller-concentration and strategic groups on the other, let us examine such empirical evidence as we possess on linkages between international exposure and the state of competition. The evidence presented below points toward the following conclusion : International exposure has frequently, if not ineluctably, vivified the competition experienced by French manufacturing enterprises.

3. IMPORT DISCIPLINE

Imports are especially likely to enhance competition when (1) the domestic industry does not function competitively, (2) the domestic buyer and the foreign seller do not belong to the same parent company, and (3) foreign sellers don't align their prices and terms of sale on those established by domestic rivals. To what extent do these conditions obtain in French markets?

3.1. Frequency of Intrafirm Trade

It is not difficult to cite instances of intrafirm trade in the European setting. In the automobile industry, the EC Commission found that "Ford Britain purchases from Ford Germany RHD [right-hand drive] cars manufactured by the latter. These purchases account for a substantial proportion of Ford Germany's total production and exports."[29]

Where direct evidence is lacking, it is sometimes possible to infer intra-firm trade from a combination of industry-level data on international trade with company-level data on the geographic distribution of subsidiaries. For example, France imports bauxite, alumina, and aluminum from French Guiana, New Caledonia, and Greece. Pechiney, France's major producer of aluminum, operates subsidiaries in all three countries. The imports in question are thus likely to be traveling within the Pechiney family of companies.

Although illustration is easy, the fact remains that systematic information on the importance of captive trade does not exist. Without direct evidence, the best we can do is argue that captive imports will not be important when (1) French companies in the relevant industry have engaged in little foreign investment, and (2) the relevant French industry contains few subsidiaries of foreign companies.

3.2. Frequency of Price Alignment

In large measure, the increased exposure of French companies to international trade is attributable to increased trade within the EC. And yet, even at the EC level, production can be sufficiently concentrated in a few companies to warrant suspicion of oligopolistic behavior. Under such circumstances, the competitive consequences of imports and exports are far from obvious. For a variety of reasons, leading producers may conspire to allow international trade, but only on terms unlikely to disturb national price levels. Several antitrust cases brought by the EC Commission reveal that oligopolistic cooperation does occur at the EC level. One in particular, the sugar case,[30] illustrates clearly how increased exposure to international trade need not entail increased exposure to competition.

Within the EC, the geographic distributions of consumption and production of sugar do not coincide: France and Belgium tend to produce more sugar than they consume; Italy, the Netherlands, and

Luxembourg tend to consume more sugar than they produce. In the northern and southern parts of West Germany, production exceeds consumption; but in the western part of the country, the opposite holds.

At the time of the commission's investigation, in each region of the community, a small number of refiners accounted for most production of white sugar. In Belgium, one company[31] controlled 85% of production; in the Netherlands, two companies[32] accounted for all production; in Italy, three groups of companies[33] controlled 90% of production; in France, five companies[34] accounted for 75% of production;[35] in Germany, production was most concentrated in the south, where one company[36] accounted for 70% of refinery output.

Not only were the individual production areas characterized by high concentration, but joint ventures served to link producers from different areas. Thus the Raffinerie Tirlementoise, Béghin, Eridania, and Süddeutsche Zucker all owned shares (directly or indirectly) in the Compagnie Européenne de l'Industrie Sucrière. This joint venture in turn controlled Say, one of the other major producers in France.

On July 1, 1968, the EEC replaced its member states as regulator of raw and refined sugar. In organizing their markets for sugar, member states had generally relied on regulation and subsidy rather than on competitive supply and demand. Although the EEC preserved many features of the national systems, including price supports for raw and refined sugar, it also wished to establish a regime of free trade in sugar within the community as a whole. While regulated by their national governments, refiners in regions where production exceeded sales tended to send their excess to countries outside the EEC.

During the first year of its authority to regulate sugar, the EEC found that little trade occurred within the community - even though France and Belgium produced substantially more sugar than they consumed; even though Italy, the Netherlands, and western Germany consumed more than they produced; and even though prices in the deficit regions exceeded prices in the surplus regions by amounts in excess of transport costs.

After the first year, trade within the community increased. Upon close examination, however, the commission found that such trade hardly served to increase competition in the regional markets for refined sugar. In most cases, trade took the form of refiners in surplus areas selling refined or raw sugar to refiners in deficit areas. The latter would sell the sugar under their own labels and at their own prices. Only with the explicit approval of refiners in deficit areas would refiners in surplus areas export to buyers who were not themselves refiners. When they did sell to nonrefiners, they charged prices above those charged to refiners. To the extent that refiners in surplus areas distributed their sugar through independent wholesalers, they warned those wholesalers not to export to deficit areas within the community until they had secured the approval of local refiners. Meanwhile, refiners in deficit areas warned their wholesalers not to buy sugar in surplus areas, or at least not to sell such sugar without prior approval of the refiners as to the terms. Both importing and exporting wholesalers were told that failure to comply with these arrangements would entail refusal by the refiners to supply them with sugar. Given the dominant positions, unilateral or collective, of the refiners, the wholesalers had reason to take such threats seriously; and they did.

Until the commission took action against this system, community markets for refined sugar exhibited substantial amounts of trade but precious little competition. For example, during the four years between 1968 and 1972, Belgium exported 88,800 tons of white sugar to Germany. Of that amount, 68,100 tons, or 77%, was designated by the EC Commission as "controlled" - unlikely to affect market prices in Germany - because it satisfied one of the following criteria : It was sold to a German refiner; it was sold to a German user but with the prior approval of a German refiner; it was sold to a German user at a price above that charged to German refiners; or it was sold to customers vowing either to denature the sugar or to reexport it outside the EC.[37]

Small wonder, then, that refiners in deficit areas maintained their control over local prices despite the arrival of imports. Small wonder also that certain countries could import substantial amounts of sugar without experiencing corresponding amounts of competition in domestic sugar markets. For the companies themselves, the purpose of the system was to preserve the authority of each group of refiners in its home area.[38]

How typical is the situation in sugar? Has increased exposure to international trade failed across the board to increase the intensity of competition in European markets? To answer these questions, it is useful to return to our French evidence on import exposure and export propensity between 1959 and 1980. In 1959, imports accounted for 34% of French consumption of sugar and sugar products.[39] Only one manufacturing industry (bulk organic chemicals) could claim greater exposure to imports at that time. Between 1959 and 1980, the incidence of imports on domestic sugar consumption declined by 17 percentage points. In fact, sugar was the only manufacturing industry to register a decline in exposure to imports. In 1980, however, imported sugar still accounted for 16% of domestic consumption.

The very fact that sugar was the only manufacturing industry to register a decline in import exposure between 1959 and 1980 suggests that the experience of the industry is hardly typical. To paint a more general picture, we may employ a palette of studies linking prices to imports at the industry level. Specifically, these studies correlate exposure to imports with the degrees to which (1) price levels are explained by cost levels, (2) prices change over time, (3) price changes are explained by changes in cost or demand, and (4) prices converge across countries. Let us discuss each type of evidence in turn.

3.3. Imports and Price-Cost Margins

In competitive markets, prices tend to approximate marginal costs. In monopolistic and oligopolistic markets, prices tend to exceed marginal costs. If exposure to imports intensifies competition, then we would expect price-cost margins to correlate negatively with exposure to imports (1) in a cross section of national industries and (2) in particular industries over time.

The first of these negative correlations has been observed in a cross-section of French manufacturing industries.[40] It has also been observed in a cross-section of large French manufacturing companies.[41]

At the industry level, time-series analysis of the relationship between price-cost margins and import-exposure has not been conducted frequently.[42] In the French setting, the major intertemporal study of profitability during the period surrounding formation of the EEC was undertaken at a more aggregate level.[43] Christian Sautter studied rates of return to capital during the period 1954-74. He found that the direction of change in profitability depended on the measure of profitability used.[44] His preferred measure suggested that competition increased after formation of the EEC: Between 1954 and 1960, profitability rose moderately; between 1960 and 1974, it declined fairly steadily and very sharply. In 1960, the return to the aggregate of French productive assets was roughly 29%; by 1974, it had declined by almost one-third to 20%.[45]

3.4. Imports and Price Changes at the Industry Level

Exposure to imports should affect changes as well as levels of prices. To the extent that import-exposure increases elasticities of supply at existing prices, upward shifts of market-demand are not as likely to result in upward movements of price. Over time, therefore, we might expect to observe a negative correlation at the industry level between import-exposure and increase in price. Table 16 reports the distribution of economic activities according to change in price during the five years following creation of the EEC (1959-64). In 12 of the 79 activities, accounting for 25% of output, domestic prices rose at least 30%. On the other hand, in 11 activities, accounting for 5% of output, prices actually declined during this half-decade. Table 17 presents corresponding information for the period 1959-1969.

These movements in prices can be linked to changes in exposure to imports. Among all 79 activities, the correlation between change in price and change in import-exposure differed negatively

TABLE 16 : Distribution of Industries by Change in Price, 1959-1964.

Change in Price	Number of Industries	Share of Output 1959	1964
dp < -20	2	0.2	0.1
-20 ≤ dp < -10	4	1.4	1.5
-10 ≤ dp < 0	5	4.2	3.9
0 ≤ dp < 10	12	9.5	8.8
10 ≤ dp < 20	28	32.9	30.5
20 ≤ dp < 30	16	28.2	30.1
30 ≤ dp < 40	10	21.8	22.7
40 ≤ dp	2	1.8	2.4
All	79	100.0	100.0

Notes : DP=(100)((Q64/QR64)/(Q59/QR59)-1), where Q is output (production distribuée) in current prices, and QR is output in the prices of 1970. Q64 is output in 1964. Shares of production are calculated in current prices. Industries are defined according to NAP-S79.

Source : INSEE, input-output tables in current prices and in the prices of 1970, level S (unpublished).

TABLE 17 : Distribution of Industries by Change in Price, 1959-1969.

Change in Price	Number of Industries	Share of Output 1959	1964
dp < -20	3	0.5	0.3
-20 ≤ dp < -10	5	1.8	1.9
-10 ≤ dp < 0	4	3.8	3.6
0 ≤ dp < 10	6	4.3	3.4
10 ≤ dp < 20	10	9.6	7.9
20 ≤ dp < 30	13	18.9	17.8
30 ≤ dp < 40	15	24.2	21.9
40 ≤ dp < 50	7	6.8	6.5
50 ≤ dp < 60	3	8.5	10.6
60 ≤ dp < 70	6	6.4	6.8
70 ≤ dp < 80	4	13.4	15.8
80 ≤ dp	3	1.9	3.6
All	79	100.0	100.0

Notes : dp=(100) ((Q69/QR69)/(Q59/QR59)-1), where Q is output (production distribuée) measured in current prices and QR is output measured in the prices of 1970. Q64 is output in 1964. Shares of output are calculated in current prices. Activities are defined according to NAP-S79.

Source : INSEE input-output tables in current prices and in the price of 1970, level S (unpublished).

from 0.[46] Such evidence is consistent with the view that exposure to imports did indeed promote competition.

3.5. Imports and the Sensitivity of Price to Cost and to Demand

In competitive markets with imperfectly elastic supply curves, prices should change each time cost curves or demand curves shift. In other words, prices should respond sensitively to shifts in cost and demand. In contrast, for a variety of reasons, markets supplied by powerful sellers can be expected to exhibit some modicum of price-inertia.[47]

David Encaoua and Philippe Michel have studied the elasticity of French prices with respect to costs and demand.[48] They found that exposure to imports correlated positively with such elasticities. Their findings are consistent with the view that exposure to imports did promote competition in domestic markets.

3.6. Imports and the International Convergence of Prices

In the limit, exposure to international trade serves to extend the boundaries of economically meaningful markets beyond national frontiers. If the multinational market functions competitively, prices should differ among countries by no more than transport-cost.[49] Moreover, prices should converge toward the minimum of the levels prevailing before the international market develops.[50]

Price-convergence within the ECSC has been studied on several occasions. For coal, "the opening of the common market had an immediate effect... Prices continued to come together until 1956. ... Then Belgian prices break out of the mould and create a divergence which is narrowed again by 1958. French devaluation [in 1957] creates another divergence."[51] In steel, "the picture is less sharp."[52] In 1954, the United Nations Economic Commission for Europe asserted: "The approach to uniformity of prices is more striking than the continuing differences."[53] Four years later, however, the high authority lamented: "In a great number of cases, the difference between the published prices of different groups of producers is much greater than the cost of transportation between the corresponding basing points."[54]

More recently, the EC Commission has studied price behavior in the European automobile industry. It has found that model-specific prices tend to differ systematically among member countries. In 1975, prices were lowest in Denmark and highest in Italy. The difference between the two was 16%. Seven years later, prices were still lowest in Denmark but highest in Britain. British prices exceeded those in Denmark by 45% and those in Italy (the country with the second-highest level of prices) by 22%.[55]

This pattern of prices cannot be explained in terms of transport costs: Cars produced in England are sold for less abroad than at home.[56] Nor, in the view of the commission, can international differences in prices be explained by corresponding differences in government price control.[57] According to London's Institute of Fiscal Studies, if Britons had been able to purchase the cars they actually acquired in 1981 at Belgian rather than British prices, they would have saved 1.3 billion pounds - 0.6% of GDP.[58]

The commission's investigation reveals how the automobile companies have succeeded in maintaining such price differentials, especially those between Britain and other parts of the EC.[59] The cost of producing an automobile is higher in England than in continental Europe. As a result, companies with production facilities in both places may decide to produce cars on the continent, export them to England, and sell them at prices above the cost of local manufacture.[60] Such a strategy requires that cars produced on the continent meet British tastes and regulations. Since many Britons want their steering columns on the right, while most others want their columns on the left, this requirement of the strategy cannot be considered nontrivial.

Ford produces automobiles in Germany as well as in England. Its German subsidiary produces a large number of cars equipped with right hand drive. Nominally destined for English military and diplomatic personnel residing in Germany, some of these satisfy German regulations. Others meet Britain's technical requirements. Ford's German subsidiary exports "a considerable percentage of its production"[61] to Britain in the form of right-hand drive cars. Ford's English subsidiary then distributes the cars in its home market at prices related to the English cost of production. Although Ford's contracts with its distributors permitted them to acquire Ford automobiles from Ford wholesalers and retailers in other EC countries, English retailers of Fords did not avail themselves of this opportunity. As a result, international trade exerted no direct downward pressure on the prices of Fords in England.

Aware of international differences in prices, many English customers sought to buy abroad their cars with right hand drive.[62] Under Ford Germany's standard agreement with its German distributors, Ford undertook to provide the distributors with any model Ford produced. This included, of course, the right-hand-drive cars that Ford Germany was exporting to Ford UK. The German distributors were all too willing to sell such cars to British nationals.

On April 27, 1982, Ford AG informed its principal dealers that as of May 1, 1982, it would cease to supply them with right-hand-drive vehicles. Even Britons residing in Germany would have to purchase such vehicles from a British subsidiary. In other words, Ford AG moved to stop the arbitrage.

The actions of Ford were unusual only to the extent that they resulted from right-hand-drive production on the continent. Other manufacturers employed different tactics to discourage purchase of automobiles in Belgium by customers residing elsewhere in the EC. Some delayed delivery to Belgium of cars meeting the technical specifications of other countries; some established wholesale prices for such cars that exceeded the corresponding prices of vehicles with Belgian specifications; and some established warranties that discriminated against those seeking after-sales service outside the country where their car was purchased. Upon intervention of the EC Commission, several companies abandoned these practices.[63]

Unlike its European rivals, however, Ford chose to fight the commission before the court of justice.[64] Ultimately, the court accepted the commission's view that Ford's system of selective distribution violated article 85(1) of the EEC treaty and failed to qualify for exemption under article 85(3). The reason was simple: Ford's refusal to supply English-type cars to German dealers impeded parallel imports and hence contravened the public interest.[65] Rather than sacrifice its system of selective distribution, Ford agreed to supply right-hand-drive cars to its German dealers.

In keeping with its position in the Ford case, the commission has announced a general strategy for dealing with geographic differentials in auto prices.[66] Companies setting list prices for a given vehicle that differ among member countries by more than 12% will lose their presumptive right to employ selective networks of dealers.[67] As the Ford experience suggests, selective distribution is important to the manufacturers: They are likely to suffer price convergence (just enough) to keep it.

3.7. Convergence on Prices in "Competitive" World Markets

Convergence of prices within the EC is especially likely to signal competition if the level upon which prices converge corresponds to the level observed in "competitive" world markets. Such correspondences have not been studied systematically.[68] We have reason to believe, however, that French prices sometimes repose well above those prevailing outside the EC.

The French government has signalled clearly its willingness and ability to exclude aggressive, extra-community competitors from its domestic markets. Its treatment of video cassette recorders during the first half of the 1980s provides a case in point. Alarmed by the success of Japanese manufacturers in supplying French markets for consumer electronics, the French government applied dubious customs procedures to delay imports of VCRs from Japan: All such imports had to clear customs in Poitiers, a remote and lightly staffed customs house. Working to rule, the inspectors insured that the Japanese products would trickle to market at an agonizingly slow pace. France abandoned the tactic only after it induced the EC to develop a community-wide policy on VCR imports. The Japanese concluded that the best way to supply the European VCR market was to form joint ventures with European firms to assemble in Europe components that the Japanese produced in Asia. At the components level, then, European exposure to imports remained; but the degree of competition in VCR markets is hardly the greater therefor.[69]

The VCR episode is not the only case of France protecting itself from suppliers outside the community. In fact, many times, the French have insulated themselves from suppliers outside the EC to a greater extent than has the community as a whole: For example, France maintains a quota on Japanese automobiles that is far more restrictive than that of any other EC country save Italy.[70]

It is important, however, to recognize the limits of such behavior. France may be able to restrict imports from Japan - just as it once restricted inward investment from the United States: but it cannot always oblige other EC countries to follow suit. If the Japanese or the Americans then export to or produce in other EC countries, and if companies in those other member countries respond to the competition by improving their own products and technology, then the French do not escape the competitive effects of Japanese or American enterprise: The competitive advantages of extra-community rivals become embodied in intra-community rivals, who enjoy relatively free access to the French market. In other words, French companies may be obliged to meet indirectly the standards of competitive world markets - as long as other EC countries adopt a liberal stance towards imports and investment originating outside the community.[71]

3.8. Conclusion

Systematic evidence does suggest that exposure to imports is associated with quasi-competitive pricing behavior. As a result, it is consistent with the hypothesis that imports did stimulate competition. If it is important not to exaggerate the positive effects of trade on competition, it is also important not to exaggerate the compatibility of pervasive arbitrage with substantial market power.

4. EXPORT DISCIPLINE

I suggested above that increased reliance on export markets is especially likely to signal increased competitive pressure when the foreign markets in question are not colonial in nature. In this section, I shall demonstrate that most French exporters have ceased to rely on colonial markets; they must compete to succeed in the markets which they supply.

4.1. Aggregate Evidence

Since World War II, the distribution of French exports by destination has undergone remarkable change. Early in the postwar period, France relied heavily on the French Overseas Union (FOU) for export markets (table 18). In 1952, 42% of all French exports went to FOU. Roughly half of such exports went to North Africa,[72] one-quarter to the rest of Africa,[73] and one-fifth to Indochina.[74] Algeria alone accounted for over 10% of French exports in 1952.

After 1952, FOU declined in importance as a destination for French exports. Between 1952 and 1962, the share of FOU in French exports declined by 50%; between 1962 and 1972, it declined again by 50%. In just two decades, then, the share of FOU in French exports fell from over 42% to under 10%. In 1972, the whole of FOU absorbed a smaller share of French exports than had Algeria alone in 1952. Since 1972, FOU has absorbed between 9.3% and 11.5% of French exports. Its importance as a destination in 1984 was identical to its importance in 1972.

The importance of each FOU member as a destination of French exports began to decline around the time it received its (political) independence. Indochina was the first market to constrict: Accounting for 8.2% for French exports in 1952, Indochina never absorbed as much as 1% of French exports after 1958. The next markets to shrink were Tunisia and Morocco. Each attained its independence in 1956. Between 1952 and 1957, their importance in French exports declined from 9.8% to 5.9%. Since Algeria's independence in 1962, Morocco and Tunisia have accounted for under 4% of French exports.[75]

TABLE 18 : The Destination of French Exports, 1952-1984
Percentage of total exports

Year	FOU	North Africa	Other Africa	Indo China	Algeria	OECD	Europe	EC6	Germany
1952	42.2	22.4	9.9	8.2	12.6	43.2	38.0	15.9	5.6
1953	37.0	20.1	8.7	6.6	11.3	46.9	40.5	18.6	7.0
1954	37.2	19.9	10.3	5.5	11.8	45.6	40.5	21.9	8.4
1955	31.8	19.1	8.7	2.5	11.9	51.7	45.8	24.4	10.5
1956	32.8	20.8	8.9	1.5	13.6	51.8	45.2	25.3	10.5
1957	35.0	21.9	9.4	1.8	16.0	49.9	43.6	25.1	10.8
1958	37.5	24.8	9.6	1.3	19.2	46.6	39.1	22.2	10.5
1959	31.8	21.6	7.1	0.6	17.0	53.5	43.4	27.2	13.1
1960	30.0	20.6	6.9	0.9	15.9	55.0	47.5	29.8	13.7
1961	26.1	16.4	7.5	0.7	12.3	59.6	52.2	33.5	15.2
1962	20.8	11.2	7.3	0.6	7.6	64.7	57.3	36.8	17.3
1963	19.6	10.3	7.2	0.5	6.9	66.3	59.4	38.3	16.6
1964	18.0	8.8	7.0	0.3	5.5	67.9	60.8	38.8	17.4
1965	16.2	7.7	6.1	0.3	5.1	69.9	62.1	40.9	19.3
1966	14.6	6.5	5.7	0.4	4.0	70.9	62.5	42.3	19.3
1967	14.3	6.0	6.0	0.3	3.6	70.3	61.8	41.3	17.3
1968	13.5	5.7	5.5	0.4	3.7	70.0	61.5	43.0	18.6
1969	12.1	4.9	4.8	0.5	3.1	73.1	65.4	47.8	20.6
1970	11.8	5.0	4.6	0.3	3.2	73.7	66.1	48.8	20.8
1971	10.3	4.2	4.3	0.3	2.5	74.7	67.1	49.4	21.5
1972	9.3	3.5	4.2	0.2	1.8	76.5	68.9	49.9	21.3
1973	9.2	3.9	3.9	0.1	2.1	76.1	69.0	48.6	19.6
1974	9.8	4.8	3.7	0.1	2.9	74.1	66.8	46.1	17.5
1975	11.5	6.0	4.2	0.1	3.6	66.8	61.0	41.0	16.3
1976	10.4	4.9	4.3	0.1	2.6	67.6	61.4	42.5	16.9
1977	10.7	5.1	4.4	0.1	2.8	67.8	60.9	41.7	16.7
1978	9.5	4.1	4.1	0.1	1.9	68.6	61.3	42.5	16.8
1979	9.5	4.1	4.1	0.1	1.9	69.6	62.9	42.6	16.8
1980	9.4	4.1	4.1	0.1	2.3	67.2	61.1	41.0	15.4
1981	9.3	4.3	3.8	0.1	2.2	64.4	57.0	37.2	14.2
1982	9.8	4.3	4.1	0.0	2.2	65.3	57.5	37.7	14.2
1983	9.5	4.3	3.7	0.1	2.6	66.7	58.1	38.0	15.0
1984	9.3	4.4	3.3	0.0	2.8	68.0	57.7	37.3	14.1

Notes : FOU=French overseas union, as defined in Adams, Restructuring the French Economy, appendix 6; EC6=original European Economic Community .

Sources: 1952-74 : Annuaire Statistique de la France, various issues; 1975-84 : International Monetary Fund, Direction of Trade Statistics, 1980 and 1986 editions.

Algeria illustrates dramatically the evaporation of France's colonial markets. Between 1955 and 1958, Algeria's share of French exports escalated along with Algeria's war for independence. At the end of that three-year period, Algeria accounted for nearly one-fifth of all French exports. Thereafter, its role declined precipitously. Between 1958 and 1962,[76] Algeria's share of French exports dropped from 19.2% to 7.6%. By 1966, Algeria's share had declined to 4.0%. Since 1966, it has remained below 4% - falling occasionally under 2%.

Corresponding to the decline of colonial markets was the rise of "competitive world markets." In 1952, France exported almost as much to FOU as it did to countries now comprising the OECD (table 18). North Africa's 3 members of FOU imported 140% as much from France as did the 5 countries joining France that very year to form the ECSC. Germany bought less than half as much from France as did Algeria.

The primacy of FOU disappeared in 1961. From that year onward, France has exported more to charter members of the common market than it has to charter members of FOU. It has also sent more to Germany than it has to Algeria. European members of today's OECD buy twice as much from France as do members past and present of FOU. The entire OECD accounted for 60% of French exports.

In 1972, the importance of the OECD, of the original common market, and of Germany as destinations for French goods reached a peak. At that time, the OECD accounted for 76.5%, the original common market for 49.9%, and Germany for 21.3% of French exports. Thus, in 1972, Germany alone bought more French goods than did the entire original overseas union.

After 1972, the geographic structure of French exports changed again. The importance of Germany declined by one-third, and the importance of the whole original common market declined by one-quarter. In part, these changes reflected the EC enlargements of 1973 and 1981;[77] for even in 1984 - 12 years after the highwater mark of 1972 - the OECD took two-thirds of French exports, as compared with 43.2% in 1952.

4.2. Industry-Level Evidence

To what extent, however, did France come to rely on "competitive world markets" for all types of exports? Has it become (as some predicted it would) the breadbasket of the common market -supplying food to the "real" industrial countries of the community while dispatching manufactures to its colonies past and present? In other words, should we stop short of concluding from the aggregate figures that most French manufacturers now export to competitive world markets, subjecting themselves thereby to "export discipline?"

TABLE 19 : Importance of French Exports to the OECD, 1983. Percent

SITC Code	Section Name	XI/XT	XIOECD/XI
0	Food and animals	13	68
1	Beverages and tobacco	3	85
2	Inedible crude materials, exc. fuel	4	92
3	Mineral fuels, lubricants, etc.	4	86
4	Animals and vegetable oils, etc.	0	58
5	Chemicals & related prods.	13	74
6	Manufactures classed by material	19	71
7	Machinery and transport equipment	34	61
8	Miscellaneous manufactures	9	72
9	Commodities and transactions nec	1	56
0/9	All	100	69

Notes : XI=French exports of goods in the relevant SITC section(s). XT=total French exports. XIOECD=French exports to OECD countries of goods in the relevant SITC section(s). SITC=standard International Trade Classification, revision 2.

Source : Organisation for Economic Cooperation and Development, Foreign Trade by Commodities, 1983, series C, vol. I : Exports (OECD, 1985).

To examine the uniformity across industries in the propensity to direct exports toward "competitive world markets," I calculated for each French industry the share of exports destined for the OECD.[78] During 1983, in the aggregate, 69% of French exports went to the OECD (table 19). Among the four manufacturing sections of the SITC,[79] only machinery and transport equipment sent less than 70% of its exports to the OECD - and even there the ratio exceeded 60%. In each of the other manufacturing sections, reliance on the OECD as a destination for exports exceeded that exhibited by producers of food.[80] At this level of industrial

TABLE 20 : French Exports to OECD Countries, 1952-1983. Percent

SITC Code	Section Name	XIOECD/XI 1952	1958	1963	1968	1973	1978	1983
0	Food, animals	34	39	58	73	76	77	67
1	Beverages, tobacco	50	63	79	80	81	80	80
2	Crude materials nec	83	82	86	85	86	85	84
3	Mineral fuels,etc.	42	51	68	87	91	87	79
4	Animals, veget. oils	32	16	42	63	61	57	56
5	Chemicals & related	39	39	54	59	65	67	67
6	Manufactures by mat'l	33	42	64	68	72	68	67
7	Machinery	26	39	55	54	65	58	54
8	Misc. manufactures	35	37	63	70	75	70	67
9	Not elsewhere class.	12	20	31	46	50	68	53
0/9	All	37	44	62	65	71	67	64

Notes : XIOECD=French exports to OECD countries of goods in the relevant SITC section(s). XI=French exports to all destinations of goods in the relevant SITC section(s). SITC=Standard International Trade Classification; 1952 and 1958: original version; 1963, 1968, and 1973: revision 1; 1978 and 1983: revision 2. OECD comprises the original OEEC plus Canada and the United States; it excludes Australia, Finland, Japan, New Zealand, and Spain.

Sources: 1952: OEEC, Foreign Trade, series II: Foreign Trade by Areas and by Commodity Categories (Sept. 1953). 1958: OEEC, Foreign Trade, series B: Analytical Abstracts, Jan.-Dec. 1959, no. 1. 1963: OECD, Foreign Trade, series C: Trade by Commodities, Jan.-Dec. 1963, vol. I: Exports. 1968: OECD, Statistics of Foreign Trade, series B: Analytical Abstracts, Jan.-Dec. 1968, no. 1. 1973: OECD, Statistics of Trade, series C: Trade by Commodities, Market Summaries: Exports, Jan.-Dec. 1978. 1983: OECD, Forgeign Trade by Commodities, 1983, series C, vol. I: Exports.

detail, it would be difficult to argue that French agriculture catered to rich countries while French manufacturers supplied the third world.

Table 20 traces variations over time in the importance of the OECD as a customer for French exports.[81] Between 1952 and 1973, the share of exports headed to the OECD increased in every industry.[82] With one small exception, the relative importance of the OECD rose substantially. Especially noteworthy was the experience of machinery and transport equipment. In 1952, only one-quarter of such exports were absorbed by the OECD. In 1973, however, 65% of such exports went to the OECD. After 1973, in most industries, the role of the OECD declined. Nevertheless, in all manufacturing sections, the importance of the OECD remained substantially greater than it had been back in 1952.

When industries are defined more narrowly,[83] the OECD no longer bought uniformly great and rising shares of French exports (table 21). Among the 35 manufacturing industries, seven[84] sent less than half their exports to the OECD. One-third of French manufacturing exports were attributable to 11 industries sending less than 60% of their exports to the OECD. In such cases, a

TABLE 21 : Distribution of French Manufacturing Industries by Reliance on OECD Countries for Export Markets, 1983.

Importance of OECD	Number of Industries	XI/XMFG (%)
0.0 ≤ XIOECD/XI < 0.3	0	0
0.3 ≤ XIOECD/XI < 0.5	7	20
0.5 ≤ XIOECD/XI < 0.6	4	13
0.6 ≤ XIOECD/XI < 0.7	7	19
0.7 ≤ XIOECD/XI < 0.8	10	28
0.8 ≤ XIOECD/XI < 0.9	7	20
0.9 ≤ XIOECD/XI	0	0
All	35	100

Notes : Industries are manufacturing divisions of the Standard International Trade Classification, revision 2. Manufactures are goods classified to sections 5 through 8 of the SITC. XIOECD=French exports to OECD countries of goods in the relevant SITC division(s). XI=French exports to all destinations of goods in the relevant SITC division(s). XMFG=French exports of all manufactures to all destinations.

Source: OECD, Foreign Trade by Commodities, 1983, series C, vol. I: Exports.

large propensity to export did not necessarily entail exposure to competitive world markets. On the other hand, 17 industries sent over 70% of their exports to the OECD.[85] Given the number and importance of the industries exporting heavily to the OECD, one must conclude that only some manufacturing industries still fail to rely on rich market economies to absorb the bulk of their exports.

Table 22 reveals the identities of the 7 manufacturing industries which sent less than half their exports to the OECD in 1983. It also reports the reliance in 1983 of each such industry on the original FOU for export markets. In a few cases, the habits of the old economic régime persisted: Manufacturers of metal products sent over one-fifth, and manufacturers of drugs sent over one-third, of their exports to FOU. On the other hand, in each of the machinery industries, FOU bought less than 20% of

TABLE 22: French Manufacturing Industries Least Reliant on OECD Countries for Export Markets, 1983. Percent.

Industry Code	Name	XI/XMFG	XIOECD/XI	XIFOU/XI
54	Medicinals, pharmaceuticals	2.0	50	36
69	Manufactures of metal nec	3.9	50	21
57	Explosives	0.1	48	21
79	Transp. eq. exc. road veh.	5.4	47	7
73	Metalworking machinery	0.8	46	10
74	Gen'l indus. machinery	5.8	45	18
76	Telecomm. & sound equip.	2.0	37	16

Notes :Industries are manufacturing divisions of the Standard International Trade Classification, revision 2. Manufactures are goods classified to sections 5 through 8 of the SITC. XI=French exports to all destinations of goods in the relevant SITC division(s). XMFG=French exports of all manufactures to all destinations. XIOECD=French exports to OECD countries of goods in the relevant SITC division(s). XIFOU=French exports to the French overseas union (see table 18) of goods in the relevant SITC division(s).

Source : OECD, Foreign Trade by Commodities, 1983, series C, vol. I: Exports.

French exports. In fact, manufacturers of transport equipment other than road vehicles sent a smaller proportion of their exports to FOU than did French exporters as a group. If these four machinery industries did not send a majority of their exports to the OECD, neither did they continue to rely on the once-sheltered markets of the overseas union.

4.3. Reliance of France's Clients on French Exports

I have employed the countries of the OECD as proxies for "competitive world markets" on the presumption that each was supplied by producers of many nationalities: In effect, I have assumed that even at the level of particular products, no small group of exporters could claim to dominate trade with an OECD country.

In their incarnation as colonies, members of FOU purchased most of their imports from France. As a result, French exporters faced little foreign competition in those markets. In their incarnation as imperial alumni, however, the FOU countries have diversified their sources of foreign supply. Even in the old colonies, French exporters now face serious competition from counterparts in other OECD countries.

Algeria provides the most import example of economic decolonization. In 1958, when Algeria's share of French exports reached its postwar maximum, France accounted for 84% of all Algerian imports and 91% of Algerian imports from the OECD (table 23). Imports from FOU, controlled no doubt by French companies, accounted for another 5% of Algerian imports. While Algeria received $962 million in imports from France, it obtained $7.3 million in imports from the Netherlands - its second largest source of foreign merchandise. It is difficult to imagine a developing country more dependent on an economic overlord.

Twenty-five years later, two decades after independence, Algeria no longer exhibited such reliance on France. The French share of Algerian imports had declined to 23%. Imports from the old FOU dropped to less than 1% of the Algerian total. In round numbers, then, Algerian imports from areas under French influence dropped from 90% in 1958 to 25% in 1983. The French share of Algeria's imports from the OECD declined from over 90% to under 30%. Germany had replaced the Netherlands as Algeria's second largest source of imports, accounting for almost half the value of imports attributable to France. If France remained the leading source of Algerian imports, French producers could no longer consider the Algerian market safe from foreign competition. From the French perspective, Algeria has not been a sheltered market for a quarter of a century.

Algeria is an extreme case, due, no doubt, to the terms under which France surrendered sovereignty over the area. Other members of the old FOU, along with certain clients of current importance who had not belonged to the union, do rely substantially on France

TABLE 23: Geographic Origins of Algerian Imports,1958 and 1983. Percent.

Exporting Area	IJ/IOECD 1958	1983	IJ/I 1958	1983
France	91	28	84	23
FOU	...	...	5	1
OECD	100	100	92	84

Notes : IJ=Algerian imports from the relevant exporting area. IOECD=Algerian imports from OECD countries, I=Algerian imports from all source countries. FOU=French overseas union (see table 18).

Source : 1958: International Monetary Fund, Directory of Trade, 1962 Edition. 1983: International Monetary Fund, Direction of Trade Statistics, 1986 Yearbook.

- at least for certain goods. To appreciate this phenomenon concretely, let us examine the dependence of all importing countries on French exports in the context of a single industry - telecommunications and audio equipment.[86] This is the SITC manufacturing division in which French exporters relied least heavily on OECD markets as of 1983. It, therefore, is the manufacturing industry most likely to have exhibited a predilection for "soft" export markets.

Table 24 reports for 1983 the mean ratio of French to OECD exports of telecommunications and audio equipment toward each of three destinations: the OECD, the French overseas union, and all other countries.[87] Among all importing countries, the mean dependence on France was 21%. This global mean corresponded closely to that within the group of countries belonging neither to the OECD nor to FOU.[88] On the other hand, it reflected poorly the corresponding means for the other two groups of countries. The OECD countries - my proxy for "competitive world markets" - bought just 5% of their imported telecommunications and audio products from French exporters. In contrast, members of the old FOU purchased 55% of such imports from France. In short, FOU remained an environment in which French exporters accounted for a large share of imports; the OECD constituted the opposite; and countries belonging neither to FOU nor to the OECD comprised an intermediate case.

TABLE 24: France's Position Among Exporters of Telecommunications and Audio Equipment, 1983. Percent unless otherwise specified.

Importing Area	Number of Countries	XJF/XF	XJF/XJOECD
OECD	22	37	5
FOU	31	16	55
Other	130	47	22
All	183	100	21

Notes : Telecommunications and audio equipment comprises goods assigned to SITC division 76. XJF=French exports of such goods to the relevant area(s). XF=French exports of such goods to all areas. XOECD=OECD exports of such goods to the relevant area(s).

Source : OECD, Foreign Trade by Commodities, 1983, series C, vol. I: Exports.

The three groups of countries differed not only in mean dependence on France but also in intragroup variation in such dependence. Among OECD clients, the French share of relevant exports never exceeded 8%.[89] Among clients in FOU, 6 countries[90] relied on France for less than one-quarter of relevant imports. Meanwhile, 5 countries depended on France for over four-fifths of such imports. Notice that three of the six countries exhibiting low dependence on France required force to obtain their independence, and another[91] left on strained terms. In contrast, Martinique and French Guiana, two of the three countries relying on France for over 90% of relevant imports, remained under French sovereignty.[92] Looking finally at countries belonging to neither the OECD nor the overseas union, some variation in dependence on France did exist: Of the 130 countries in this group, 18 imported no telecommunications or audio equipment from France. For another 33, the ratio of French to OECD exports was less than 1%. At the other end of the spectrum, for three countries,[93] the French share of relevant exports exceeded 40%. In two of these cases, the ratio was 44%; in the other,[94] it was 61%.

Although I have not performed similar analyses of other manufacturing divisions of the SITC, I suspect that these figures on French exports of communications and audio permit us to draw several conclusions regarding the impact of exports on the competitive pressures faced by French exporters. First, exports to the OECD are exports to "competitive world markets." French sellers do not dominate exports of most products to rich market economies. Second, certain members of the old FOU no longer rely heavily on France to satisfy their import needs. In particular, Algeria and Indochina have shed most vestiges of their erstwhile dependence. Third, other members of FOU - especially those that remain legally linked to France - continue to rely heavily on France for imports. Finally, countries belonging neither to the OECD nor to the original FOU exhibit a degree of dependence on France that lies between those displayed by the other two groups. Some of these countries exhibit dependence as pronounced as that to be found in the overseas union; but most fall well below that level.[95]

4.4. Exports and the Sensitivity of Prices to Cost and Demand

If the foreign markets supplied by French exporters were competitive, and linked fairly tightly to the domestic market, then the propensity of an industry to export should correlate positively with the sensitivity of its domestic price to shifts in cost or demand. David Encaoua and Philippe Michel have observed just such a correlation after formation of the EEC.[96]

4.5. Conclusion

The declining importance of colonial and quasi-colonial markets, the opening of former colonies to imports from developed countries other than France, and the rising importance to French exporters of "competitive world markets" have all served to increase the vigor of competition experienced by French exporters. The timing of these changes is worth juxtaposing with the timing of the increased propensity to export. Recall that the propensity to export did not rise until the late 1960s. It was precisely between 1959 and 1966, however, that the destination of French exports was changing so radically. We may conclude, therefore, that changes in French export behavior, first in terms of destinations and then in terms of incidence on production, served throughout the period since 1959 to increase the intensity of competition experienced by French sellers.

5. CONCLUSION

To this day, France imposes quotas on certain imports, employs fastidious customs procedures, and discriminates in public procurement against goods produced abroad. Moreover, to this day, the European Communities have failed to create a single internal market. Public and private barriers continue to impede international trade and investment, sheltering the EC as a whole from the outside world, and one EC country from another.

Nevertheless, fundamental changes in the international relations of the French state have been accompanied by fundamental changes in the exposure of French business to foreign competition. Foreign goods have come to account for major shares of French consumption and French producers export major fractions of domestic output. Virtually all manufacturing enterprises are now exposed to foreign rivals, and this is reflected in French entrepreneurial behavior. The evidence discussed in this paper should give pause to those in the United States who argue that France remains a protectionist country despite its participation in the European Communities.

NOTES

1 Space prevents me from discussing international investment. See Restructuring the French Economy, chap 4.

2 Europessimism - the lament that members of the European Communities are coming to rely less heavily on each other rather than more so - is discussed in Eric Stein, "The European Community in 1983: A Less Perfect Union?" Common Market Law Review, vol. 20 (December 1983), pp. 641-656.

3 Unfinished nonferrous metals (27%), edible oils and fats (33%), sugar (34%), and bulk organic chemicals (36%).

4 Imports accounted for over two-thirds of domestic consumption in air and sea transport (68%), nonferrous metallic minerals (88%), and crude petroleum (95%).

5 Coal (+27 percentage points), fish (+38 percentage points), ferrous minerals (+59 percentage points) and natural gas (+71 percentage points).

6 In all but one of these eight industries (air and sea transport), the decline was slight - between 3.2 and 0.6 percentage points. In air and sea transport, IM declined by 9 percentage points.

7 Shoes (+30 percentage points), knitwear (+35 percentage points), woven textiles (+36 percentage points), household electronics (+52 percentage points), and manmade fibers (+56 percentage points).

8 Sugar.

9 The rate of duty (t) is measured as (100)(T)/(M), where T=duty collected and M=imports cif.

10 At the .01 level of statistical significance in a one-tail t-test (r=0.49, N=46).

11 See George W. Stocking and Myron W. Watkins, Cartels in Action: Case Studies in International Business Diplomacy (Twentieth Century Fund, 1946).

12 Manmade fibers, knitwear, yarn and thread, leather products, and shoes.

13 Fish, natural gas, ferrous minerals, nonferrous metallic minerals, crude petroleum, and air and sea transport.

14 Transport related services (21%), nonmetallic minerals (27%), nonferrous metallic minerals (41%), ferrous minerals (54%), and air and sea transport (94%).

15 All but miscellaneous manufactures and wood; in both of these industries, EX fell by less than 5 percentage points.

16 Among the industries where it increased substantially were electrical equipment (+20 percentage points), office equipment and professional electronics (+23 percentage points),

unfinished nonferrous metals (+25 percentage points), bulk organic chemicals (+30 percentage points), and aerospace equipment (+37 percentage points). Each of these industries accounted for over 35 billion francs of output in 1980.

17 Air and sea transport (-13 percentage points), nonferrous metallic minerals (-16 percentage points), and ferrous minerals (-27 percentage points).

18 Land and Fresh water transport, agricultural products, and fish.

19 The maximum was +14 percentage points in fish.

20 Note the jump in 1970 following the devaluation of 1969. The timing of this jump should remind us that increases in the propensity of French manufacturers to export cannot be attributed solely to governmental deregulation of international trade. Nevertheless, it should be remembered that imports as well as exports were increasing rapidly and across the board during this period, suggesting the importance of trade liberalization in our context.

21 The numerator of EX includes exports to all destinations. To the extent that exports to community countries fell, absolutely or in relation to other exports, the data discussed in the text are compatible with the declining importance of the community as a market for its members. We shall have occasion below to examine the geographic composition of French exports.

22 In 1959, only two industries, accounting for two percent of manufacturing output, could claim the same.

23 Manmade fibers, aerospace equipment, military products, sugar, and bulk organic chemicals.

24 Manufacturing industries producing at least 50 billion francs of output in 1980 and exporting at least 30% of that output were: crude steel (35%), automobiles (38%), office equipment and professional electronics (38%), mechanical equipment (38%), and unfinished nonferrous metals (41%).

25 The concept of strategic group is discussed in Howard H. Newman, "Strategic Groups and the Structure-Performance Relationship," Review of Economics and Statistics, vol. 60 (August 1968), pp. 417-428.

26 Unless the two parts of the multinational enterprise produce nonsubstitutable goods.

27 See William James Adams, "Producer-Concentration as a Proxy for Seller-Concentration: Some Evidence from the World Automotive Industry," Journal of Industrial Economics, vol. 29 (December 1980), pp. 185-202.

28 A few recent studies have attempted to overcome this problem. See David Encaoua and Bernard Franck, "Performances Sectorielles et Groupes de Sociétés," Revue Economique, vol. 31 (May 1980), pp. 397-429; and David Encaoua and Alexis Jacquemin, "Organizational Efficiency and Monopoly Power: The

Case of French Industrial Groups," European Economic Review, vol. 19 (September 1982), pp. 25-51 See also INSEE, Les Groupes de Sociétés dans le Système Productif Français, Année 1974, Collections de l'INSEE, E71 (INSEE, 1980). Unfortunately, no benchmarks exist for earlier postwar years.

29 Re the Agreement of Ford Werke AG (No. 2), before the EC Commission (83/560/EEC); [1984] 1 C.M.L.R. 596, 599.

30 Re the European Sugar Cartel, before the EC Commission; [1973] C.M.L.R. D65. Also Coöperatieve Vereniging 'Suiker Unie' UA and others v. E.C. Commission, cases 40-48/73, 50/73, 54-56/73, 111/73, and 113-114/73 before the EC Court of Justice; [1976] 1 C.M.L.R. 295.

31 Raffinerie Tirlemontoise.

32 Suiker Unie and Centrale Suiker.

33 Eridania, the Padano group, and Agricola Industriale Emiliana.

34 Sucre-Union, Béghin, Say, Générale Sucrière, and Lebaudy.

35 Ten smaller companies contributed the balance of output.

36 Süddeutsche Zucker.

37 [1976] 1 C.M.L.R. 295,435. It should be noted that deliveries to German refiners accounted for only 4,500 tons, or 7% of the total amount of "controlled" trade. It should also be noted that of the 20,700 tons of uncontrolled exports to Germany, small Belgian refineries outside the orbit of Raffinerie Tirlemontoise accounted for 11,300 tons(55%).

38 As the refiners themselves put it, "chacun chez soi."

39 The industry in question (NAP-S402) includes raw and refined sugar, but not confectionary products.

40 See Antoine A. Auquier, French Industry's Reaction to the European Common Market (Garland Publishing, 1984), chap. 3. See also Frédéric Jenny and André-Paul Weber, Concentration et Politique des Structures Industrielles (La Documentation Française, 1974). It has also been observed in Belgium, Canada, the United Kingdom, and the United States. For examples, see Alexis Jacquemin, Elisabeth de Ghellinck, and Christian Huveneers, "Concentration and Profitability in a Small Open Economy," Journal of Industrial Economics, vol. 29 (December 1980), pp. 131-144; Richard E. Caves, Michael E. Porter, and A. Michael Spence, Competition in the Open Economy: A Model Applied to Canada (Harvard University Press, 1980); Philip P. Turner, "Import Copmpetition and the Profitability of United Kingdom Manufacturing Industries," Journal of Industrial Economics, vol. 29 (December 1980), pp. 155-166; and Thomas A. Pugel, "Foreign Trade and US Market Performance," Journal of Industrial Economics, vol. 29 (December 1980), pp. 119-130.

41 See William James Adams, "International Differences in Corporate Profitability," Economica, vol. 43 (November 1976), pp. 367-379.

42 In the American setting, this may be attributed to failure of import-exposure to vary sufficiently over time. Although cross-section in design, the study of Lawrence B. Krause, "Import Discipline: The Case of the United States Steel Industry," Journal of Industrial Economics, vol. 11 (November 1962), pp. 33-47, focuses on price changes rather than price-cost margins.

43 Christian Sautter, "L'Efficacité et la Rentabilité de l'Economie Française de 1954 à 1974," Economie & Statistique, no. 68 (June 1975), pp. 5-21.

44 When measured essentially as (Y-T+I)/K, where Y=income, T=taxes on income, I=interest paid, and K=fixed investment - each valued at constant prices - the return to capital in the macroeconomy remained roughly constant between 1954 and 1974. On the other hand, when measured as (Q-W)/K, where Q=value-added and W=remuneration of labor - each valued at constant prices - profitability first rose and then declined, as described in the next section of text.

45 See Sautter, "L'Efficacité et la Rentabilité de l'Economie Française de 1954 à 1974," p. 13, figure III.

46 At the .001 level of statistical significance (r=-0.38) during 1959-64, and at the .01 level of statistical significance (r=-0.36) during 1959-69 in one-tail t-tests .

47 See Simon Domberger and Philip Murphy, Industrial Structure, Pricing, and Inflation (St. Martin's Press, 1983).

48 David Encaoua and Philippe Michel, Dynamique des Prix Industriels en France (Economica, 1986), pp. 148-158, 164-176, and 187-188.

49 And remaining tariffs.

50 I say converge "toward" rather than converge "on" to allow for upward sloping market-supply curves in the low-cost countries.

51 William Diebold, Jr., The Schuman Plan: A Study in Economic Cooperation 1950-1959 (Praeger, 1959), p. 279.

52 Diebold, The Schuman Plan, p. 279.

53 Diebold, The Schuman Plan, p. 279.

54 Diebold, The Schuman Plan, p. 282. Two features of coal and steel signal the need for caution when interpreting the evidence on price-convergence. First, most evidence pertains to list prices; despite the community's requirement of open pricing, discrepancies between list and transactions prices did exist and may have varied in magnitude among member countries. Second, both industries are structured oligopolistically - even at the community level; price-convergence does not imply convergence on a competitive price.

55 See "Cheaper Cars and Drugs?" The Economist, April 16, 1983, p. 50.

56 For example, in a 1983 survey of model-specific pre-tax prices, the European federation of consumers groups (BEUC) found that the price of an Austin Metro 1000 L was 49% greater in Britain than in Belgium. The British price also exceeded those in France and Germany. See "Cars: Autosuggestion," The Economist, October 29, 1983, p. 52.

57 See "Cheaper Cars and Drugs?" The Eonomist, April 16, 1983, p. 50: "The EEC commission has at long last completed its investigation into the huge gap between high British car prices and lower continental ones. Not surprisingly, it has dismissed claims by carmakers that price differences of more than 40% (as between Britain on the one hand and Belgium or Denmark on the other) can be explained away by exchange-rate or inflation differentials, divergent tax structures, transport costs or government price regulations." The position of the manufacturers is articulated by François Perrin-Pelletier in William James Adams and Christian Stoffaës, eds., French Industrial Policy (The Brookings Institution, 1986).

58 See "Car Prices: Another Billion," The Economist, October 2, 1982, p. 52.

59 The facts in this paragraph are taken from Re the Agreement of Ford Werke AG (No. 2), before the EC Commission (83/560/EEC); [1984] 1 C.M.L.R. 596.

60 Such a strategy may or may not maximize profit, depending (partly) on constraints associated with terminating local production.

61 Ford of Europe Inc. and Ford Werke AG v. E.C. Commission, cases 228-229/82 before the EC Court of Justice; [1984] 1 C.M.L.R. 649,652.

62 Companies arose to spare such customers the inconvenience of having personally to fetch their cars abroad.

63 For example, see Re Fiat Auto SpA, before the EC Commission; [1984] 2 C.M.L.R. 497. See also Re Alfa Romeo Cars, before the EC Commission; [1985] 1 C.M.L.R. 480.

64 General Motors had also fought the commission on the issue of whether it abused the monopoly granted to it by the Belgian government for certifying that General Motors cars produced in Europe and purchased abroad by Belgian residents conformed to Belgian specifications. The alleged abuse consisted of charging prices for this service that were unrelated to cost and high enough to erase the advantages of arbitrage. Although the court annulled the commission's decision against General Motors, it did say that exercise of a dominant position, even one granted by government, would violate article 86 of the EEC treaty if it curbed parallel imports. See General Motors Continental NV v. Commission of the European Communities, case 26/75 before the EC Court of Justice; [1975] ECR 1367.

65 Ford Werke AG and Ford of Europe Inc. v. E.C. Commmission, cases 25/84 and 26/84 before the EC Court of Justice; [1985] 3 C.M.L.R. 528.

66 See commission regulation (EEC) no. 123/85 of 12 December 1984; OJEC, L 15, 18 January 1985. See also the explanatory notice sent by the commission to manufacturers; OJEC, C 17, January 18, 1985.

67 The 12% figure applies to differentials that exist for a year or more; the corresponding figure for differentials lasting less than a year is 18%; OJEC, C 17, January 18, 1985, p. 5.

68 It would be interesting to correlate our indicators of price behavior (price-cost margins, elasticities of price with respect to cost, and changes over time in price) not only with exposure to all imports but also with a geographic breakdown of such exposure. In particular, it would be interesting to distinguish the impact of exposure to EC rivals from the impact of exposure to rivals outside the community. Unfortunately, French input-output data - the best source of information on trade in relation to production and consumption, does not separate intra- from extra-community trade. In his study of French exposure to international competition, Auquier did distinguish EEC from other imports. He observed that imports from the EEC exerted the stronger positive effect on competition, as measured (negatively) by price cost margins. See Auquier, French Industry's Reaction to the European Common Market,chap. 3.

69 Joint ventures of this type have caused new problems for EC commercial policy. Components travel from Asia to Europe at low prices, permitting products assembled by the joint ventures to be sold at commensurately low prices. The EC takes the position that "underpricing" of components is tantamount to dumping of final products; and it has threatened in such cases to impose antidumping levies on goods assembled within its borders if value-added within the EC fails to exceed a specified share of total product value.

70 See Louis T. Wells, Jr., "Automobiles," in Raymond Vernon, ed., Big Business and the State: Changing Relations in Western Europe (Harvard University Press, 1974).

71 In this regard, it is interesting to note that during the 1960s, France's appetite for deterrence of inward American investment abated when it became apparent that the Americans would simply locate elsewhere in the community if refused a spot in France.

72 Algeria, Morocco, and Tunisia.

73 Cameroon, Comoro Islands, French Equatorial Africa, French West Africa, Madagascar, Réunion, and Togo.

74 Cambodia, Laos, and Viet Nam. The remainder of such exports flowed to French territories in the Americas (principally French Guiana, Guadeloupe, Martinique, St. Pierre and Miquelon) and in Oceania (principally French Polynesia, New Caledonia, New Hebrides, Wallis and Futuna).

75 The next countries to receive their independence issued from colonies in western, central and eastern Africa. Most of these countries obtained their independence peacefully in 1960; and

the evolution of French exports to the region reflected the form and substance of these political events.

76 The year of Algerian independence.

77 Enlargement of the EC was not the whole story, however, for the importance of both OECD Europe and the entire OECD also declined.

78 Industries are defined as one-digit sections and two-digit divisions of the standard international trade classification (SITC).

79 Sections 5 through 8.

80 Section 0.

81 In table 20, due to limitations of the primary data, "OECD" excludes Australia, Finland, Japan, New Zealand, and Spain. OECD is here defined as the original OEEC plus the United States and Canada.

82 Industries are still defined as one-digit sections of the SITC.

83 That is, at the two-digit (division) level of the SITC.

84 Accounting for one-fifth of French manufacturing exports.

85 Especially reliant on the OECD for export markets were (together with the percentage of their exports flowing to the OECD): office machines and automatic data processing equipment (86%), nonferrous metals (85%), organic chemicals (85%), photographic, optical and timing equipment (82%), paper (81%), texiles (81%), and inorganic chemicals (80%).

86 SITC 76.

87 Within each group, countries were weighted in proportion to their importance in French exports of telecommunications and audio equipment.

88 Given the weighting scheme employed, this convergence is attributable not simply to the large fraction of trading nations that falls in this residual group but also to the importance of the group as a purchaser of division 76 goods from France.

89 Among OECD countries, Spain depended most, and Canada least, on French exports of telecommunications and audio equipment.

90 Kampuchea, Vanuatu, Viet Nam, Algeria, Mauritania, and Guinea.

91 Guinea.

92 The third of these countries (Comoro Islands) did not receive its independence until the 1970s.

93 Yemen, Iraq, and Sierra Leone. Iraq's dependence on France should not be analyzed independently of its agreement to supply France with oil on preferential terms.

94 Sierra Leone.

95 Although France is no longer the dominant supplier of imports to its former colonies, it continues to be their principal source of inward direct investment. On January 1, 1971, France still accounted for 61% of the Algerian, Moroccan, and Tunisian subsidiaries of multinationals based outside the United States. The corresponding figure for the rest of French Africa was 58%. See James W. Vaupel and Joan P. Curhan, The World's Multinational Enterprises: A Soucrcebook of Tables Based on a Study of the Largest U.S. and Non-U.S. Manufacturing Corporations (Harvard University Graduate School of Business Administration, 1973), cross-tabulation 21.1.1.

96 See David Encaoua and Philippe Michel, Dynamique des Prix Industriels en France (Economica, 1986), pp. 148-158, 164-176, and 187-188. Moreover, Antoine Auquier found a negative correlation between price-cost margin and propensity to export in a cross-section of manufacturing industries. See his French Industry's Reaction to the European Common Market (Garland Publishing, 1984), p. 318.

The Convergence of International and Domestic Markets
D.B. Audretsch, L. Sleuwaegen, and H. Yamawaki (Editors)

5. EXPORTING THE CAPITAL MARKETS : COMPARATIVE ADVANTAGE AND CAPITAL MARKET IMPERFECTIONS*

Richard E. Baldwin
Columbia University Graduate School of Business

0. INTRODUCTION

The recent informal discussion of high technology industries has often stressed the role of capital market "quality" as a determinant of comparative advantage (Scott and Lodge, (1985)). For instance, European firms argue that the access US firms have to venture capital is a significant advantage. On the other hand, Wellons (1985) argues that the structure of Japan's financial system gives Japanese firms an edge. These arguments have tended to be rather vague and informal due in part to the lack of a manageable model linking capital market imperfection and economic performance.

Capital market imperfection has been the basis of arguments advanced in several other areas as well. For example the lack of risk-sharing markets in LDCs is one element in the "big push" and balanced growth literature (Rosenstein-Rodan, 1943). The lack of such markets also seems to be behind some of the justifications for government intervention in the industrialization of LDC's. In yet another literature Kindleberger (1969), Hymer (1976) and Aliber (1970) point out that differences between countries' capital markets can lead to multinational corporations (MNCs).

* I gratefully acknowledge the helpful comments of Paul Krugman, Rudi Dornbusch, Lars Svensson, Trosten Person, Nils Gottfries and Rob Gertner. Funding was provided by the Alfred Sloan Foundation.

Considering the widespread use of capital market imperfection as an explanation of economic phenomena, the lack of a model that focuses on this link is surprising. Indeed there seems to be no formal model with which to evaluate the arguments mentioned above. This paper provides a simple general equilibrium model that allows explicit consideration of the link between capital markets and the behavior of firms. We use the model to examine the effects that differences between countries' capital markets have on the pattern of merchandise trade. The impact that such differences have on the gains from trade and optimal commercial policy are also studied. One model in the trade literature does look at a related issue. Grossman and Razin (1983) present a model of the link between the diversification of a firm's income stream and its choice of technique. Working with a Helpman-Razin type model[1] in which assets are not traded internationally, they show that the diversification of a firm's income stream may affect its choice of the capital-labor ratio used in production.

The classic study of capital markets and trade is Helpman and Razin (1978). Their model, which is based on the Diamond (1967) stock market model, assumes that capital markets are perfect in the sense that investors avail themselves of all risk-sharing possibilities in the stock market (at least domestically). Our model, on the other hand, looks at trade under uncertainty with imperfect capital markets. The advantage to focusing on capital market imperfection is that it allows a direct definition of capital market quality in terms of the degree of imperfection.

Instead of using the Diamond stock market model, our model draws on the Mayshar-Rotemberg[2] model of capital market imperfection. The Mayshar-Rotemberg model, which itself is based on the capital asset pricing model (CAPM), defines capital market imperfection in terms of the diversification of shareholders. That is, in a perfect capital market, investors are diversified to the full extent of the stock market. Imperfect capital markets are characterized by investors who are less than fully diversified. In the Mayshar-Rotemberg model investors choose to be less than perfectly diversified due to the presence of transaction costs.

The idea behind our model is simple. We assume that countries' capital markets differ in the extent to which they allow risk to be diversified, and that capital markets are not integrated internationally. We then establish a link between the diversification opportunities in a country's capital market and the output decision of firms. The link is based on the connection between shareholders and firms. If a firm acts in the best interest of its shareholders, its production decision must take into account its shareholders' risk aversion and the risk diversification possibilities available to them. Specifically, we make the fairly standard assumption that firms maximize the utility of their shareholders.[3] We then demonstrate that the resulting equilibrium price of a competitive firm's output is equal to marginal costs plus a risk premium. The risk premium turns out to be a simple function that is decreasing in the "quality" of a country's capital market and increasing in the firm's level of production. Capital market "quality" is here defined as the extent to which a capital market allows shareholders to diversify risk (this definition is made more rigorous below). Thus a country with a "good" capital market will have small risk premiums.

In a world where this link holds and international trade in assets is absent, differences between the "quality" of countries' capital markets will influence the pattern of merchandise trade. Indeed, since a firm's equilibrium price equals marginal cost plus a risk premium, the trade effects of capital markets differences will be similar to the trade effects emphasized by standard comparative cost theory. In particular we show that differences between capital markets lead to trade in goods between otherwise identical countries. Moreover in a two-countries, two-goods model, we demonstrate that the country with the "better" capital market exports the "risky" good. Analogues to the Heckscher-Ohlin, Stolper-Samuelson and Rybczynski theorems are also shown to hold.

Since the model provides a framework for analysing the impact of capital markets on the economic behavior of firms, it might be usefully applied to several other areas. For instance, the framework might be used to examine the link between capital market imperfection and firms' attitudes towards risk. In the model, the degree of risk aversion displayed by firms is a continuous function of the degree of capital market imperfection. A companion paper, Baldwin (1985), uses a similar model to show that international differences in capital markets would give rise to MNCs.

The model in this paper is in no way intended as a general model of the trade effects of imperfect capital markets. The model was constructed to be as tractable as possible while still capturing a number of important features of the link between capital market imperfections and firm behavior.

The first section presents the model. The second derives the autarky equilibrium prices, quantities and utilities. The third section calculates the trading equilibrium and shows that free trade is welfare improving. We also demonstrate that analogues to the Hecksher-Ohlin, Stolper-Samuelson and Rbyzsynski theorems hold. The fourth section analyzes the role for government policies. In the last section, we briefly consider the generality of the results.

1. THE MODEL

The model is a simple general equilibrium trade model with two countries (Home and Foreign), two sectors (manufacturing and agriculture) and one factor of production (labor). To concentrate on the effects of capital market differences, the countries are assumed to be identical except in their capital markets. Constant returns to scale and perfect competition are assumed throughout. Demand shocks are the only source of uncertainty in the model.

The manufacturing sector consists of m differentiated varieties denoted as Y_i , $i = 1,\ldots,m$. In keeping with the assumption of perfect competition, we assume that there are n firms producing each variety in each country. There are, therefore, nm firms in each country. For simplicity the agricultural good, A, is assumed to be a homogeneous good. We also assume that A is produced not by firms but directly by labor. Therefore only shares of manufacturing firms are traded on the stock market. This assumption simplifies the analysis of the stock market equilibrium.

We assume that there are two classes of consumers (workers and firm owners). This assumption simplifies the calculation in two ways. It allows us to give the firm owners (who we assume are the only ones who hold shares) a utility function that is amendable to the mean-variance analysis of the finance literature. Moreover, it allows us to give the workers a utility function that results in simple demand equations for manufactured goods. Firm owners are assumed to consume only the agricultural good, A, so that the mean and variance of their income may be derived without reference to a price index. The utility function of owners is:

$$(1) \qquad U^{o} = E(A^{o}) - \delta \, Var(A^{o}),$$

where A^{o} is an owner's consumption of A. Workers have a random-tastes type of utility function, namely the utility of workers in state s is:

$$(2) \qquad U^{w}(s) = A^{w} + \sum_{i=1}^{m} [\alpha Y_i^{w} - (\beta/2)(Y_i^{w})^2 + v_i(s) \, Y_i]$$

where Y_i^{w} and A^{w} are a worker's consumption of variaty i and A, and $v_i(s)$ is the realization of the random variable v_i in state s. The $v_i(s)$ are the variety-specific demand shocks. We assume that they are independently and identically distributed (i.i.d.) across varieties, with mean zero and variance σ^2. This implies that the covariance between the demand shocks of any two varieties is zero.

Turning to the production side, we choose units of Y_i and A so that the production functions are $y_i = L_i /c$, and $A = L_a$, where L_i and L_a are labor inputs into Y_i and A, c is the unit labor input coefficient for a typical variety of manufactured goods, and y_i is the output of a single manufacturing firm producing variety i.

Models with uncertainty must make assumptions about the stochastic timing of agents' decisions. Here it is assumed that all resources, i.e. labor, must be in place before the state of nature is known. This implies that firms cannot change their outputs according to the actual price that occurs in each state. Rather they must optimize on the expected price.[4] Consumers, however, can observe the state before buying. When the state occurs, trading takes place and prices adjust to clear the markets. These assumptions would put our model in the Helpman-Razin (1978) classification of Ex Post Commodity Trading models. To summarize, the output of firms is constant across states, but the equilibrium prices fluctuate due to demand shocks.

The capital market in this model is a stock market. Due to demand shocks, owning a firm is risky. In order to diversify this risk, firm owners exchange shares with each other on a stock market. Shares are listed only on their domestic stock market and there is no international trade in shares. All other risk sharing possibilties are assumed away.[5] We assume that each firm owner is endowed with one whole Y_i firm. As we shall see, since the demand shocks are i.i.d., the profits of firms producing different varieties are also i.i.d. Given this, the optimal portfolio is trivial to calculate. Treating the shares of all firms producing the same variety of Y_i as one type of share, firm owners will split their holdings equally among as many types of shares as possible.

This is where the concept of capital market imperfection comes into play. Mayshare (1979) and Rotemberg (1984) show that rising transaction costs lead investors to hold stock in fewer firms, i.e. to become less diversified. We rely on this intuitive result and define the index of capital market quality as the number of manufacturing firms among which firm owners split their wealth. We do not write out the Mayshare problem, rather we simply assume that S and S^* are the number of firms represented in a typical portfolio in the Home and Foreign countries. We say the capital markets are imperfect since S and S^* are less than m. Lastly we assume that the Home capital market is more imperfect than is the Foreign capital market, i.e. $S < S^*$.

2. AUTARKY EQUILIBRIUM

This section calculates the autarky equilibrium for the Home and Foreign countries. We derive the autarky supply and demand equations and introduce a diagram which facilitates the analysis.

Workers and owners choose state-dependent consumption plans to maximize utility subject to endowments. The resulting aggregate autarky demand curves for all varieties of manufactured goods are linear in price and have additive demand shocks. These demand curves are identical apart from variety-specific additive demand shocks. More precisely, the aggregate inverse demand curve for a variety of Y is:

$$p_i(s) \,/\, p_a(s) = \alpha - (\beta/k)\, Y_i + v_i(s), \tag{3}$$

where $p_i(s)$ and $p_a(s)$ are the prices of Y_i and A in state s, and k is the number of workers per country. The demand function for A is:

$$A(s) = \Big[\, k\underline{L} - \sum_{i=1}^{m} [p_i(s)\, Y_i(s)] + \Big[\sum_{f=1}^{nm} \pi_f(s)\Big]\Big] \,/\, p_a(s) \tag{4}$$

where $\underline{L}$ and $\pi_f(s)$ are the labor endowment per worker, and the profits of firm f in state s. By symmetry of the two countries, equations (3) and (4) are the autarky demand curves for both the Home and Foreign countries. The demand for A can be simplified to, $A(s) = (k\underline{L} - mcY)/p_a(s)$ since the expenditure term cancels out the revenue component of profits.

The objective function of firms is the weighted utility of shareholders. Specification of these objective functions requires knowledge of the mean and variance of profits. Normalizing the wage to unity, the profits of firm f in state s are $\pi_f(s) = (p_i(s) - c)\, y$, where lower case y refers to the output of a single firm. The output of Y firms does not vary across states. Given that the demand shocks are additive, the mean and variance of profits are $E(\pi) = (E(p) - c)y$, and $Var(\pi) = y^2\sigma^2$ for every variety.

Firms are assumed to take the price of their output as given. In this case, it is easy to show that the objective functions of Home and Foreign firms can be written as[6] :

$$(5) \qquad V^h = E\,[(p(s) - c)y] - (\delta/S)\ \mathrm{Var}\,[(p(s) - c)y]$$

$$(6) \qquad V^f = E\,[(p^*(s) - c)y] - (\delta/S^*)\ \mathrm{Var}\,[(p^*(s) - c)y],$$

where we drop the variety subscript since in equilibrium all varieties are symmetric. A typical Home firm maximized (5) with respect to y. The first order condition is: $0=(E[p]-c)-2(\delta/S)\sigma^2 y$. Adding up the first order conditions of the n firms producing each variety, the Home supply function of a typical variety of Y is:

$$(7) \qquad E[p] = c + 2(\delta/S)\sigma^2(Y/n).$$

Similarly, the Foreign supply curve is:

$$(8) \qquad E[p] = c + 2(\delta/S^*)\sigma^2(Y/n).$$

Having derived the autarky supply and demand curves for the manufacturing sector, we turn to the A sector to close the model. The total amount of labor employed in the manufacturing sector is $m(cY^h)$, where Y^h is the total Home production of a single variety of manufactured goods. By full employment the labor employed in the A sector is $(k\underline{L} - mcY)$. Since the unit input coefficient of A is one, this amount is also the output of A. The demand curve for A is $A(s) = [(k\underline{L} - mcY)/p_a(s)]$. Clearly then, equilibrium in the A market requires that $p_a(s)$ equal unity in all states.[7]

The residual nature of the A sector allows the equilibrium to be characterized with the help of a partial equilibrium diagram of the manufacturing sector, Figure 1. By equation (7) the Home supply curve for a typical variety of Y is a function of its expected price. We graph this as HH. Similarly, taking expectations of equation (3) shows that demand for Y can be expressed as a function of expected price.[8] This we graph as DD. The autarky equilibrium expected Home price for Y is p^h and the output is Y^h. The actual price of a variety of Y varies from state to state according to the demand equation (3). The price of A is unity and the output is $(k\underline{L} - mcY^h)$. Similarly, the Foreign supply curve, FF, is given by (8), and the Foreign autarky demand coincides with DD. The autarky equilibrium for the Foreign economy is described by p^f and Y^f.

FIGURE 1 : Autarky equilibrium for home and foreign markets

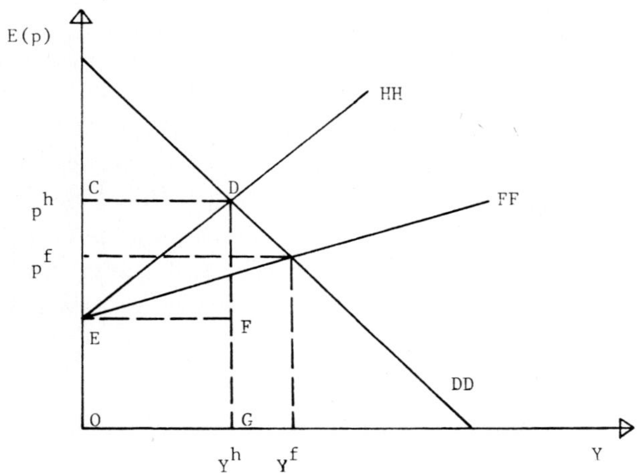

In this model changes in consumer and producer surplus measure changes is the sum of expected utilities of consumers. To see this note that in equilibrium the sum of expected utilities of the k workers in the Home country is:

$$(10) \qquad kE[U^w] = m\,[\alpha Y_i - (1/2)(\beta/k)Y_i^2 - cY_i - E(\sum_{f=1}^{nm} \pi_f)] + k\underline{L},$$

since the total A consumption by workers is $k\underline{L} - mcY - E(\Sigma\pi_f)$. The first two terms in the square brackets are the area under the demand curve. The next term is the resource cost, i.e., the rectangle EFGO in Figure 1. Expected profits are the rectangle EFDC. Thus, the expression inside the square brackets is just the consumer surplus derived from consumption of a typical variety of Y. The $k\underline{L}$ term represents the value of the total labor endowment. Turning to the owners, the sum of the utilities of the nm firm owners is nm times $[(E(p) - c)y - (\delta/S)\sigma^2y^2]$. Using the first order condition we see that this equals m times $[(E(p) - c)Y/2]$. This corresponds to the triangle EDC in Figure

1, which is the producer surplus. By symmetry, consumer and producer surplus are also appropriate welfare measures for the Foreign country.

3. TRADING EQUILIBRIUM

The trading equilibrium can be described with the help of Figure 2. HH and FF are still the relevant supply functions. The world supply curve, the sum of HH and FF is drawn as RR. Likewise, world demand is the sum of autarky demand curves, which we draw as WW. It is easy to show that the expected trading equilibrium price, p^w, lies between the two autarky prices. Home and Foreign outputs of a variety of manufactured goods are Y^h and Y^f respectively. Since both countries consume at level X, the

FIGURE 2 : The trading equilibrium

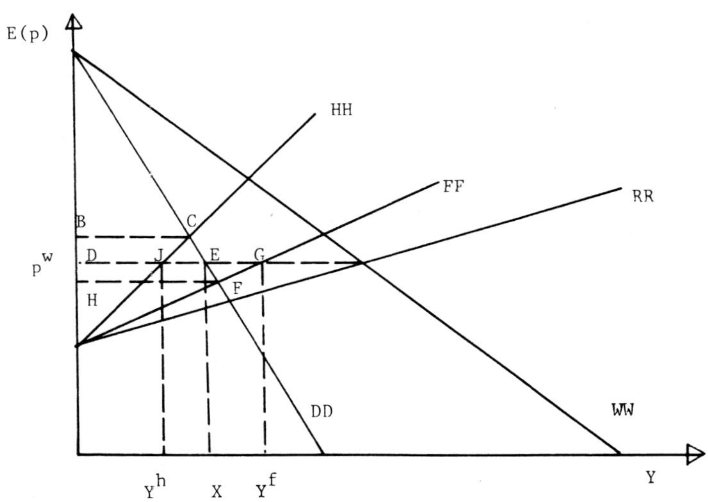

Foreign country exports Y. The Home country's budget constraint implies that the Home country exports A. We have therefore shown that capital market differences cause trade between countries that have none of the "standard" reasons for trading.

It is worthwhile to look at this result more formally. Substituting the trading equilibrium price into (8) and (9) shows that (Y^h/Y^f) equals (S/S^*). In other words, the ratio of output of Y in the Home and Foreign countries is proportional to the relative capital market imperfection of the two countries. Since Home and Foreign workers are identical, each country consumes $(Y^h + Y^f)/2$ of each variety. Because the physical quantity of exports is production less consumption, the expected volume of Home exports of a variety of Y (which we refer to as X) is:

$$(11) \qquad X = (Y^h/2)\,[1 - (S^*/S)].$$

Here X is negative since $S < S^*$. This means the Home country imports some of all varieties of Y. This equation gives us our first results : the country that is comparatively well "endowed" with diversification possibilities exports the "risky" good.[9] This can be interpreted as an analogue of the quantity version of the Hecksher-Ohlin (H-O) theorem. From Figure 1, it is clear the the expected autarky price of a variety of Y is higher in the Home country than in the Foreign country, so relative autarky prices predict the pattern of trade in the standard H-O manner.

Equation (11) is testable since all variables are observable in the trading equilibrium. To get a more realistic equation, we could allow the countries to differ also in cost functions and owners' risk preferences. In this case the expression is:

$$(12) \qquad X = [\ (Y^h/2)[1 - (L\delta/\delta^*)(S^*/S)]\ ] - [\ (c - c^*)/[4(L\delta^*/S^*)(\sigma^2/n)]\ ]$$

Equation (12) allows us to separate the influences of relative capital market imperfection (the first term in large square brackets) and the standard comparative cost advantage (the second term) on the trade pattern. Given that capital markets have an independent influence, trade might run "uphill". That is, if the Home economy had a small comparative cost advantage in Y (i.e., $c < c^*$), but the Foreign country had a much better capital market, the Home country might import Y.

Figure 2 also enables us to consider the welfare effects of trade. Home workers' expected utility increases by m times the trapezoid BCED. Due to the rise in the expected price of Y they face, Foreign workers' expected utility is decreased by m times DEFH. The utility of Home firm owners decreases by m times DBCJ. Finally, Foreign firm owners gain by m times DGFH. Adding up the gains and losses we see that both the Home and Foreign countries gain from trade. The gains for Home and Foreign economies are m times CJE and EFG respectively. This result can be interpreted as an analogue to the Stolper-Samuelson theorem. Trade is welfare improving, but not all factors gain. Firm owners in the country that has the higher risk-sharing potential to labor ratio gain from trade while workers in that country lose. The direction is reversed for the Home country.

A type of Rybczynski theorem also holds in this model. Consider an increase in the diversification of the optimal Home portfolio, i.e., an increase in S. In Figure 2 this can be represented as a flattening of the supply schedule HH. Clearly, under both autarky and trade, Home output of each variety of Y increases. Since there is only $k\underline{L}$ labor in the economy, an expansion of the Y sector inevitably leads to a contraction in the A sector.

4. COMMERCIAL POLICY

Due to imperfect risk-sharing markets, the trading equilibrium is not pareto optimal. Indeed it is not even constrained pareto optimal in the Diamond (1967) sense, since the economy's risk-sharing potential is not fully exploited. Given this, government policies could improve welfare. This paper will deal with two such policies for the Home country.

Since $S < m$, shareholders (and therefore firms) do not face the social shadow price of risk. As a result, too little of each Y_i is produced in both the trading and autarky equilibria. This suggests that a subsidy to Y might improve welfare. We shall see however, that this conclusion is incorrect. The second policy to be considered stems from the fact that taxation of risky assets can affect risk taking behavior. The policy we examine is in the spirit of Bulow and Summers (1984).

Before analysing these policies, we note that since the Home country faces a downward sloping demand for its exports, the standard optimal tariff is not zero. Since this issue has nothing to do with imperfect capital markets, we do not address such a policy. One set of policies that does deserve attention are schemes to reduce capital market imperfection. Typically first-best policies address market imperfections at their root. Such policies, however, would require an explicit model of the source of the imperfection, and are therefore beyond the scope of this paper.

Consider the effects of the trading equilibrium of a subsidy to the Y sector. Suppose, for reference, the Foreign country has a perfect capital market, i.e. $S^{*} = m$, but the Home country has $S < m$. This situation is depicted in Figure 3. Since the countries are identical, the constrained optimum for the Home economy would be attained if HH coincided with FF. A production

FIGURE 3 : The effect of a subsidy on the trading equilibrium

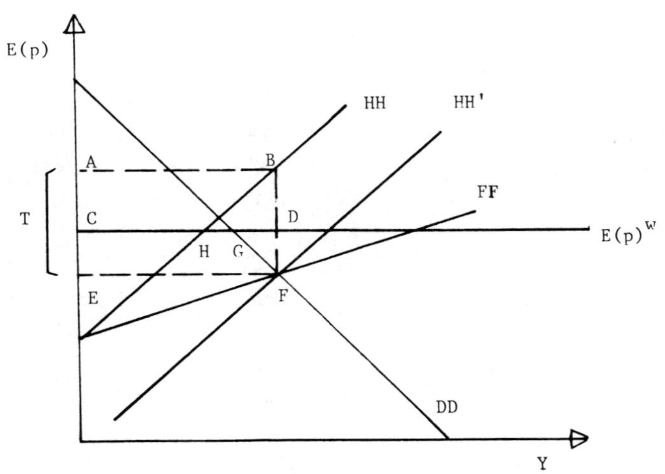

subsidy to Y firms (denominated in A goods and paid for by a lump-sum tax on workers) would correspond to a vertical shift down in the HH schedule. If the size of the subsidy was T in Figure 3, HH′ would be the effective supply schedule. Clearly the constrained optimal quantities and prices would result.

Such a policy, however, would entail a reduction in the sum of expected utilities. The workers would lose the difference between the increase in consumer surplus, CGFE, and the total subsidy, ABFE. The owners would gain ABHC, which means the net loss would be BHGF. The reason for this loss is that firm owners still evaluate the risk of producing Y at the private shadow price. The subsidy moves them to the right price and quantity, yet the increase in their expected income due to the subsidy is partially offset by the disutility of the greater riskiness of producing more Y. Nonetheless, the subsidy payment reduces the expected utility of workers by the full amount. In other words, the production subsidy fails to improve expected welfare since it does not cause firms to face the social price of risk. The next policy we consider accomplishes this.

The second policy is a tax-cum-subsidy on the profits of unintegrated Z firms. The basic idea is that a tax-cum-subsidy can provide additional risk-pooling possibilities when capital markets are imperfect. Suppose the government taxes all firms' profits at a rate of t, and shares out the resulting tax revenue according to expected tax payments. By symmetry, the subsidy received by every firm is (1/nm) of the tax revenue collected in each state of nature. Under this scheme, each firm's tax payment net of the subsidy it receives has an expected value of zero. In "good" states a firm is a net contributor, while in "bad" states it is a net recipient. Such a policy would reduce the variance of profits without changing their expected value.

One easy way to think about this policy is to view the subsidy as a "security" held by the firm. Since taxes are collected from all firms, the security embodies all the risk-pooling possibilities in the economy. In the same vein, we interpret t as the share of the firm's "wealth" held in the new security. Since the tax-cum-subsidy does not affect expected profits but reduces the variance of profits, the optimal tax rate is 100 percent. This policy would allow investors to obtain all risk-pooling possibilities in the economy by holding shares in only one Y firm. The policy would also result in a constrained pareto optimal equilibrium. This tax-cum-subsidy, in a sense, takes the place of the imperfect capital market. Note that this policy would have no effect in a country with perfect capital markets.

One obvious objection to this scheme is that if the government can costlessly and accurately tax profits, why is the capital market not perfect? First, any fully satisfactory answer would require a model with a more complete description of the capital market failure. The Mayshar-Rotemberg model relies on transaction costs at the source of capital market imperfection. A more appealing approach might be to assume that investors must gather information on firms in which they invest. Under this extension of the model, we note that it may be cheaper for the government to observe profits than for private investors. Governments collect taxes for a large number of reasons. If there are fixed costs in gathering information but small costs in using it, private investors may find it opimtal to be less well informed than the government.

5. HOW GENERAL ARE THE RESULTS?

The model is not meant as a general model of trade with imperfect capital markets. Its usefulness is in that it allows explicit consideration of capital markets as a source of comparative advantage. Further theoretical research is certainly needed to determine whether the results holds in a more general model. More importantly, empirical research is needed to determine whether differences in capital market quality have a significant impact on the pattern of trade.

Informally, the result that capital market quality affects the trade pattern seems theoretically robust. In both the CAPM and Diamond stock market models, firms consider the diversification possibilities of their investors when making their choices. The CAPM predicts that firms invest up to the point where the value of the marginal product of capital equals the safe rate plus a risk premium. The premium is $E(r_m)Cov(F,r_m)/Var(r_m)$, where r_m is the excess return on the market portfolio and F is the value of the marginal product of capital.[10] In other words, the risk premium on a project is a function only of the undiversifiable risk. Although the relationship is complicated and the concepts are hard to define, it seems reasonable to expect firms in economies with better diversification possibilities to face smaller risk premiums. Clearly this would affect the pattern of trade.

In the Diamond model, firms choose output to maximize the stock market value of profits. This value depends, inter alia, on the degree of diversification of the portfolio held by shareholders. Indeed, in a Diamond-type model with representative shareholders, firms choose to produce at a point where the marginal product of capital equals the marginal costs times a risk premium that is greater than one. Defining U′ as the marginal utility of shareholders and Ø as the multiplicative productivity shock faced by the firm, the premium (assuming E[Ø] = 1) is equal to (1-Cov(U′,Ø)). If the utility function is concave, the covariance is negative since consumption is positively correlated with the productivity shock. It seems plausible that as shareholders become more diversified, their consumption would depend less on any one firm's Ø. The covariance might then be expected to rise towards zero. While the general equilibrium analysis would be complicated, it seems that even in a Diamond-type model greater diversification of shareholders would lead to greater output of risky goods. Given this informal reasoning, it seems that the results from our model about the trade pattern would hold in a more general theoretical setup.

The policy results, on the other hand, seem to depend more heavily on the exact nature of the model. Nonetheless the reason there is a role for policy is that the firms do not face the social shadow price of risk. The tax-cum-subsidy leads to an extreme result in this simple model. In general the collection of taxes and the distribution of subsidies are costly and may lead to socially useless rent-seeking behavior. These costs would have to be balanced against the risk-pooling benefits of such a policy. The general point, however, is that cross-subsidization can have risk-pooling effects when risk-sharing markets are imperfect. This result would appear to have some general validity.

NOTES

1 Helpman and Razin (1978).

2 Mayshar (1979) and Rotemberg (1984).

3 See Grossman and Hart (1979) for references.

4 We offer two informal interpretations of this assumption. One is that productive capacity must be in place before the state is known. The other is that goods must be on the store shelves before the state is known.

5 Specifically we rule out horizontal integration.

6 We shall see that the equilibrium price of A is unity in all states. Therefore the price of A does not appear in the shareholders' indirect utility function. Because there are S shareholders per firm, each holding 1/S of the stock, the manager faces the typical firm owner's utility function. This is $U^o = (1/S)E[\Sigma\pi_f] - (\delta/S^2)\Sigma Var[\pi_f]$, where the summation is over the S firms in a firm owner's portfolio. For the ith firm this reduces to $V = (1/S)E[\pi_i] - (\delta S^2)Var[\pi_i] + G$, where G is the contribution of other firms' profits to U^o. Since (1/S) and G are a positive constants to the firm, maximizing (5) is equivalent to maximizing V.

7 The key is that A enters linearly into workers' utility functions and is the only good consumed by firm owners. These assumptions imply that the marginal rate of substitution of Y_i and A in consumption does not depend on the quantity of A consumed. For workers, $[(dU/dY_i)/(dU/dY_i)/(dU/dA)] = \alpha - \beta Y_i + v_i(s)$, for firm owners it is trivially true. This means the price of A does not change as the consumption of Y_i changes.

8 The usual Jensen's inequality problem does not arise here since only the price of Y is stochastic.

9 We say that Y is the risky good since taking labor as the numeraire, the price of Y is stochastic while that of A is not. Choice of numeraire in uncertainty models is not innocuous however.

10 See Bulow and Summers (1984) for details.

REFERENCES

ALIBER, R. (1970), "A Theory of Direct Foreign Investment", in Kindleberger (ed), The International Corporation, Cambridge: MIT Press.

BALDWIN, R. (1985), "Capital Markets as a Cause of Multinational Corporations", MIT mimeo.

BULOW, J. and L. SUMMERS (1984), "Taxation of Risky Assets", Journal of Political Economics.

DIAMOND, P.A. (1967), "The Role of a Stock Market in a General Equilibrium Model with Technological Uncertainty", American Economic Review, vol. 57, pp. 759-776.

DIXIT, A and J. STIGLITZ (1977), "Monopolistic Competition and Optimal Product Diversity", American Economic Review, vol. 67, pp. 297-308.

GROSSMAN, G.M. and A. RAZIN (1983), "Direct Foreign Investment and the Choice of Technique under Uncertainty", Princeton mimeo.

GROSSMAN, S. and O. HART (1979), "A Theory of Competitive Equilibrium in Stock Market Economies", Econometrica, vol. 47, pp. 293-329.

HELPMAN, E. and A. RAZIN (1978), A Theory of International Trade Under Uncertainty, New York, Academic Press.

HYMER, S. (1976), The International Operation of National Firms : A Study of Foreign Investment, Cambridge, MIT Press.

KINDLEBERGER, C. (1969), American Business Abroad, New Haven, Yale University Press.

MAYSHAR, J. (1979), "Transaction Costs in a Model of Capital Market Equilibrium", Journal of Political Economy, vol. 87, pp. 673-700.

ROSENSTEIN-RODAN, P.N. (1943), "Problems of Industrialization of Eastern and South-Eastern Europe", Economic Journal.

ROTEMBERG, J.J. (1984), "Financial Transaction Costs and Industrial Performance", Sloan School of Management Working Paper, #1554-84.

SCOTT, B. and G. LODGE (eds) (1985), U.S. Competitiveness in the World Economy, Cambridge, Harvard Business School Press.

WELLONS, P.A. (1985), "Competitiveness in the World Economy: The Role of U.S. Financial System", in Scott and Lodge (eds), U.S. Competitiveness in the World Economy, (Cambridge, Harvard Business School Press, 1985).

III

DETERMINANTS OF TRADE ADVANTAGE

The Convergence of International and Domestic Markets
D.B. Audretsch, L. Sleuwaegen, and H. Yamawaki (Editors)

6. AN EMPIRICAL INVESTIGATION OF UK MANUFACTURING'S TRADE WITH THE WORLD AND THE E.E.C. : 1968 AND 1980

Bruce Lyons
University of East Anglia, Norwich

0. INTRODUCTION

The aim of this paper is to explain international trade in manufactured products. Such trade is becoming increasingly important yet it has been largely ignored in both the empirical and, until recently, in the theoretical trade literature. This lack of investigation is particularly regrettable because manufactured imports (exports) comprised 76% (81%) of total U.K. imports (exports) in 1980, and many other advanced countries are probably not dissimilar.[1] The traditional image of the U.K. exchanging manufactures for agriculture and raw materials is now very much a thing of the past. Furthermore, most of this trade is with advanced countries who can be expected to have factor endowments and other attributes similar to those of the U.K. Table 1 shows that three quarters of manufactured trade is with other OECD countries, and half of this is with the original six members of the EEC. A more detailed breakdown would also show that most 3-digit industries both import and export at least 10% of their output.

In the light of these facts, it is less surprising that test of various formulations of the Ricardian and Heckscher-Ohlin trade models have shown that comparative advantage is at least disappointing in the explanation of trading patterns (see Stern, 1975). The evidence of Table 1 suggests the <u>Similarity</u>, rather than the <u>difference</u>, between the U.K. and its major trading partners as a major impetus for trade. It is the argument of this paper that comparative advantage theory provides an insufficient basis for the explanation of such trade, and that an industrial organisation approach may prove more productive. The recent literature on monopolistic competition and international trade provides an appropriate framework emphasising, not national attributes, but those product and market characteristics that make for a high volume of both imports and exports. This literature gives the starting point for our empirical investigation which

TABLE 1 : U.K. Manufacturing Trade with Advanced Countries in 1980

Area of origin : or destination	EEC6	EEC8	USA	Japan	OECD	World
Share of total imports	41.8%	47.9%	13.2%	4.3%	82.5%	100%
Share of total exports	32.0%	39.8%	8.3%	1.4%	67.8%	100%
Imports as % domestic disappearance	9.6%	11.0 %	3.0%	1.0%	18.9%	22.9%
Export as % domestic production	7.5%	9.3%	1.9%	0.3%	15.9%	23.4%

Source : See Appendix

will be shown to provide substantial backing for this approach to the modelling of international trade flows.

Section 1 of the paper summarises the various trade hypotheses and explains how they are to be tested empirically. Section 2 outlines the statistical framework and presents the results of the regression analysis of U.K. manufactured trade in 1968 and 1980, with a further breakdown of trade with the original six EEC countries and the rest of the world. A final section provides a brief comparison with some previous studies and presents our conclusions.

1. THE DETERMINANTS OF IMPORT PENETRATION AND EXPORT PROPENSITIES

The approach of this paper is to group the determinants of trading propensities into three broad categories, such that for the i'th industry :

$$(1) \qquad S_{mi} = f(CA_i, F_i, D_i) \text{ with } f_1 < 0,\ f_2 < 0,\ f_3 > 0$$

and

$$(2) \qquad S_{xi} = g(CA_i, F_i, D_i) \text{ with } g_1 > 0,\ g_2 < 0,\ g_3 > 0$$

where, S_m is important penetration, S_x is the export propensity, CA is a vector of variables determining comparative advantage, F is a vector of variables causing trading frictions, and D is a vector of product and market characteristics which promote international trade. (The i subscripts are dropped in the following paragraphs).

Equations (1) and (2) provide a useful framework in that they emphasise how some factors, CA, primarily affect the balance of trade,[2] whilst others, F and D, mainly affect the volume of trade.[3] Thus, the D factors may lead to international trade when there is no comparative disadvantage (advantage). The remainder of this section elucidates the components of the CA, F and D vectors, and concludes with a brief discussion of the relevance of each for the U.K.'s trade with Europe and with the rest of the world. Details on the empirical specification of the variables used in the econometric analysis are given in Appendix A3.

1.1. CA : Comparative advantage

1.1.1. Factor Intensities

The Heckscher-Ohlin theorem suggests that specialisation takes place in order to economise on relative factor scarcities. More specifically, if a country is relatively abundant in capital, it should export capital intensive products and important labour intensive products. However, faith in the empirical relevance of this version of the theory was severely jolted by the famous work of Leontief, who showed the U.S.A. to be exporting relatively labour intensive products. Many explanations of the Leontief paradox have been put forward. For instance, the U.S.A. has vast agricultural resources which significantly alter its pattern of trade, and further explanations are outlined below. However, it is worth noting here that institutional arrangements and government policies can undermine the assumption on which the model is based. Highly developed capital markets make finance internationally very mobile, and Melvin (1979) has shown how profits taxation can severely affect relative prices in the U.S.A..[4] In the U.K., investment subsidies and labour taxes may also significantly affect relative factor prices, particularly in those declining regions where traditional comparative advantages has been eroded and grants may have artificially raised capital intensity. On the other hand, there are frequent complaints in the U.K. that there is a shortage of risk capital and that the banks do not work closely enough with industry. Monetary policy and government spending may also significantly affect the cost of capital and trades unions may raise the real wage. In spite of these problems, we include the capital labour ratio, KL, among our determinants of comparative advantage. Also, the raw material import content of industrial output, RMM, should reflect the disadvantage of being distant from important supplies.

1.1.2 Human skills

Perhaps the most important result of Leontief's empirical work, was the empirical recognition of the obvious fact that labour throughout the world is not homogeneous. Consequently, the factor intensity model must be adjusted to include differences in labour skills and abilities. This may be done by including variables to directly reflect the relative abundance of different skill groups, their educational qualifications, or the market value of their talents. The various human capital measures, HK, are detailed in the Appendix. However, it should be noted that those measures based on returns (wages or value added) are afflicted by market imperfections, while those based on training usually ignore that received "on-the-job".

1.1.3 Technology

Sophisticated nations develop new products first, not only because of their scientific and technological capacity, but also because the latent demand for new products first becomes apparent in their easily observed, and therefore crucial, home markets. New products are then exported to less advanced countries which eventually undertake production once the technological problems have been ironed out and a more standardised product is developed. (Hume, 1758; Posner, 1961; Vernon 1966). As a measure of product novelty, we include research and development intensity, RDS. The data refer only to the U.K. is no longer at the forefront of product development and if U.K. R&D reflects the world ranking of industries, then it may be associated with comparative disadvantage.

1.1.4. Size

The size of a country becomes important if there are economies of scale and either trading costs or national tastes. In the former case, large countries are relatively favoured because a larger fraction of their output is not subject to costly trade; so it pays for specialisation to take place in that country. In the case of particular national tastes, it may be that a small country cannot expect to be able to influence the rest of the world; whereas a large country, in catering for its own tastes, can gain sufficient scale economies to sell its products abroad (Dreze, 1960). Scale economies are represented in our model by minimum efficient plant size relative to domestic output, MES. If the U.K. is a relatively large market, and if it has a disproportionate influence on world tastes, it is expected to have a comparative advantage in high MES products (and <u>vice versa</u> if not). Trading costs and product differentiation (which may be associated with national tastes) are discussed below.

1.2. F : Trading Frictions

Transport costs, TRS, are the most obvious friction that discourages international trade. Given that a product is traded, the optimal volume of trade falls with TRS. As with other frictions, high values of TRS may also encourage direct investment or licensing as alternative modes of foreign entry.

Tariff and non-tariff barriers to trade are well known to exist, but less easy to measure objectively. It will therefore be left to an analysis of the residuals of our regression equations to see whether or not industries known to be internationally protected have lower trading propensities.

Another important, yet less well understood, element of trading frictions is due to market costs such as advertising, ADS. Entry barriers are discussed in more detail below, but briefly, foreign entrants have to overcome consumer goodwill, and the market specific costs that this entails may discourage international trade. Note that ADS is based on U.K. data, so its use in the export equations assumes international similarities in the industrial ranking of advertising intensities (a similar assumption must be made about many of the other variables employed in our empirical work). Also ADS is a flow variable measured over one year, whereas the stock of advertising capital would be more appropriate.

1.3. D : Product and Market Characteristics

This section considers the roles of product differentiation, entry barriers and market power in determining international trade. In order to focus clearly on these product and market characteristics, for the moment we abstract from comparative (and absolute) advantage. Firms in all countries are thus assumed to face identical cost conditions; though there may be additional costs of trading across national frontiers, in which case imports have a higher delivered cost than do domestic sales. An industry is defined as a collection of products that are close, but possibly imperfect substitutes in consumption, and which have a similar production technology. Therefore, although products may be differentiated, it is assumed that <u>in principle</u> any product could be produced equally well and cheaply anywhere in the world. It is this that distinguishes the following arguments from the neo-technology view discussed under 1.1.3. above.

1.3.1 Product Differentiation

In recent years, there has been a burgeoning of international models set in the context of monopolistic competition (eg Dixit and Norman, 1980; Krugman, 1980; Lancaster, 1980). The starting point for nearly all such models is the existence of economies of scale. In their absence, all varieties of product can be made locally at no disadvantage, and world trading propensities would be unaffected. Consider, then, an industry where each firm makes a differentiated product, there are scale economies, consumers have a basic preference for variety, and the pattern of tastes is identical in every country. If there are no trading costs, then each firm sells to every country as product varieties are exchanged to reduce production costs. In such circumstances each country's export propensity is one minus its share of world consumption, and import penetration is all but its share in world production.[5] Since comparative advantage, or possibly random historical factors, determine the relative shares of consumption and production for each country, in the absence of any advantage we can expect substantial and relatively balanced trade in differentiated products.[6] Instead of asking the usual question "Why trade?", it thus becomes appropriate to ask "Why not trade?".

The introduction of trading costs can modify trading propensities in two ways. Firstly, the volume of trade is reduced as consumers throughout the world substitute away from more expensive imports in favour of slightly less appropriate, but cheaper domestic products. Industries with only minor scale economies or little underlying consumer preference for variety may even cease to trade internationally. Secondly, proportionately less of the output of a product produced in a large domestic market needs to incur trading costs, and this leads to a comparative cost advantage. Product differentiation, trading costs, and economies of scale combine to favour production in larger economies.[7]

Having outlined the main predictions of monoplistic competition models of international trade, the next step is to make them empirically operational. Trading costs have already been treated in 1.2. above. Economies of scale, represented in our empirical work by MES, enter both as a precondition for trade in differentiated products, and as a possible sourve of comparative advantage if the U.K. market is relatively large (or small). As a precondition, it should be noted that industries which do trade need not trade much more intensively just because they have greater scale economies. Nevertheless, a monotonic relationship between scale economies and trade would still result if relatively more industries find trading costs are worth overcoming as returns to scale increase.

The key empirical problem in examining the role of product differentiation in international trade lies in the specification of the underlying consumer preference for variety. This is extremely difficult because substantial conceptual as well as direct measurement problems arise. One approach might be to measure cross-elasticities of demand between products, and another to measure the economic distance (in characteristics space) between them. However, apart from the empirical difficulties, neither measure would be independent of the number of products supplied, and thus of the amount of trade taking place. We must therefore rely on very indirect measures based on some plausible associations with demand or supply parameters.

Durable goods, DUR, are expected to be positively associated with the underlying demand for variety. They are often lumpy investments fulfilling a key role in the production or consumption process (e.g. a lathe or a stereo). Such goods may have many variants to suit individual needs, but few close substitutes outside this range of products. In such circumstances producer or consumer surplus may be more sensitive to specification than to price as compared with non-durable goods (e.g. raw material inputs or washing powders). This association may be seen as either a behavioural one (because of infrequent purchasing of lumpy investment), or as one deriving (coincidentally) from the inherently heterogeneous nature of such products.

Industries subject to rapid change and development may be reflecting not only technological feasibility, but also demand factors (necessity being the mother of invention). Research and development intensive industries, RDS, are thus expected to be heavily traded (RDS is a domestic measure, though the world intensity might be more appropriate for this and other variables in this section).

Caves et. al (1980) suggest that advertising is typically applied to relatively simple and homogeneous products which cannot be distinguished by obvious characteristics. If this is a true reflection of the role of advertising, there may be a greater underlying demand for variety in physically differentiated, low advertising, ADS, industries. However, we should note that this is not the more standard view of advertising which is that it is both a symptom and a sourve of product differentiation (Comanor and Wilson, 1967). As such it should be expected to be positively associated with trade.

Products made to detailed specifications require more skilled and educated labour, which is not necessary for more standardised products once production runs have been set up. Complexity and variety tend to go hand in hand, so human capital, HK, is expected to be associated with more traded products.

These proxies for the underlying demand for variety, together with those for scale economies and trading costs, combine to define the empirical role of product differentiation in our model of international trade.

1.3.2. Entry barriers

In developing the relevance of entry barriers for international trade, it is necessary to distinguish between barriers to the establishment of new productive capacity and barriers to the establishment of new markets. Both are faced by entrants in each country, but it can be argued that there is a comparative advantage to being foreign in overcoming marketing barriers. Thus, ceteris paribus, industries with high production barriers will be more traded, and those with high marketing barriers will be less traded on international markets.

Imports (exports) can enter the domestic (foreign) market in a more limited, and therefore less disruptive, manner than can domestic entrants in industries subject to substantial scale economies. Also, since foreign suppliers already produce for their domestic markets, they will be less troubled by the capital market premiums and imperfections that make the costs of capital and new technology more expensive to new suppliers. Furthermore, production set up costs discourage the use of direct investment and licensing as alternative modes of entry into foreign markets. Production entry barriers are represented by MES, KL, and RDS in our empirical work. MES and KL, may jointly pick up the capital requirement barrier, since the more appropriate concept of the capital requirement for a firm of minimum efficient size had to be rejected as adding too much multi-collinearity to our regression analysis. The stock of accumulated patents and knowledge is expected to be related to the flow of research and development activity, RDS.

In constrast, foreign firms have no such advantage in setting up distribution and servicing networks, or in breaking down the accumulated goodwill of existing suppliers. Although foreign firms can always employ local marketing agencies, they may find themselves at a comparative disadvantage in understanding and exploiting a market which has substantial set up costs in a country with a different language and alien socio-cultural environment.[8] Advertising intensity, ADS, is the only variable we have to measure such barriers, and it is discussed further in (b) above.

1.3.3. Market power

The theoretical relationship between market power and trading propensities is extremely complex (see e.g. White, 1974; Papgoulatos and Sorensen, 1976). If one country can supply at a lower cost than the world price (inclusive of trading costs), then a monopolist can limit price against imports; but if there is uncertainty as to domestic demand or the world supply price, the higher domestic price charged by the monopolist permits a greater probability of import penetration than arises with the competitive industry. Unless the "monopolist" is really a cartel which has difficulty in changing its agreed price or else there is a ratchet effect, this model does not explain sustained import penetration once the monopolist appreciates his misjudgements. However, it does suggest import share instability and a higher average level of import penetration.

On the export side, a price discriminating monopolist facing increasing costs and competitive world market will export more than his competitive counterpart. However, if he is not permitted to sell at a lower price abroad, he will export either at the competitive level, or not at all if exploiting the domestic market alone gives him greater profits. Trading costs are essential for the above results, for in their absence arbitrage ensures that behaviour is the same under both market structures.

Trade may also arise from the outcome of a non-cooperative oligopoly game (Brander, 1981; Lyons, 1981) out of which import penetration is the side effect of crude price raising behaviour. This case suggests that both exports and import penetration may arise at the same time even when cost and demand conditions are perfectly anticipated. As domestic firms become more collusive, they may develop the stance of Stackelberg leadership against imports, and if those imports are in perfectly elastic supply, we return to the monopoly model.

The above analysis treats domestic and foreign firms as operating independently of one another. This need not, in fact, be the case. Even without joint ownership, a domestic firm may either treaten retaliation against an aggressive importer in his own home market, or more amicable international competitive trade.[9] Competitive trade may be less easily constrained in third markets where there is no local manufacturing capacity.

As extreme case of international interdependence is given by multi-national firms. MNF's indulge in a great deal of trade but this is not because they compete with their own subsidiaries in the product market. Partly, they are filling out product range, and much is marketed through 'sales only' subsidiaries. Other trade is vertical, using intrafirm supplies rather than resorting to the international (or national) market. Inasmuch as MNF's use their monopsony power in input markets (including the inputs of labour and government subsidies), this might raise trading propensities as a bargaining device. However, the correlation between multinationals and trade may be non-casual; for instance if product differentiation leads to both. It is an empirical matter to demonstrate how much of the MNF effect is pure substitution, trade diversion, and trade suppression. Unfortunately, it is also something that is not taken up here but must await other papers. Data has only just been collected and it has yet to be incorporated into our empirical framework.

As well as its more direct implications, market power is often associated with high profits, regional behaviour, and these features may also influence international trade. Profits provide lower cost funds with which to set up risky and expensive export facilities. They also provide the wherewithal to lobby governments for subsidies and protection from foreign competition. Regional concentration makes the vote catching possibilities of conceding tariffs etc all the more attractive to a politician. It has often been noted that delivery is an important non-price factor in international markets. If profits can be used to buy good industrial relations with higher wages of better conditions, or if excess capacity is held as a strategic variable to deter entry, delivery times may be improved. However, inasmuch as large plant size and market power are related, the abominable strike record of large plants in the U.K. will work in the opposite direction. Finally, sales maximising behaviour increases the relative attractiveness of exporting if foreign demand is perceived as being more elastic.[10]

In summary, simple arguments suggest that market power will be associated with higher import penetration, but there is no straightforward relationship with exports. Once transnational firms and international collusion are acknowledged, market power may lead to geographic market segmentation which could reduce world trade, at least between major producing nations. Other factors, such as the existence of monopoly profits, could result in fewer imports and higher exports.

Standing back from this complex plethora of hypotheses, our first conclusion must be that the effect of market power may differ substantially between different industries. Since we can only hope to pick up average relationships in cross-section regression analysis, a wealth of important detail will be lost. Nevertheless, we include the concentration ratio, CR, as the standard proxy for market power (the Herfindahl index gave similar results). Other sources of market power may include the variables already listed as entry barriers, particularly RDS as the of temporary monopolies, and also those variables associated with low price elasticities (i.e. the underlying demand for variety).

1.4. Endogeneity

A major reservation to the use of a number of the measures described in this section is that some may be endogenously related to trade in the long run. For instance, trade might bankrupt the least efficient or lowest quality firms, alter the domestic supply of variety (therefore, possibly, firm numbers) and influence the return on R & D. International trade also alters the returns to investment in human, physical and marketing capital, lobbying for tariff protection, and even manipulating human tastes.

In the face of such a shortage of truly exogenous variables it is tempting to abandon all hopes of empirical analysis. However, we prefer the alternative of pressing ahead whilst bearing these possibilities in mind. This view is supported by some evidence relating to the rapid increase in world trade in recent years. This increase was occasioned largely by lowering trade barriers and third world development, but it has had little immediate and obvious impact on our "independent" variables. For instance, both import and export propensities in our sample to have almost doubled through the 1970's, whilst the average concentration ratio has remained quite unchanged.[11] Either trade affects concentration very slowly, or there have been coincidentally offsetting forces at work; and it is very difficult to imagine a significant source for such concentration reducing forces in the last 15 years.

1.5. The U.K., E.E.C. and Rest of the World

The U.K. and the main E.E.C. countries are at similar stages of economic development. As compared with the rest of the world, factor intensities including human capital, technology and even national size differ relatively little. It is therefore to be expected that comparative advantage will be less of a feature of intra-E.E.C. trade than it is for trade with the rest of the world. There are also fewer tariff distortions within the E.E.C. However, inasmuch as tariffs have traditionally been used to compensate for comparative disadvantage, the suggestion that comparative has less of a role to play within the community, may possibly have to be reversed. Transport cost will be quantitatively less important, but may still play an important part in determining the overall volume of E.E.C. trade.

It is expected that intra-E.E.C. trade will emphasize product and market factors. In particular, countries at similar stages of development tend to both demand and produce similar goods. This follows both from Linder's (1961) argument that close with a market is necessary for producers to set up in business, and from monopolistic competition models (eg Helpman, 1981) which show trade in differentiated products to be greatest between countries with a similar factor abundance. The U.K. probably has a demand pattern and factor abundance closer to that of the original E.E.C. countries than it does to the rest of the world; so product and market characteristics are expected to be more important then they are for non-European trade.

2. EMPIRICAL INVESTIGATION OF U.K. TRADE IN MANUFACTURED GOODS

2.1. The Statistical Model

The basic theory relates to the determination of import penetration as a proportion of domestic output, S_m, and of exports as a proportion of domestic output, S_x. A problem with using such ratios as dependent variables in linear regression is that the estimated model may predict values less than zero or greater than 100%, which conflicts with the economic model that trade ratios must lie within those bounds. In statistical terms, such estimates must be inefficient. A logistic transformation of S_m and S_x is therefore applied and the following model estimated.

$$(3) \qquad S = \frac{100}{1 + \exp(-X\beta - u)}$$

where, S is the trade ratio, S_m or S_x,

exp (...) is the exponential function,

X is a vector of independent variables representing CA,F and D,

ß is a vector of coefficients,

and u is a vector of errors agreeing with the standard OLS assumptions. It is straightforward to rearrange equation (3) into a form amenable to OLS estimation :

$$(4) \qquad \log_e (S/[100 - S] = X\beta + u$$

A characteristic of the logistic transformation is that small changes in X have little impact on trade when S is "low" or "high". Thus, the model captures the fact that, for instance, if transport costs are almost prohibitive, a small change in them will make little difference to trade (costs will still be almost prohibitive and trade will be very low). At the other extreme, if transport costs are negligible not alter the very high level of import penetration. In between such extremes, the independent variables may have a more substantial impact. This logistic function is sketched in Figure 1.

FIGURE 1 : The Logistic Curve

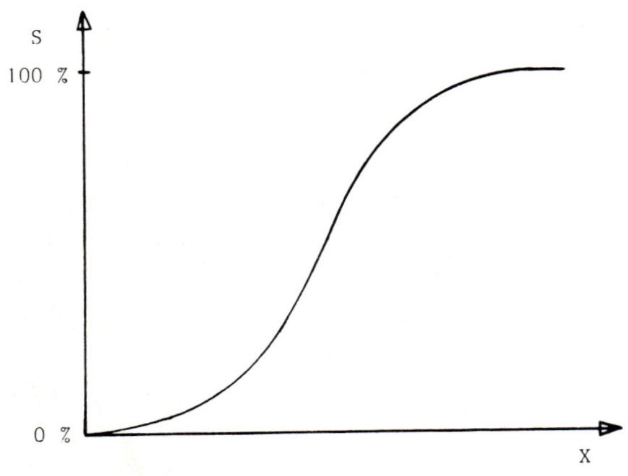

For convenience of presentation, estimates of ß in the tables that follow have been multiplied by 10. Bearing this in mind, it is easily shown that the partial effect of a small change in the j'th independent variable, x_j, is given by

$$\frac{\partial S}{\partial x_j} = \frac{\beta_j (100 - S)S}{1000}$$

Evaluated at the mean value of both S_m and S_x in our 1980 sample (26%), the effect on the trade ratio, S , of raising s_j is thus given approximately by doubling the reported coefficients in tables 2 and 3. This provides a reasonable approximation for industries with trading propensities between 20% and 80%, but outside this range the partial effects may be considerably smaller.[12]

Equation (4) is applied to cross-section data on 111 3-digit industries in the U.K. manufacturing sector. separate estimates are made for both import and export ratios for 1968 and 1980. Greater data availability for 1980 permits a geographical breakdown between trade with the original 6 E.E.C. countries (which account for over a third of U.K. trade in manufactures) and that with the rest of the world. full details of the sample of industries, data sources, and definitions of the variables are given in the Appendix.

2.2. Empirical Results

Table 2 presents estimates based on import penetration in 1968 and 1980 (M68 and M80 respectively), and exports in each year (X68 and X80). Table 3 gives more detailed results for the 1980 sample. For ease of comparison, regressions (3.1) and (3.2) simply repeat (2.3) and (2.7). The remaining regressions relate to imports to and exports from the original 6 E.E.C. countries (EM and EX), and trade with the rest of the world (NEM and NEX).

The most striking result to emerge from an overview of both tables is that all statistically significant coefficients have the same sign in all regressions whether they relate to imports or exports, trade with the E.E.C. 6 or the rest of the world, 1968 or

TABLE 2 : Explanation of U.K. Manufacturing Import and Export Propensities 1968 and 1980

	TRS	ADS	MES	DUR	RDS	CR	KL	QUB	WSL	CONSTANT	$\bar{R}^2$ (F stat)
(2.1)M68	-2.56	-1.39	6.83	1.91	0.98	-0.26	0.53	0.252		-16.4	.4252
	(4.65)°	(2.51)*	(4.00)°	(0.79)	(2.20)*	(4.35)°	(3.43)°	(2.34)*		(4.74)°	(11.17)°
(2.2)M68	-2.64	-1.03	6.97	1.49	1.33	-0.24	0.60		0.326	-13.9	.3943
	(4.68)°	(1.89)$^{+}$	(3.98)°	(0.60)	(3.06)°	(3.80)°	(3.26)°		(0.05)	(2.26)*	(9.95)°
(2.3)M80	-2.69	-0.98	7.52	6.10	1.06	-0.21	0.24	$2.6x10^{-4}$		37.6	.4301
	(4.64)°	(1.72)$^{+}$	(4.37)°	(2.52)*	(2.23)*	(3.53)°	(4.37)°	(0.00)		(10.72)°	(11.38)°
(2.4)M80	-2.64	-1.11	7.51	5.95	1.22	-0.19	0.27		-2.20	45.0	.4425
	(4.59)°	(2.01)*	(4.42)°	(2.49)*	(2.71)°	(3.08)°	(4.68)°		(1.51)	(7.61)°	(11.92)°
(2.5)X68	-2.00	-1.21	6.44	6.58	0.19	-0.084	-0.076	0.550		-27.7	.5057
	(3.88)°	(2.35)*	(4.03)°	(2.91)°	(0.46)	(1.47)	(0.52)	(5.46)°		(8.58)°	(15.07)°
(2.6)X68	-2.26	-0.52	6.90	5.26	0.84	0.05	-0.10		11.31	-31.0	.3802
	(3.92)°	(0.94)	(3.86)°	(2.07)*	(1.90)$^{+}$	(0.79)	(0.54)		(1.77)	(4.94)°	(6.03)°
(2.7)X80	-2.87	-0.78	5.37	6.17	0.73	-0.06	0.09	0.27		29.8	.4658
	(5.42)°	(1.51)	(3.42)°	(2.79)*	(1.68)$^{+}$	(1.13)	(1.78)$^{+}$	(2.66)°		(9.30)°	(12.99)°
(2.8)X80	-2.94	-0.43	5.63	5.86	1.09	-0.04	0.10		0.53	30.9	.4296
	(5.37)°	(0.82)	(3.47)°	(2.57)*	(2.54)*	(0.66)	(1.78)$^{+}$		(0.39)	(5.47)°	(11.36)°

111 observations; absolute t-ratios in brackets; 2-tailed significance tests : ° 1%
* 5%
+ 10%

TABLE 3 : Explanation of U.K. Manufacturing Trade with the World, the Original 6 EEC Countries and the Rest of the World : 1980

	TRS	ADS	MES	DUR	RDS	CR	KL	QUB	JMM	WDL	GRD	CONSTANT	$\bar{R}^2$ (F Stat)
(3.1)M80	-2.69	-0.98	7.52	6.10	1.06	-0.213	0.242	2.6×10^{-4}				37.6	.4301
	(4.64)°	(1.72)$^+$	(4.37)°	(2.52)*	(2.23)*	(3.53)°	(4.36)°	(0.00)				(10.72)°	(11.38)°
(3.2)M80	-2.62	-0.87	6.87	5.40	1.07	-0.215	0.243	-0.023	0.234			37.6	.4387
	(4.54)	(1.53)	(3.91)°	(2.21)*	(2.27)*	(3.59)°	(4.41)°	(0.21)	(1.60)			(10.83)°	(10.55)°
(3.3)EM	-2.39	-0.72	4.03	6.14	0.387	-0.147	0.242	0.247				-27.5	.4202
	(4.78)°	(1.48)	(2.72)°	(2.94)°	(0.95)	(2.83)°	(5.06)°	(2.61)°				(9.13)°	(10.97)°
(3.4)EM	-2.37	-0.62	4.08	3.59	0.247	-0.173	0.244	0.214		2.3×10^{-3}		-27.1	.4420
	(4.83)°	(1.28)	(2.80)°	(1.53)	(0.61)	(3.31)°	(5.20)°	(2.27)*		(2.23)*		(9.14)°	(10.68)°
(3.5)NEM	-2.40	-0.87	5.82	4.56	1.21	-0.224	0.178	-0.114				-11.5	.3467
	(4.01)°	(1.49)	(3.28)°	(1.82)$^+$	(2.47)*	(3.60)°	(3.10)°	(1.01)				(3.18)°	(8.30)°
(3.6)NEM	-2.30	-0.72	4.94	3.62	1.22	-0.227	0.179	-0.146	0.315			-11.4	.3679
	(3.90)°	(1.24)	(2.75)°	(1.45)	(2.54)*	(3.70)°	(3.17)°	(1.29)	(2.10)*			(3.20)°	(8.11)°
(3.7)NEM	-2.28	-0.63	5.02	2.69	0.507	-0.220	0.181	-0.091	0.318		0.181	-13.1	.3696
	(3.85)°	(1.08)	(2.79)°	(1.02)	(0.64)	(3.58)°	(3.21)°	(0.74)	(2.13)*		1.13)	(3.39)°	(7.45)°
(3.8)X80	-2.87	-0.78	5.37	6.17	0.727	-0.062	0.090	0.267				29.8	.4658
	(5.42)°	(1.51)	(3.42)°	(2.79)°	(1.68)$^+$	(1.13)	(1.78)$^+$	(2.66)°				(9.30)°	(12.99)°
(3.9)EX	-2.89	-0.68	3.34	2.98	0.676	-0.123	0.087	0.251				25.8	.4063
	(5.79)°	(1.38)	(2.29)$^+$	(1.43)	(1.66)$^+$	(2.36)*	(1.81)$^+$	(2.65)°				(8.54)°	(10.41)°
(3.10)NEX	-2.57	-0.47	3.52	6.37	0.439	-0.032	0.078	0.270				-22.7	.4621
	(5.53)°	(1.04)	(2.56)*	(3.28)°	(1.16)	(0.67)	(1.75)$^+$	(3.06)°				(8.08)°	(12.81)°
(3.11)NEX	-2.56	-0.43	3.54	5.26	0.378	-0.044	0.079	0.256		1.0×10^{-3}		-22.5	.4624
	(5.51)°	(0.94)	(2.57)*	(2.37)*	(0.99)	(0.88)	(1.77)$^+$	(2.86)°		(1.02)		(8.00)°	(11.51)*

1980. This suggests considerable support for modelling trade in manufactured good in terms of trade creating and frictional factors rather than as a function of comparative advantage. Furthermore, most coefficients are of a similar order of magnitude in all equations, though, as will be noted below, there are several exceptions to this proposition.

Turning to the more detailed results, transport costs, TRS, provide a remarkably consistent trading friction, always significant at the 1% level, and always with a coefficient lying between 2 and 3.

Advertising, ADS, also acts as a trading friction by raising market penetration costs. However, although the sign and size of the coefficient estimates are quite consistent, the standard error is large in the 1980 sample, particularly for exports. This is probably explained by the fact that we only had data for U.K. advertising in 1968. This introduces two problems : firstly, that relative advertising intensities may have changed substantially in the twelve years up to 1980 export equations, then, we have to rely on both intertemporal and international similarities if the true relationship is to be found. Furthermore, current advertising may be poor proxy for the goodwill accumulated over many years of advertising. Bearing these problems in mind, the result that advertising is a trading friction may be much stronger than it at first sight appears.

Economies of scale, MES, provide a substantial stimulus to international trade. Along with transport costs, MES is the most economically and statistically significant variable in our model. For 1980, the size of the import coefficients is a little larger than in the 1970's which led to disadvantage in large scale production.

Durable goods, DUR, are more traded than non-durable as customers search for the most appropriate capital goods.[13] DUR is rather less significant for NEM and EX, which may be explained by the relative strength of the European engineering industries.

RDS, research and development, has had a fairly consistent effect over the years, raising imports rather more than it does exports. It is much more important for NEM than it is for EM, which probably reflects the technological advance of the U.S.A. in those industries where the U.K., but not so much the EEC 6, concentrates her research efforts (aerospace and electronics). Investigation of the impact of the source of finance of the R & D, such as regession (3.7) which includes GRD, the proportion of R & D financed by the government, failed to reveal anything of interest due to substantial collinearity with RDS.

Industrial concentration, CR, significantly reduces imports, but little affects total exports in both years. This contrasts with (weak) positive simple correlations between concentration and import penetration, and concentration and the export propensity. Exactly the same result is found when H replaces CR in these regressions and simple correlations (though the statistical significance of H in the regression is lower). In the statistical sense, this reversal is undoubtedly caused by the significant positive correlations between CR (or H), and MES, QUB, KL and RDS. Only RDS and QUB within the second group are as strongly correlated. Economically speaking, it is probable that in simple correlations concentration captures the true role of scale economies, and perhaps entry barriers and product differentiation, rather than market power.

The concentration effect is thus seen to be very sensitive to the specification of the trade equations and should be treated with caution. Nevertheless, the result in tables 2 and 3 are consistent with the view that high CR does not raise efficiency, or else exports would also be higher, but it does provide lobbying powers to suppress imports via tariffs, subsidies, "voluntary" export restraints, specification requirements, or more covert collusive (or non-collusive) means. There is an interesting contrast between trade with the EEC 6 and that with the rest of the world. CR significantly reduces both EM and EX about equally, which is consitent with geographic market segmentation in more concentrated industries. In contrast, a greater reduction in imports is found for rest of the world trade, perhaps because lobbying is most effective against non-E.E.C. imports. CR has no effect on exports to more distant markets, NEX, where collusive agreements are less easily arranged.

The capital labour ratio, KL, gives no support to the naive formulation of the Heckscher-Ohlin theorem. Although the 1968 import and export equations have opposite signs, the KL coefficients in the latter are quite insignificant and by 1980 KL raises export as well as imports.[14] The geographical breakdown in table 3 suggests a slightly greater impact of KL on E.E.C. 6 trade than it has on that with the rest of the world. The evidence is thus consistent with KL acting as a production entry barrier which deters local entry but consequently induces trade between similar, nearby countries. Overall, Britain appear to stand at some comparative disadvantage in capital intensive industries (coefficients are higher in the import than export regressions), perhaps due to her poor per capita investment record.

Many different human capital measures were tried, but only two are reported here. The even numbered regressions in table 2 report the result using WSL, average wages and salaries, and the odd numbered regressions employ QUB, a measure of educational attainment amongst employees. The WSL results are very similar to those using value added per man; and the QUB results bear a similarity to the other training and socio-economic class based measures reported in the Appendix. The WSL results are poor, particularly as a causation problem was expected to reinforce any human capital effect - industries with a comparative advantage should be able to concede higher wage claims in imperfect labour markets. QUB does not suffer from such problems, but available data were rather more aggregated. Human capital raises both imports and exports, a result which is consistent with the view that production complexity leads to trade, rather than that human capital is a source of comparative advantage.[15] This view has a particular strength for trade with the E.E.C. 6 where educational attainment is relatively homogeneous, and it is conformed by the European trade equations (3.3) and (3.9), where the coefficients on QUB are almost exactly the same. The coefficients in the NEM and NEX equations, on the other hand, have opposite signs, and thus human capital based comparative advantage may have a part to play in trade with less similar countries.

Greater availability of data for 1980 permits the study of several additional factors that may have a bearing on trading propensities. The first is to consider the impact of Japanese trade. It has often been observed that in the relatively few areas in which the Japanese excel, they drive home their advantage with extremely competitive behaviour, unlike some western firms who are content to take profits. We therefore constructed the variable JMM, the Japanese share of total imports,[16] to test the proposition that import penetration is greater than is predicted by our basic model if the Japanese are relatively substantial competitors. Note that JMM has no identity type relation with import penetration, if fact, measurement error in non-Japanese imports would tend to lead to a negative correlation between the two. Regressions (3.2) and (3.6) suggests there is some truth in the hypothesis, particularly in relation to non E.E.C. 6 imports. An unreported regression with EM as the dependent variable gives a positive coefficient on JMM (β = .127, t = 1.00), so the Japanese effect is not merely the substitution of European imports.

It is becoming increasingly appreciated that reliability, delivery and service are crucial to international competitiveness. A dissatisfied workforce may make less reliable products, as well as voicing its displeasure in the form of strike action. More directly, the proportion of working days lost through strikes, WDL, will lead to delivery delays. The only significant impact of WDL was found to be on EM, and this is largely at the expense of DUR. This is consistent with the view that strikes encourage a switch to nearby European suppliers, particularly for durable goods where customers may hold lower stocks and bear less loyalty to suppliers from whom they buy only occasionally.[17] As a cautionary note, regression (3.11) is reported. Although WDL is statistically insignificant in the logistic functional form, it is positive and significant for total exports and particularly non-EEC 6 exports in linear regression - in fact its size and significance exceeds that in the linear import regression. Thus, the influence of strikes appears to be very sensitive to the specification of functional form.[18]

A number of other variables were experimented with, but none was statistically significant in any import or export equation. High values of the raw material import content of an industry, RMM, were expected to adversely affect comparative advantage. On reflection, however, the measure chosen was probably inappropriate, being dominated by high value "agricultural" imports such as tobacco and furs. The proportions of women and part-timers in the workforce had been expected to be inverse human capital measures since both categories are less permanent members of the workforce, and so have a lesser incentive to acquire skills. It may be that QUB captures most of this already. Finally, the identity of the purchaser was expected to affect trade. Consumers may value difference for its own sake more highly than industrial purchasers; or the latter may require more detailed specifications for rigid production processes. If one of these outweighted the other, it would be an incentive to look to the world markets for variety, and raise trade in industries dominated by that group of customers trade. Alternatively, if locally produced products tend to reflect local, idiosyncratic tastes in consumer goods, this may reduce export potential unless the U.K. is a world trendsetter. None of these hypotheses gains any confirmation (more accurately, the overall group of hypotheses) when the share of consumers expenditures, CE, is appropriately measured.[19]

As a guide to the economic, as opposed to the statistical, significance of the above variables, it is helpful to examine the approximate percentage point change in the 1980 values of S if the independent variables increase by one standard deviation. Based on the 1980 mean, TRS reduces trade (both import penetration and the export propensity) by 10% and MES raises trade by 10%; ADS reduces trade by 5% and RDS raises trade by 5%; CR and KL raise imports by 10%; QUB raises exports (and European imports) by 6%; and durable goods, DUR, have an average 12% points more trade. In 1980, the sample range of S_m was [0.4%, 88%], and the range of S_x was [0.3%, 96%] with mean 26% for each. The economic import of such variables is therefore far from negligible.

Overall, tables 2 and 3 <u>confirm the view that international trade in manufactured goods has much less to do with comparative advantage, than it does with product and market characteristics.</u> As expected by the similarity of the U.K. and EEC 6 economies, this view gains strongest confirmation in the EM and EX equations. Regressions (3.3) and (3.9) bear a strikingly close resemblance, while the coefficients in the NEM and NEX regressions (3.5) and (3.10) are only a little less impressively similar (except for QUB, as explained above). It is quite probable that a further breakdown between the more advanced and the less developed non-EEC 6 countries would provide some useful insights (particularly since the USA and Japan are lumped in with Zaire and Bangladesh as "non-European"!).

The residuals of the basic 1980 regressions were investigated to see which industries did substantially better or worse than our model predicts. Amongst the more traded products, higher than prediced imports were found in photographic chemical materials (for which Japan accounts for 8½ % of imports) and weaving. Mining machinery had lower imports, and textile machinery had higher exports than predicted. The U.K. has a traditional expertise in these industries and the residuals may reflect export diversion and marketing drives since the domestic mining industry was expanding at the time and the domestic textile industry was contracting. The nationalised coal industry also has a purchasing bias in favour of local suppliers. Outliers in the EEC and non-EEC regressions reflect the import of cane sugar from the West Indies and paper and board from Scandinavia and Canada. Interestingly, none of the U.K.'s more protected industries 'except weaving) is in the outliers list. This may reflect either the impotence of controls or that protection is applied mainly in response to a local industry's comparative disadvantage.

Finally, estimation was repeated with three different sub-samples : (i) the food, drink and tobacco industries were excluded (ii) only industries where exports exceeded imports were included, and (iii) only industries where imports were greater than or equal to exports were included. None of these sub-samples leads to a major revision of the results reported above. Sub-sample (i) made ADS significant (negative) in all the import regressions, but QUB insignificant in the EX regression. The general picture to emerge from sub-samples (ii) and (iii) was that the estimated standard errors increased substantially, and the statistical significance of many variables was reduced, but the sign pattern remained the same.

3. CONCLUSIONS

The main argument of this paper has been that international trade in manufacturers, particularly among developed nations, depends more on product and market characteristics than it does on traditional sources of comparative advantage. Economies of scale, product differentiation and trading costs work together with entry barriers and market power to determine the total volume of both imports and exports. This hypothesis receives strong support from the empirical work reported in the previous section, and the detailed conclusions need not be repeated here.

Previous empirical studies are difficult to compare because of the diversity of countries, time periods and independent variables employed, but there follows an attempt at a brief summary. Only Pagoulatos and Sorensen (1976) adopt a symmetric approach to imports and exports, finding that her large domestic market gave the U.S.A. a comparative advantage in industries with high scale economies, that transport costs reduce trade, concentration raises trade, R & D reduces imports, and that a proxy for product differentiation has a positive effect on exports. For Canada, Baumann (1976) and Caves et. al (1980) found some evidence for scale economies raising both imports and exports. Their product differentiation proxies tended to raise trade, but the concentration effect differed between the two studies. Raw materials and R & D intensities were favourable to exports but advertising and capital intensities reduced imports. There was also some evidence for tariff effects trade, but their finding that consumer goods industries exported less must be questioned (see the Appendix). Glejser et. al. (1977) show Belgian exports to be reduced by each of concentration, a consumer goods dummy and domestic sales (as scale economies are attained in the home market); while Carlsson and Ohlsson (1976) find that seven factor endowment variables help explain Swedish exports. In the only other U.K. study of import and export penetration, apart from R & D raising both, Cable and Rebelo (1980) find very weak relationships except when looking at trade with the LDC's. Taken as a whole, these six studies suggest broad support for the relevance of scale economies, transport costs and, through various proxy measures, of product differentiation. Concentration has a mixed effect, and factor intensities show through sometimes but rarely as definite comparative advantage measures reducing imports and raising exports. Finally, several of the above studies[20] include measures of the activity of multinational firms and find them to raise trading propensities. Along with a finer breakdown of non-European trade, further investigation of the trade raising effects of multinationals is clearly an area for further research.

APPENDIX : Sample Selection and Variables in the Regression Analysis

A1 Sample Industries

The main published data source is the Census of Production (hereafter COP) for 1968 and 1979, published by the B.S.O. in 1972 and 1982. 144 MLH (3-digit) industries are given in the 1968 COP, but 33 were eliminated from our sample on the following grounds : (i) industries with "miscellaneous" in their titles and other catch-all groups which cannot be expected to behave as one industry, (ii) the ferrous metals industries which are nationalised and may not exhibit market behaviour, (iii) service and construction industries (MLH's 341, 423; 474 and 485) which cannot be visibly traded (iv) industries where international transfer pricing and re-export problems are severe (MLH's 262, 351 and 396), and (v) MLH 422.2, canvas goods and sacks etc., which was the only remaining industry that did not import and export in both years (no imports in 1968). For this 111 industry sample, the 1980 unweighted average imports as % domestic disappearance for the EEC 6 was 10.3% and for the world it was 26.4%. Exports as % domestic production were 8.3% and 26.1% for the E.E.C. 6 and the world. As can be seen by comparing these figures with the total manufacturing average given in Table 1, the sample is only slightly biased towards more traded goods (which was to be expected from our sample selection criteria). The sample covers 75.6% of all manufactured imports and 72.3% of exports. Similar figures for trade with the EEC 6 are 71.1% and 73.4%.

A2 Sample Years

1968 was chosen because of the detailed COP available for that year. However, the year may have been affected by differential effects of the November 1967 devaluation of sterling. The second sample is for 1980, the latest year for which trade data were available. Differential effects of the severe recession may have affected these results. Also, the 1980 COP was based on a new industrial classification, so the 1979 COP was used when necessary; and since more recent COP's have been less comprehensive, 1968 COP data was sometimes used for both sample years. 1980 does have one advantage, which is a regional breakdown of the trade data by MLH industry.

A3 Definition of Variables and Data Sources

All trade data were purchased from the B.S.O. (only total imports and exports for 1980 have been published in Business Monitor MQ12). The original EEC 6 countries are Germany, France, Italy, the Netherlands, Belgium and Luxembourg. All variables are expressed as percentages.

S_m = imports/(total sales less exports plus imports). sales data from 1968 COP and Business Monitor PQ1002 (1st quarter 1981) for 1980.

S_x = exports/total sales.

EM and EX are based on similar ratios, except the numerator is replaced by EEC 6 data. The same applies to NEM and NEX.

JMM = imports from Japan/total imports

TRS = transport costs/sales : 1968 COP. Also used for 1980.

ADS = advertising expenditures/sales : 1968 COP (aggregation of data meant the same ratio had to be applied to all constituent MLH's in some cases). Also used for 1980.

MES = minimum efficient plant employment size/total employment : source Lyons (1980). Also used for 1980.

DUR = 1 if typical purchasers were expected to buy no more frequently than once per year, = 0 otherwise. DUR is dominated by the engineering industries.

RDS = research and development expenditures/sales : C.S.O. Studies in Official Statistics No. 27 Table 11. 1972/3 data, the most recent year available at the time of computations, is used for 1980 sample (aggregation of the data meant the same ratio had to be applied to all constituent MLH's in some cases).

CR = the five firm concentration ratio : obtained from B.S.O. for 1968 and 1979 COP.

KL = capital/labour : employment from COP 1968 and 1979; 1968 capital obtained by disaggregating the Blue Book Order level figures using total energy consumption expressed in therms, based on official conversion factors and energy data from 1968 COP; 1980 capital stock kindly given by Dick Allard who calculated perpetual inventory figures with the assistance of the Office of Fair Trading. Only direct capital requirements are calculated. This is appropriate if all intermediate products are traded. Failing that, indirect requirements should have also been included to find the relevant factor intensities. It should be no surprise to observe that Leontief's work did include all indirect requirements calculated from the full input-output matrix.

HK = human capital variables : QU and CL measures are obtained from the Census of Population 1971; OPR, WSL and VAL are from 1968 and 1979 COP. QU variables are only available at the Order level, though CL were less aggregated. Both are expressed as a percentage of the workforce.

QU1 = post-A level qualification e.g. degree, HND.

QU2 = A-level or equivalent e.g. HNC, but not including QU1. Various combinations were tried : QU = QU1 + QU2; QUA = 2*QU1 + QU2; QUB = 3*QU1 + QU2.

CL1, CL2 and CL3 were based on the socio-economic groups of the occupational mix in the industry.

OPR = proportion of operative in total employees.

WSL = average wages and salaries per employee.

VAL = value added per head (this variable was particularly badly affected by the 1979 recession).

WDL = working days lost per 1000 employees, average for 1978-80: Employment Gazette, July 1982.

WOM = percentage of woman in the labour force, 1977 : Business Monitors PA 211-PA496.

PART = percentage of part-time employees in the labour force, 1977 : Source as for WOM.

RMM = direct import content of raw materials/industrial output, 1974: Input-Output Tables, PA1004.

CE = consumers' expenditures/(total sales less exports plus imports), 1968 and 1974 : Input-Output Tables. Note the appropriate deflator of consumers' expenditures is not total sales nor total sales plus imports (used by Baumann, 1976 and Caves et al, 1980), either of which can be shown to lead spurious correlations by including exports in the denominator.

NOTES

1 1985 figures show a drop to 69 % and 67 % for manufacturing's share of imports and exports ; part of which can be accounted for by the peaking of North Sea Oil production.

2 In general equilibrium, of course, any factor affecting the balance also affects the volume.

3 Once more, this is just a general tendency. For instance, high transport costs can give a large country a comparative advantage.

4 Melvin (1970, 1972) also discusses the effects of commodity taxation and tariffs.

5 If q=domestic production, c=domestic consumption, Q=world production (inclusive of q), C=inclusive world consumption, and Q=C, we can write domestic imports, m=c-aq, where a=c/C is the country's share of world consumption. Thus, m/c=1-(q/Q). Also, exports x=q-aq, so x/q=1-(c/C).

6 The present argument should be distinguished from one relating to economies of scale in the production of homogeneous products. The latter combination implies national specialisation, but no intra-industry trade. The homogeneous product case raises the variance of trading propensities but does not suggest a regression relationship with scale economies unless there are size effects as discussed in 1.1.4. above (Caves et. al., 1980, p. 70).

7 Note the similarity between this and the Drèze argument summarised in 1.1.4. above. However, Drèze emphasises the ability of large countries to influence world tastes, while the present argument rests on cost advantages.

8 For instance, the limited British successes in selling to that most alien of marketing environments, Japan "have been largely confined to specialities and high-quality goods. Mass-produced articles are notably absent ... as they are from a wide range of Western products sold in Japan" (Allen, 1978, pp.40-41). Apart from reflecting the role of product differentiation, speciality goods require a lower investment in mass marketing arrangements.

9 An interesting case study of such behaviour is Courtaulds in the 1960's. See Cowling et al. (1980), pp.82-84 for evidence based on a Monopolies Commission investigation.

10 Davies and McGuinness (1982) show that this may even involve pricing at less than marginal cost.

11 In fact industrial concentration rose most rapidly in the two decades prior to the 1970's - a period when import penetration grew much less rapidly. According to the NEDC, import penetration in manufacturing was 8.8 % in 1957 to be compared with our sample figures of 14.1 % in 1968 and 26.4 % in 1979.

12 The maximum effect of a change in x_j is at S=50 % where reported ß should be multiplied by 2.5. For S=28 % or 72 %, ß should be multiplied by 2, for S=18 %, or 82 % ß should be

multiplied by 1.5; and for S=11 % or 89 % ß requires no adjustment. Outside this range the effect of a small change in xj rapidly diminishes. In our 1968 sample, the mean value of Sm is 14 %, and Sx is 17 %;so the appropriate multiple is a little over one.

13 No obvious explanation for the insignificance of DUR in the M68 equations (2.1) and (2.2) presents itself, though it is consistent with the view that Britain once had a comparative advantage in durable goods industries and this was being eroded through the 1960's and 1970's.

14 No particular notice should be taken of the changing size of the coefficient in the import equations, since capital is valued at different prices in each period, and also grew in physical terms.

15 The fact that QUB is insignificant in the M80 equation may be due to problems similar to those relating to ADS. QUB is taken from the 1971 census of population, a date nearer to 1968 than 1980, and there may have been inter-temporal changes. Also QUB relates to U.K. production and if foreign production methods differ, it will be more appropriate to exports than imports.

16 Values of JMM greater than 10 % are found in sythetics, machine tools, office machinery, watches and clocks, electrics, motor cars, motor cycles and pottery. Only the last of these has lower than average import penetration.

17 Alternatively it may be due to a spurious correlation between strikes and the engineering industries.

18 Perhaps it should be emphasised that unless speicfically reported our results are <u>not</u> sensitive to a change to a simple linear functional form with S as the dependent variable.

19 Appropriate measurement is discussed briefly in the Appendix.

20 Cable and Rebelo (1980), Caves et al. (1980) and Glejser et al. (1977).

REFERENCES

ALLEN, G.C. (1978), <u>How Japan Competes : a Verdict on Dumping</u>, I.E.A. Hobart Paper 81.

BAIN, J.S. (1956), <u>Barriers to New Competition</u>, Harvard University Press.

BAUMANN, H. (1976), "Structural determinants of Canada's pattern of trade", <u>Canadian Journal of Economics</u>, vol. IX, pp. 408-423.

CABLE V. and REBELO (1987), "Britain's pattern of specialisation in manufactured goods with developing countries and trade protection", <u>World Bank Staff Working Paper</u> No. 425.

CARLSSON, B. and L. OHLSSON (1976), "Structural determinants of Swedish foreign trade", European Economic Review, vol. 7, pp. 165-174.

CAVES, R.E., M.E. Porter, A.M. SPENCE with J.T. SCOTT (1980), Competition in the Open Economy; a Model Applied to Canada, Harvard University Press.

COMANOR, W.S. and T.A. WILSON (1967), "Advertising, market structure and performance", Review of Economics and Statistics, vol. 49, pp. 423-440.

COWLING, K. et al (1980), Mergers and Economic Performance, Cambridge University Press.

DAVIES, S.W. and A.J. MCGUINESS (1982), "Dumping at less than marginal cost", Journal of International Economics, vol. 12, pp. 169-182.

DIXIT, A.K. and V. NORMAN (1980), Theory of International Trade, Cambridge University Press.

DREZE, J. (1960), Quelques reflections sereines sur l'adaptation de l'industrie belge au Marche Common, Comptes Rendus des Travaux de la Societe Royale d'Economic Politique de Belgique, no. 275.

GLEJSER, H., A. JACQUEMIN and J. PETIT (1977), Exports in an imperfect competition framework : an analysis of 1446 small country exporters.

HELPMAN, E. (1981), "International trade in the presence of product differentiation, economies of scale and monopolistic competition: a Chamberlin-Heckscher-Ohlin approach", Journal of International Economics, U11, pp. 305-340.

HUME, D. (1758), "Of the jealousy of trade", Essay VI, Green, T.H. and T.H. Grose (eds) (1964), The Philosophical Works, Vol.3, Scientia Verlag Aalen.

KENEN, P.B. (ed.)(1975), International Trade and Finance : Frontiers for Research, Cambridge University Press.

KIERZKOWSKI, H. (ed.)(1983), Monopolistic Competition and International Trade Oxford University Press.

KRUGMAN, P. (1980), "Scale economies, product differentiation and the pattern of trade", American Economic Review, vol. 70, pp. 950-959.

LANCASTER, K.J. (1980), "Intra-industry trade under perfect monopolistic competition", Journal of International Economics, vol. 10, pp. 151-175.

LINDER, S.B. (1961), An Essay on Trade and Transformation, Wiley : New York.

LYONS, B.R. (1981b), "Industrial behaviour, the technology of demand, and the pattern of international trade between identical countries", Recherches Economique de Louvain, vol. 47, pp. 243-258.

LYONS, B.R. (1983), "The pattern of international trade in differentiated products : an incentive for the existence of multi-national firms", Kierzkowski, H. (ed).

MELVIN, J.R. (1972), "The effects of tariff preferences on Canadian imports : an empirical analysis", Canadian Journal of Economics, vol. 5, pp. 48-69.

MELVIN, J.R. (1979), "Short-run price effects of the corporate income tax and implications for international trade, American Economic Review, vol. 69, pp. 756-774.

PAGOULATOS, E. and R. SORENSEN (1976), "Domestic market structures and international trade : an empirical analysis", Quarterly Review of Economics and Business, vol. 16, pp. 45-60.

POSNER, M.V. (1961), "International trade and technical change", Oxford Economic Papers, vol. 13, pp. 323-341.

STERN, R.M. (1975), "Testing trade theories", Kenen,P.B. (ed.).

VERNON, R. (1966), "International investment and international trade in the product cycle", Quarterly Journal of Economics, vol. 80, pp. 190-207.

WHITE, L.J. (1974), "Industrial organisation and international trade : some theoretical considerations", American Economic Review, vol. 64., pp. 1013-1020.

The Convergence of International and Domestic Markets
D.B. Audretsch, L. Sleuwaegen, and H. Yamawaki (Editors)

7. DEVELOPING COUNTRY EXPORT COMPETITIVENESS IN MANUFACTURED GOODS

Harry P. Bowen
Stern School of Business, New York University
and
National Bureau of Economic Research

0. INTRODUCTION

Growth since the mid-1960s in developing country exports of manufactured goods has generated considerable interest in uncovering the source of their competitive success and in particular, the source of the relatively better performance of certain developing countries. In this regard, researcher's have explored numerous issues including inward versus outward looking policies, the role of external market conditions, and the efficacy of "export-led" growth (e.g., Love (1984), Michaely (1977), Riedel (1984) and Tyler (1981)). While such factors have undoubtedly contributed to the growth in developing country exports, analysts have tended to ignore a more fundamental source of expanded trade performance, namely, changes in the pattern of developing country resource supplies over time. Although a number of studies have correlated export success and capital-labor intensity across industries and found the negative relationship expected on the basis of the factor abundance theory (e.g., Boatler (1975), Donges and Riedel (1977) and Helleiner (1976)), these analyses beg the question of the extent to which changes in resource supplies have influenced the success of developing countries as exporters of manufactured goods.

In part, the absence of a systematic study of the relationship between developing country (LDC) trade performance and their resource supplies derives from difficulties in applying the traditional method for studying the determinants of a country's trade performance, namely, a cross-section regression of industry trade balances on input requirements. While such regressions could be used to study the determinants of LDC trade performance, in reality their application is hampered by incomplete or nonexistent data on input requirements in such countries. Using data on U.S. input requirements is one way to compensate for the lack of such data in LDCs, but the appropriateness of U.S. data to LDCs is often subject to question. Equally important is that the results from such regressions may contain little, if any, information about an country's underlying resource supplies. (Leamer and Bowen (1981)).

That resource supply changes may explain LDC competitiveness can be inferred from the results of studies such as Balassa (1979), and especially Leamer (1984). But while these studies indicate that trade patterns conform to resource supply patterns world-wide, they use regression methodologies that only permit inferences about the trade pattern and resource supplies of an "average" country, not that of specific countries. This absence of country specific information leaves unanswered the question of possible differences among countries in the relationship between trade performance and resource supplies.

In response to the above issues, this paper investigates the relationship between changes in LDC trade performance and changes in their resource supplies. The analysis uses the methodology developed by Bowen (1983) whereby net trade in a commodity in which a country is most internationally competitive is regressed on national factor supplies across countries. This approach has three advantages. First, resource supplies are the explanatory variables and thus the results permit direct inferences about the influence of resource supplies on trade performance. Second, the procedure does not use industry input data and thus makes no commitment to U.S. technology. Finally, the results are specific to a particular country so that one can study the extent of differences among countries in the relationship between trade performance and resource supplies.

The remainder of the paper is organized as follows. Section 1 presents the theoretical model which forms the basis for the empirical work and develops the procedures employed in the study. In Section 2 the results of estimating an export performance equation for each of thirty-six developing countries in both 1966 and 1980 are presented and then used in conjunction with data on the pattern of LDC resource supplies to infer the influence of resource supply changes in determining changes in LDC trade performance. In Section 3 a direct study is made of the contribution of resources changes to changes in trade performance by estimating equations relating changes in trade performance to changes in resources supplies between 1966 and 1980. The results of this analysis are then used in Section 4 to examine if differential growth in resource supplies over time offers an explanation for differences in the trade performance of the NICs versus that of other LDCs. Section 5 contains concluding remarks.

1. THEORY AND MODEL SPECIFICATION

The theoretical foundation for the analysis conducted here is the model of multicountry, multifactor trade developed in Bowen (1980), Leamer and Bowen (1981) and Leamer (1984). Assuming equal numbers of goods and factors as well as the assumptions sufficient for factor price equalization, the model implies that the net trade of country i can be expressed as a linear function of its excess factor supplies:[1]

(1) $$T_i = A^{-1} (E_i - \alpha_i E_w)$$

where T_i = Kx1 vector of net trades.
A = KxK matrix of factor input requirements.
E_i = Kx1 vector of factor supplies in country i.
E_w = $\Sigma_i E_i$, a Kx1 vector of world factor supplies.
α_i = country i's share of world expenditure.

For estimation purposes it is convenient to consider the following reduced form variant of (1):

(2) $$T_i = RE_i \quad .$$

The KxK matrix R has elements $r_{jk} = (a^{-1}_{jk} - w_k Q_{wj}/Y_w)$ where a^{-1}_{jk} an element of A^{-1}, w_k is the common world price of factor k, Q_{wj} is world output of good j and Y_w is world expenditure (GNP). Since $r_{jk} = \partial T_{ij}/\partial E_{ik}$, each element of R is interpreted as the total change (production minus consumption) in the net trade of good j resulting from a change in the supply of resource k, holding constant the prices of both goods and factors.

Equation (2) suggests that estimates of each r_{jk} for a given commodity j can be formed by regressing net trade in good j on factor supplies across countries. Leamer (1984) used this approach to study the relationship between the net trade in each of ten commodity aggregates and resource supplies across countries. However, a limitation of this approach in the context of the present study is that the estimated coefficients correspond to a specific commodity (or commodity aggregate) and thus do not directly indicate the effect of a resource change on the trade performance of a particular country. To use such regressions to study the trade performance of a particular country, a method is needed to convert the commodity specific estimates into country specific estimates.

One possibility is to estimate a separate equation for each commodity and then select a subset of the equations on the basis of some criteria particular to the country of interest. For example, one might select those equations corresponding to commodities in which a country has a comparative advantage. By some averaging of the estimated coefficients for each resource across the selected subset of equations, one could infer the average effect of a resource change on trade in the selected subset of commodities and thus on the country's comparative advantage.

Another possibility would be to first construct an aggregate commodity whose component commodities are those in which a country is thought to have a comparative advantage. The estimates formed by regressing net trade in this aggregate commodity on resource supplies across countries would then indicate the effect of resource changes on trade in the aggregate commodity. But by construction of the aggregate commodity, the estimates also indicate the effect of resources changes on the country's comparative advantage.

These two approaches would yield identical results if the method used to average coefficients across equations under the first approach were identical to the method of averaging that is implicit in the second approach. Inspection of (2) indicates that estimates formed using the second (aggregate commodity) approach are identical to the unweighted sum of the coefficients for each resource across the subset of equations estimated using the first approach. Given this, one advantage of the aggregate commodity approach is that it reduces the number of equations to be estimated from several to one. A second advantage is that coefficient standard errors and associated regression diagnostics are obtained directly. For these reasons the aggregate commodity approach is used here.

Since in this paper we are interested in explaining a country's export performance, the construction of an aggregate commodity requires the identification of a subset of commodities in which a country is most internationally competitive. One measure of a country's trade performance in commodity j is its level of net trade in that commodity. However, as Deardorff (1985) noted, "the volume of trade in a good depends rather obviously on the importance of that good in world markets" and therefore some scaling is required to account for this importance. Deardorff conjectured that an appropriate scaling variable would be a measure of world market size as opposed to the commonly used data on industry shipments. Actually, the model stated above suggests a scaling variable that is consistent with Deardorff's conjecture, namely, the world output of commodity j. From (2), the equation for commodity j is

$$(3) \qquad t_{ij} = \Sigma_k \, (a^{-1}_{jk} - w_k Q_{wj}/Y_w) E_{ik}$$

and dividing both sides by world output gives

$$(4) \qquad t_{ij}/Q_{wj} = \Sigma_k \, (a^{-1}_{jk}/Q_{wj} - w_k/Y_w) E_{ik} \, .$$

Whereas the model indicates that world output is an appropriate variable for removing commodity "size" effects, data on world outputs that conforms to the classification of traded goods are not available. In view of this, one can assume that world output of commodity j is proportional to world exports of commodity j (X_{wj}), $Q_{wj} = \lambda_j X_{wj}$ in which case (4) can be written

$$(5) \qquad s_{ij} = t_{ij}/X_{wj} = \Sigma_k (a_k^{-1}/X_{wj} - \lambda_j w_k/Y_w)E_i .$$

where s_{ij} can be interpreted as country i's share of the world export market for commodity j.

Adopting s_{ij} as the measure of country i's trade performance in commodity j, a ranking of such ratios across commodities for a given country is then an ordering of that country's trade performance (competitiveness). And by selecting a subset of the commodities at the top of this ranking, one can form an aggregate commodity which represents a "commodity" in which the country is most competitive. This commodity aggregate is hereafter denoted the country's export good.

For this study, data on country i's trade in country z's export good were constructed by first ranking country z's net trade to world export ratios in each of eighty-two 3-digit SITC manufacturing commodity categories.[2] From this ranking, the top ten ranked commodities were selected to represent those in which country z was most competitive. Then, for each country i, the net trade to export ratios in these ten commodities were summed to yield observations on the trade in country z's export good.[3] Algebraically, if the set m_z indexes country z's top ten ranked commodities, then country i's trade in country z's export good is computed as

$$(6) \qquad s_i^z = \sum_{j \in m_z} s_{ij}$$

Given observations on the trade in each country's export good in both 1966 and 1980, a study of the resources determining trade performance in the market for this good is made by estimating the following equation for each country in each sample year:

$$s_i^z = \beta_0 + \Sigma_k \beta_k E_{ik} + \epsilon_i \qquad (7)$$

where s_i^z = country i's share of the world export market for country z's export good.

β_k = coefficient whose sign indicates the directional change in trade performance due to a change in resource k.

E_{ik} = country i's supply of resource k.

ϵ_i = error term assumed to reflect omitted resources.

TABLE 1 : Sample of Countries

Developing Countries		Other Countries	
1)	Argentina	24)	Australia
2)	Brazil	25)	Austria
3)	Chile	26)	Belgium-Luxembourg
4)	Colombia	27)	Canada
5)	Costa Rica	28)	Denmark
6)	Egypt	29)	Finland
7)	El Salvador	30)	France
8)	Greece	31)	Germany
9)	Honduras	32)	Ireland
10)	Hong Kong	33)	Italy
11)	India	34)	Japan
12)	Israel	35)	Netherlands
13)	Korea	36)	Norway
14)	Malaysia	37)	Switzerland
15)	Mexico	38)	Spain
16)	Peru	39)	Sweden
17)	Philippines	40)	United Kingdom
18)	Portugal	41)	United States
19)	Sri Lanka		
20)	Singapore		
21)	Thailand		
22)	Turkey		
23)	Yugoslavia		

Since the error term is assumed to reflect omitted resources, it is natural to expect the variance of residual i to vary with a measure of country size and thus some form of heteroscedasticity correction is warranted. Following Leamer (1984, p 121), GNP is taken as the measure of country size and the hypothesized systematic heteroscedasticity is modeled as

$$(8) \qquad \sigma_i^2 = \delta(GNP_i)^{\gamma}$$

where δ and γ are unknown parameters. Given (8), estimation of the parameters in (7) proceeds in a three step fashion. First, (7) is estimated and the logarithms of the squared residuals derived from this unweighted regression are regressed on the logarithms of GNP in order to form estimates of the parameters δ and γ in (8). The predicted values of σ_i^2 from this auxiliary regression are then used as weights for re-estimating (7).

Data on the supply of seven resources in each of forty-one countries (see Table 1) were collected for 1966 and 1980. The resources are: net capital stock, skilled labor, semiskilled labor, unskilled labor and three types of land differentiated by climate. These data are from Bowen (1983).[4] The capital data are measured in constant 1966 U.S. dollars.

2. DETERMINANTS OF TRADE PERFORMANCE : CROSS-SECTION ANALYSIS

The detailed results of estimating (7)[5] with respect to each country's export performance using the cross-section samples in both 1966 and 1980 are summarized here by reporting the signs of the estimated coefficients. Examining only coefficient signs serves to uncover the influence of each resource on a country's trade performance and also permits an assessment of any similarities among countries in the relationship between trade performance and resource supplies. Given a high degree of similarity, the results can then be interpreted as indicating the relationship between trade performance and resource supplies of an "average" LDC. In all cases, a coefficient's sign is reported if its associated confidence level is eighty percent or higher.

Tables 2 and 3 show the coefficient signs estimated for each resource and country in 1966 and 1980, respectively. The sign patterns in both Table 2 and Table 3 suggest a high degree of similarity among LDCs in terms of the relationship between export performance and resource supplies. In 1966 the average LDC's export performance was positively related to semiskilled labor and negatively related to unskilled labor, capital and the three types of land (Table 2). The influence of skilled labor is mixed but on average exerts a negative influence on trade performance.

The suggested negative influence of unskilled labor on trade performance appears surprising since this resource is usually thought to be a source of LDC export performance. However, recall that in theory the sign of a coefficient indicates the net effect (production minus consumption) of a resource change on trade performance and the sign of this effect need not coincide with that expected under a "factor intensity" interpretation.[6] Therefore the results suggest that, on average, an increase in unskilled labor raises consumption relative to production and, in this sense, unskilled labor is "unfriendly" to trade performance in the market for the average LDC's export good. A less formal interpretation is that in 1966, country's abundant in unskilled labor were unlikely to be internationally competitive in manufactured goods.

In 1980 (Table 3) the average LDC's export performance remained positively related to semiskilled labor and the negative influence of skilled labor suggested in 1966 is now clearly evident. Unskilled labor became a generally positive determinant of export performance as did the land variables.[7] The generally negative influence of capital found for 1966 has given way to differences among countries such that the average influence of capital on LDC trade performance is problematic.

Comparing the 1966 results to those for 1980, the changed influence of each resource may be revealing the rapid emergence of LDCs in world trade. In 1966, trade in manufactured goods was dominated by developed countries and the results for that year reflect that competitiveness in the market for a commodity in which the average LDC was most competitive required a suitable supply of semiskilled labor. The subsequent emergence of developing countries in manufactured goods trade is reflected in the 1980 results by the positive influence of unskilled labor and the negative influence of skilled labor as developed countries absorbed increasing amounts of developing country manufactured goods. The differences in the 1966 and 1980 results also suggest that the emergence of developing countries in manufactured goods trade is broadly along the lines of their "comparative advantage."

TABLE 2: Export Performance Regressions - 1966

Country	Capital	Labor S	Labor SS	Labor US	Land L1	Land L2	Land L3	R^2
Argentina								.31
Brazil								.33
Brunei	-	+	+	-	-	-	-	.58**
Cameroon		-	+				+	.54**
Chile		-	+	+			+	.59**
Colombia	-		+	-	-	-	-	.59**
Costa Rica		-	+		-			.53**
Cen.Afr.Rep.								.26
Egypt	-		+	-	-			.42**
El Salvador	-		+	-	-	-	-	.56**
Greece								.30
Guatemala								.28
Honduras			+		-	-		.38*
Hong Kong		-	+		-	-	-	.41**
India	-		+	-	-		-	.48**
Israel								.30
Korea		-	+	-	-	-		.50**
Madagascar	-	+	-	-				.42**
Malawi			+		-	-	-	.46**
Malaysia		+	+	-	-	-	-	.47**
Martinique								.16
Mexico			+	-	-	-	-	.55**
Nicaragua								.30
Pakistan	-		+	-	-		-	.55**
Peru								.30
Philippines		-	+					.42**
Portugal								.30
Reunion								.20
Singapore		-	+			-	-	.37*
Spain			+	-	-			.38*
Sri Lanka		-	+				-	.39*
Thailand	-	+		-				.71**
Tunisia								.26
Turkey								.31
Upper Volta		-	+				+	.49**
Yugoslavia	-	+		-	-			.45**

S Skilled
SS Semiskilled
US Unskilled

Confidence levels: * = 95 percent, ** = 99 percent.
A sign is shown if its associated confidence level is at least 80 percent and the overall regression has an associated confidence level of at least 95 percent.

TABLE 3 : Export Performance Regressions - 1980

Country	Capital	----	Labor	----	----	Land	----	R^2
		S	SS	US	L1	L2	L3	
Argentina	-		+	-		+		.35*
Brazil	-		+	-	+			.61**
Brunei								.20
Cameroon								.17
Chile		-	+	+	+	+	+	.72**
Colombia		-	+					.48**
Costa Rica		-	+					.35*
Cen.Afr.Rep.								.28
Egypt		-	+	+				.42**
El Salvador		-	+					.33*
Greece		-	+			+	+	.40*
Guatemala								.28
Honduras		-	+	+	+		+	.63**
Hong Kong	+	-	+	+				.46**
India	+	-	+	+				.48**
Israel								.14
Korea		-	+					.46**
Madagascar	+		-	+	+		-	.62**
Malawi	+	-	+	+	+	-	+	.75**
Malaysia	-	-	+					.35*
Martinique		+	-	-	-	-		.58**
Mexico								.16
Nicaragua	+	-	+	+		+		.47**
Pakistan	+	-	+	+			-	.57**
Peru								.30
Philippines		-	+					.47**
Portugal		-	+					.43**
Reunion								.27
Singapore								.20
Spain		-	+					.36*
Sri Lanka	-		+	-		-		.35*
Thailand		-	+	+				.54**
Tunisia								.27
Turkey	+	-	+	+				.37*
Upper Volta	+	-	+	+	+		-	.68**
Yugoslavia								.30

S Skilled
SS Semiskilled
US Unskilled

Confidence levels: * = 95 percent, ** = 99 percent.
A sign is shown if its associated confidence level is at least 80 percent and the overall regression has an associated confidence level of at least 95 percent.

Overall, the results suggest that an increase in the supply of semiskilled labor relative to other resources would be expected to increase trade performance in those markets in which the average LDC was most competitive. This raises the question of what the actual pattern of factor supply was for the average LDC in 1966 and how it changed over the 1966-80 period.

Following Bowen (1983), a country's factor abundance is defined by the ranking of its world resource shares. Accordingly, factor abundance for LDCs as a group was obtained by adding the world share of each resource in each country across the sample of twenty-three developing countries in each sample year. The resulting world resource shares are shown in Table 4.

TABLE 4 : Developing Country World Resource Shares

All Countries				
Year	Capital	Skilled Labor	Semiskilled Labor	Unskilled Labor
1966	11.9	30.8	41.2	98.0
1980	15.7	35.8	45.9	99.3
change	(3.8)	(5.0)	(4.7)	(1.3)
India Excluded				
Year	Capital	Skilled Labor	Semiskilled Labor	Unskilled Labor
1966	9.8	18.2	26.8	25.2
1980	13.0	21.3	31.0	24.0
change	(3.2)	(3.1)	(4.2)	(-1.2)

In both 1966 and 1980, LDCs as a group were most abundant in unskilled labor followed by semiskilled labor, skilled labor and capital. However, as the second half of Table 4 indicates, the measured abundance of unskilled labor is heavily influenced by the presence of India. With India excluded, LDCs as a group were most abundant in semiskilled labor in each year. Thus, excluding India, LDC resource abundance conforms to the above evidence that trade performance in the market for a commodity in which the average LDC is most competitive is positively related to semiskilled labor.

Although the structure of LDC factor abundance did not change over the 1966-80 period, there were differences in the rate of resource accumulation as indicated by the percentage point changes shown in Table 4. With India excluded, LDCs increased their share of semiskilled labor relative to each of the other resources and thus became relatively more abundant in semiskilled labor. The increased abundance in semiskilled labor together with the results in Table 2 and 3 implies increases in LDC competitiveness over time and is therefore consistent with the acknowledged increases in LDC trade performance since the mid-1960s.

3. CHANGES IN TRADE PERFORMANCE

The preceding cross-section analysis suggests that growth in the average LDC's export performance since the mid-1960 is the result of changes in its resource supplies, notably an increase in semiskilled labor. However, inferring time-series behavior from cross-section results has several pitfalls, and we accordingly turn attention to a direct examination of changes in LDC trade performance in relation to changes in resource supplies over time.

From (7), the change in country i's trade performance in country z's export good between 1966 and 1980 can be decomposed as

$$\Delta s_i^z = \Delta \beta_o + \Sigma_k \Delta \beta_k E_{ik}^{66} + \Sigma_k \beta_k \Delta E_{ik} + \mu_i \qquad (9)$$

where E_{ik}^{66} is the level of resource k in country i in 1966 and ΔE_{ik} is the change in resource k between 1966 and 1980.[8] Equation (9) allows for changes in the coefficients over time since these are theoretically functions of prices which are expected to change. However, implicit in (9) is the possibility of a change in the composition of a country's export good. Here this possibility is removed by defining the basket of commodities to be that in 1980. Thus, Δs_i^z is the change in trade performance in the market for a commodity in which country z was most competitive in in 1980.

Prior to estimating (9) consideration was again given to the possibility of systematic heteroscedasticity associated with country size. In this case, correction was made by first estimating (9) and then regressing the logarithms of the squared residuals from this regression on the level of 1966 GNP in order to estimate the parameters in (8). The predicted residuals from this auxiliary regression were then used as weights to re-estimate (9).

As in Section 2, the detailed results of estimating(9)[9] for each country are summarized by the signs of the estimated coefficients as reported in Table 5. In general, the R-squares associated with the change regressions are much higher, and the coefficient standard errors much smaller, than those associated with the cross-section analyses considered earlier.[10]

The results indicate that changes in trade performance in the market for the average LDC's 1980 export good are positively related to changes in semiskilled and unskilled labor and negatively related to changes in skilled labor and capital. Except for capital, these results are similar to the cross-section results obtained for 1980 (Table 3).

The strong evidence that capital exerts a negative influence on trade performance, and the general improvement in regression diagnostics, suggests that the earlier cross-section analysis may have omitted an important resource. In particular, a resource that is correlated with the level of capital across countries but uncorrelated with changes in capital over time. One possibility is the elusive "technology factor," but this explanation is unsatisfactory since one would also expect this "factor" to be highly correlated with skilled labor, and the results for skilled labor are essentially the same as those derived in the 1980 cross-section.

Another possibility is a variable reflecting mineral resources whose availability is not captured by the land variables. To check the influence of such a variable, data on Leamer's (1984) "minerals index" were constructed for 1980 and used to re-estimate (7). In no case did the inclusion of this variable alter the signs of the variables. In view of this, a less appealing but

TABLE 5 : Change in Export Performance 1966-1980
1980 Export Basket

Country	Capital	---- Labor ----			R-Sq	F
		S	SS	US		
Argentina					.41	.39
Brazil	-	-	+		.58**	2.59*
Brunei	+		+		.98**	19.56**
Cameroon		-	+	+	.61**	1.78
Chile					.41	1.28
Colombia	-	-	+	+	.87**	7.15**
Costa Rica	-		+		.65**	.79
Cen.Afr.Rep.	-	-	+		.65**	.62
Egypt	-	-	+	+	.80**	3.10*
El Salvador	-	-	+	+	.79**	5.55**
Greece			+	+	.54**	.70
Guatemala	-		+	+	.77**	5.54**
Honduras	-	-	+		.58**	.94
Hong Kong	+	-	+		.61**	1.89
India			+		.56**	.53
Israel			+		.58**	7.74
Korea	-	-	+	+	.80**	3.77**
Madagascar			+	-	.55**	1.22
Malawi	-	-	+		.46*	1.53
Malaysia	-	-	+	+	.66**	1.99*
Martinique			-	-	.62**	5.28**
Mexico	-	+			.94**	13.20**
Nicaragua			+	-	.62**	2.32*
Pakistan	-		+	+	.81**	3.28*
Peru	-	-	+	-	.56**	1.79
Philippines	-	-	+	+	.78**	2.55*
Portugal	-	-	+		.65**	2.82*
Reunion					.36	1.38
Singapore	-	-	+	-	.96**	33.72**
Spain	-		+	+	.60**	1.36
Sri Lanka	-		+	-	.92**	13.61**
Thailand	-	-	+	+	.74**	1.77
Tunisia	-	-	+	+	.71**	2.45*
Turkey			+		.85**	8.26**
Upper Volta					.28	.45
Yugoslavia		-	+	-	.60**	2.04

S Skilled
SS Semiskilled
US Unskilled

Confidence levels: * = 95 percent, ** = 99 percent.
A sign is shown if its associated confidence level is at least 80 percent and the overall regression has an associated confidence level of at least 95 percent.
The F-statistics in the last column are for testing the null hypothesis of no change in the coefficients over time.

nonetheless distinct possibility is that the capital variable contains a measurement error component that is relatively constant over time. However, in the present study there is no adequate method for determining the extent of such error.[11]

Finally, the (joint) hypothesis that the coefficients did not change between 1966 and 1980 can be rejected for all but four countries (Argentina, Chile, Reunion and Upper Volta). As noted earlier, coefficient changes were expected since they are theoretically functions of relative prices which surely changed over the sample period.

Overall, the results of this section support the earlier findings that a major source of the growth in LDC competitiveness in manufactured goods was an increase in their supply of semiskilled labor. However, there is evidence that capital accumulation is "unfriendly" to trade performance in the markets for LDC export goods. Whereas this latter result appears consistent with the predictions of the factor abundance theory, the negative influence of capital accumulation on trade performance seems inconsistent with the generally high rates of capital accumulation observed for LDCs over the sample period. One explanation for this is that capital accumulation permitted many LDCs to surpass a "threshold" level of capital needed to produce manufactured goods. Thus, while many LDCs had high rates of capital formation in the 1960s and 1970s, LDCs have nonetheless specialized in producing and exporting manufactures which used primarily semiskilled and unskilled labor. Finally, the results underscore the potential fragility of inferences about time series behavior on the basis of cross-section results.

4. DIFFERENTIAL TRADE PERFORMANCE - NICs VERSUS OTHER LDCs

The results presented in preceding sections indicate that changes in LDC resource supplies provide a consistent explanation for the growth in their competitiveness in manufactured goods since the mid-1960s. However, the bulk of LDC exports of manufactured goods emanate from only a few LDCs, the Newly Industrialized Countries (NICs). What factors account for the relative success of these countries compared to other developing countries? Are the resources determining NIC export performance different from those determining the export performance of other LDCs? To what extent has the change in NIC resource supplies differed from that of other LDCs? These questions are analyzed below.

Among the countries studied here, nine are commonly considered NICs: Argentina, Brazil, Greece, Hong Kong, Korea, Malaysia, Mexico, the Philippines and Singapore. Treating these nine countries combined as the NICs and the remaining fourteen countries as Other LDCs, Table 6 shows their respective world resource shares of capital and the three types of labor in 1966 and 1980.

In both 1966 and 1980 the NICs where most abundant in semiskilled labor and least abundant in capital. The Other LDCs (India excluded) were most abundant in unskilled labor in 1966 but in 1980 became most abundant in semiskilled labor. Although the factor abundance ordering of each group in each year is similar, the changes in the resource shares of each group were markedly

TABLE 6 : World Resources Shares of NICs and Other LDCs

Year	Capital	Skilled Labor	Semiskilled Labor	Unskilled Labor
NICs*				
1966	4.9	9.4	13.6	11.6
1980	8.2	11.9	17.5	11.1
change	(3.3)	(2.5)	(3.9)	(-0.5)
Other LDCs				
1966	6.9	21.3	27.6	86.4
1980	7.4	23.8	28.4	88.2
change	(0.5)	(2.5)	(0.8)	(1.8)
Other LDCs India excluded				
1966	4.9	8.8	13.2	13.6
1980	4.7	9.4	13.5	12.8
change	(-0.1)	(0.6)	(0.3)	(-0.8)

* Argentina, Brazil, Greece, Hong Kong, Korea, Malaysia, Mexico, the Philippines and Singapore.

different; the NICs rate of resource accumulation far exceeded that of the Other LDCs between 1966 and 1980. In particular, while the world share of each resource in Other LDCs was virtually unchanged, the NICs increased their world share of capital, skilled labor, and semiskilled labor. This pattern of resource accumulation is such that the NICs increased their abundance in semiskilled labor relative to other resources. This evidence of differential resource accumulation would explain differences in the trade performance of the NICs versus that of Other LDCs if the determinants of their respective export performance were the same.

With reference to Table 5, there are few differences in the resources determining the export performance of an average NIC versus that of an average Other LDC's. In particular, the export performance for each group of countries is, on average, positively associated with semiskilled labor and unskilled labor but negatively associated with capital and skilled labor. Since the influence of each resource in determining the export performance of these two groups of countries is essentially identical, a consistent explanation for the difference in their respective trade performance is the difference found above in their rates of resource accumulation. In particular, since both groups experienced a decrease in their world share of unskilled labor (India excluded from Other LDCs) of approximately equal magnitude, the principal source of differential export performance was the differential growth in semiskilled labor supplies.[12]

5. CONCLUDING REMARKS

This paper has presented a systematic analysis of the relationship between developing country trade performance in manufactured goods and their resource supplies over the period from 1966 to 1980. In a sample of forty-one countries, regressions were estimated for each of thirty-six developing countries which permitted identification of the resources determining trade performance in the market for a commodity in which each country was most competitive. In addition, direct analysis was made of the change in each country's trade performance in relation to changes in their resource supplies over the sample period.

The results indicated a high degree of similarity across LDCs in terms of the relationship between trade performance and resource supplies. In general, trade performance in markets in which LDCs are most competitive was found to be positively related to semiskilled labor and unskilled labor and negatively to capital and skilled labor. Examination of the actual pattern of factor supply changes for LDCs as group revealed that they became relatively more abundant in semiskilled labor over the sample period. Thus, to a large extent the growth in LDC competitiveness in manufactured goods is consistent with the predictions of the factor abundance theory.

Finally, a comparison of the NICs versus other LDCs indicated few differences in the resources determining their respective trade performance. However, as a group, the NICs were found to have increased their world share of each resource except unskilled labor whereas the world resource shares of other LDCs were essentially unchanged between 1966 and 1980. Given no differences in the resources determining the trade performance in each group of countries, the differential growth in resource supplies therefore provided a consistent explanation for the more rapid growth in NIC export performance.

What implications does this study have with regard to the future evolution of LDC trade and its impact on developed countries? Overall, the results suggest that continued accumulation of semiskilled labor in LDCs will further increase their competitiveness in manufactured goods. This increased competitiveness will further erode the position of import competing producers in developed countries with the industries most affected being those reliant on semiskilled labor.[13] In turn, this suggests that increases in LDC competitiveness will create further pressure for the relative wage of semiskilled workers to fall in developed countries.

NOTES

1 In the absence of factor price equalization, (1) can also be derived by assuming that input requirements are fixed and internationally identical. Alternatively, one can take (1) to be an approximation to the general nonlinear relationship that exists between trade and resource supplies.

2 These commodities are a subset of the one hundred and two manufacturing commodities defined by SITCs 5-8. Commodities groups excluded are SITCs 515, 661-663, 681-689, 863, 892 and 896.

3 A list of the ten commodities selected to comprise each country's export good is available from the author upon request.

4 Briefly, net capital stock is the discounted sum of gross domestic investment flows (beginning with 1948) assuming an average asset life of fifteen years. Skilled labor is number of profesional/technical workers; semiskilled labor is number of workers who are not professional/technical multiplied times the country's literacy rate; unskilled labor is the total workforce times one minus the literacy rate. Land variables are the number of hectares of a country's total land contained under one of three climate types: Land1, tropical; Land2, micro-thermal; Land3, meso-thermal.

5 The detailed results are available from the author upon request.

6 Formally, the coefficients are not pure Rybczynski effects, and thus the results do not provide a test of the factor abundance theory.

7 The positive influence of the land variables may reflect that the more successful LDCs in terms of exports of manufactures have been those with abundant natural resources.

8 The land variables do not change over time.

9 The detailed results are available from the author.

10 This contrasts with the earlier findings of Bowen (1983) in which the time-series results where generally much worse than the corresponding cross-section results.

11 However, in a different context, Bowen, et. al. (1987) could not reject the hypothesis that capital, as well as the other resource variables, are measured with error.

12 Puzzling is that the NICs rate of capital accumulation would imply decreased trade performance. Here it must be remembered that the coefficient signs indicate production minus consumption effects. Thus, the negative influence of capital reflects the general state of capital scarcity in developing countries.

13 That semiskilled labor is most likely to be affected by import competition from LDCs is also supported by an earlier study (Bowen, 1983) which found semiskilled labor to be the principal positive determinant of competitiveness in the U.S.'s import good.

REFERENCES

BALASSA, Bela (1979), "The Changing Pattern of Comparative Advantage in Manufactured Goods", Review of Economics and Statistics, vol. 61 (2), pp. 259-266.

BOWEN, Harry P., Edward E. LEAMER and Leo SVEIKAUSKAS (1987), "Multicountry Multifactor Tests of the Factor Abundance Theory", American Economic Review, vol. 77 (5), pp. 791-809.

BOWEN, Harry P. (1983), "Changes in the International Distribution of Resources and Their Impact on U.S. Comparative Advantage", Review of Economics and Statistics, vol. 65 (3), pp. 402-414.

CHENERY, Hollis and Moses SYRQUIN (1975), Patterns of Development, 1950-1970, (New York and London: Oxford University Press for World Bank).

HAVRYLYSHYN, O. (1985), "The Direction of Developing Country Trade", Journal of Development Economics, vol. 19 (December), pp. 225-281.

KEESING, Donald B. and Donald R. SHERK (1971), "Population Density in Patterns of Trade and Development", American Economic Review, vol. 61(5), pp. 956-961.

LEAMER, Edward E., Sources of International Comparative Advantage: Theory and Evidence, (Cambridge: MIT Press), 1984.

________ and Harry P. BOWEN (1981), "Cross-Section Tests of the Heckscher-Ohlin Theorem: Comment", American Economic Review, vol. 71 (5), pp. 1040-43.

LOVE, J. (1984), "External Market Conditions, Competitiveness, Diversification amid LDC Exports", Journal of Development Economics, vol. 16, pp. 279-291.

MICHAELY, M. (1977), "Exports and Growth: An Empirical Investigation", Journal of Development Economics, vol. 4 (1), pp. 49-53.

TYLER, W. G. (1981), "Growth and Export Expansion in Developing Countries", Journal of Development Economics, vol. 9, pp. 121-130.

RIEDEL, J. (1984), "Trade as the Engine of Growth in Developing Countries, Revisited", Economic Journal, vol. 94, pp. 56-73.

The Convergence of International and Domestic Markets
D.B. Audretsch, L. Sleuwaegen, and H. Yamawaki (Editors)

8. THE DYNAMICS OF EXPORT COMPETITION*

David B. Audretsch
Wissenschaftszentrum Berlin für Sozialforschung
Leo Sleuwaegen
Catholic University of Leuven and Erasmus University
Hideki Yamawaki
Wissenschaftszentrum Berlin für Sozialforschung

0. INTRODUCTION

The dynamic evolution of export performance between the EC, Japan and U.S. is examined in this paper. By considering the interaction between the export shares of these three regions over the period 1962-1985, we seek to identify whether there are markets in which exports compete and if export shares move systematically over time. Further, by examining the intertemporal behavior of export shares at a fairly disaggregated level for 165 three-digit SITC (Standard International Trade Classification) industries, we are able to determine whether the patterns of intertemporal movement of export shares are uniform or specific to industrial sectors and possibly market structure.

The contribution of this paper is to consider market shares from a dynamic perspective. While we do not adress the question of what determines the long-run steady state market equilibrium, we instead focus on the process of how a country's market share responds to those of its major trading partners and adjusts to unexpected disturbances. In the second section of this paper we

* We thank Michael Karge, Talat Mahmood and Wim Dehandschutter for their computational assistance, and Andre Sapir, Denis de Crombrugghe and Dalia Marin for their comments. Any errors and omissions are the authors responsibility.

examine the evolution in export shares over time. Rank-correlation tests are applied in the third section to identify patterns of adjustment in export share between the EC, Japan, and the U.S. In the fourth section a decomposition of variance for Japanese and U.S. export shares is calculated from a vector autoregressive system and analyzed in medium and high R&D industries. Finally, in the last section a summary and conclusion are presented.

1. EXPORT SHARES IN THE EC, JAPAN AND U.S., 1962-1984

The OECD trade statistics enable analysis of the trend in export shares at a fairly disaggregated level to be carried out.[1] Because we consider export patterns over a relatively long period, 1962-1984, only 165 industries could be included in the data sample. These industries, along with their corresponding SITC classification are listed in Appendix A. Since the focus of this paper is on competition between these three regions in the export market, we are concerned primarily with trends in the export share of each region.[2] To maintain consistency over time, we include only the original six member countries in the region consitituting the EC.[3] The export share (XS^j_{it}) in industry j and period t is defined as the exports (X) of a given region to the other two regions, divided by the total amount of exports from each of the three regions to the remaining two :

$$(1) \qquad XS^j_{it} = X^j_{it} \Big/ \sum_{i=1}^{3} X^j_{it}$$

The advantage of this export share measure is that it reflects the relative competitiveness of each of the three regions vis-a-vis the other two. One important qualification is that this measure does not at all indicate the performance of exports in markets outside these three areas. For certain products export competition in third-party markets may be, in fact, more significant than in the markets of these major trading partners. An additional qualification is that the extent of foreign direct investment is not incorporated in the export measure. Because foreign direct investment can be a substitute for exporting, this omission is likely to distort, at least somewhat, inferences regarding industries such as transportation equipment and chemicals.

A comparison of the shift in mean export shares between the EC, Japan and the U.S. over the period 1962-1984 for 22 aggregated industrial sectors is shown in Table 1. The mean export shares in the industries within each sector are compared between the three regions and between the subperiods 1962-1974 and 1975-1984. For example, the mean export share of the EC in the 30 industries comprising the food sector was 0.3476 in the early period and 0.3513 in the recent period. Because the means are unweighted, the averages for each region within a given time period do not necessarily sum to one. As the numbers listed in the parentheses indicate, the EC had the highest mean export share of the three regions in 11 of the food industries during the early period and in 9 industries in the more recent period. The number of industries included within any given sector is determined simply by summing across regions within a given time period.

Perhaps the most striking observation from Table 1 is the absence of any singular predominant pattern of the export shares between the two periods to emerge. Rather, almost every conceivable pattern in the change in export shares between the three regions can be found. While certain sectors such as food, beverages & tobacco, chemicals, paper, and instruments exhibited remarkable stability between the periods, other sectors such as photographic equipment, footwear, office machines, and non-electrical machinery experienced drastic changes in export shares.

The EC exhibited the strongest export performance in industries comprising the leather, petroleum, textiles, apparel, and footwear sectors. These sectors rank among the lowest in terms of R&D intensity. The OECD determined that the textiles, footwear, and leather industries had the smallest R&D-sales ratios (weighted by the eleven main OECD countries) in manufacturing, averaging just 0.2 percent in 1980.

Further, the EC experienced a considerable decrease in export share between the two periods in medicinals & pharmaceuticals, metal products, office machines & computers, transportation

TABLE 1 : Comparison of Mean Export Shares Between the EC, Japan, and the U.S. for 1962-1974 and 1975-1984 (number of industries with highest export share listed in parentheses)(a)

Sector	EC		Japan		U.S.	
	1962-74	1975-84	1962-74	1975-84	1962-74	1975-84
Food, beverages & tobacco	0.3476 (11)	0.3513 (9)	0.0989 (3)	0.0689 (1)	0.5335 (16)	0.6161 (20)
Crude materials	0.3942 (3)	0.3639 (1)	0.2213 (1)	0.1801 (2)	0.7689 (3)	0.4560 (4)
Petroleum products	0.3922 (0)	0.5231 (1)	0.0250 (0)	0.0158 (0)	0.5828 (1)	0.4611 (0)
Animal & vegetable oil	0.2243 (0)	0.1600 (0)	0.0861 (0)	0.0963 (0)	0.6806 (4)	0.7436 (4)
Chemicals	0.4405 (7)	0.4140 (8)	0.1516 (1)	0.1408 (0)	0.5287 (15)	0.4807 (15)
Medicinals & pharma-ceuticals	0.3913 (0)	0.2612 (0)	0.0780 (0)	0.0915 (0)	0.5287 (1)	0.6473 (1)
Leather	0.4610 (1)	0.4809 (2)	0.2277 (1)	0.1466 (0)	0.3113 (1)	0.3726 (1)
Rubber	0.5433 (2)	0.4712 (2)	0.1953 (0)	0.3517 (0)	0.2614 (0)	0.1771 (0)
Cork & wood	0.3273 (1)	0.4101 (1)	0.4012 (1)	0.1913 (0)	0.2716 (0)	0.3987 (1)
Paper	0.1517 (0)	0.2100 (0)	0.2030 (0)	0.1887 (0)	0.6453 (2)	0.6014 (2)
Textiles	0.4202 (3)	0.4472 (2)	0.4053 (3)	0.2899 (2)	0.1745 (0)	0.2070 (2)
Stone, clay & pottery	0.4827 (3)	0.5403 (2)	0.7471 (0)	0.2623 (4)	0.1437 (1)	0.1475 (0)
Iron & steel	0.4479 (4)	0.4257 (3)	0.3751 (4)	0.5025 (6)	0.1770 (1)	0.0711 (0)
Metal products	0.3610 (2)	0.2598 (0)	0.4023 (3)	0.5162 (5)	0.2367 (1)	0.2241 (1)
Non-electrical machinery	0.3318 (4)	0.3588 (5)	0.0955 (0)	0.4850 (4)	0.5782 (14)	0.3993 (9)
Electrical machinery	0.1372 (2)	0.1366 (0)	0.3826 (5)	0.6065 (9)	0.2302 (6)	0.3002 (4)

TABLE 1 (cont.) : Comparison of Mean Export Shares Between the EC, Japan, and the U.S. for 1962-1974 and 1975-1984 (number of industries with highest export share listed in parentheses)(a)

Sector	EC		Japan		U.S.	
	1962-74	1975-84	1962-74	1975-84	1962-74	1975-84
Office machines & computers	0.2267 (0)	0.1355 (0)	0.1002 (0)	0.3810 (1)	0.6733 (3)	0.4984 (2)
Trans-portation equipment	0.4414 (3)	0.2848 (3)	0.2713 (3)	0.5375 (5)	0.2873 (3)	0.2812 (1)
Apparel	0.4156 (3)	0.5273 (6)	0.4595 (4)	0.2244 (0)	0.1249 (0)	0.2983 (1)
Footwear	0.6837 (1)	0.9278 (1)	0.3110 (0)	0.0348 (0)	0.0053 (0)	0.0374 (0)
Instruments	0.3312 (1)	0.2685 (0)	0.3059 (1)	0.3790 (2)	0.3629 (2)	0.3528 (2)
Photograph equipment	0.3757 (2)	0.1945 (0)	0.2998 (1)	0.5058 (3)	0.3245 (2)	0.2998 (2)

(a) Means are unweighted averages and therefore do not always sum to one.

equipment, and photographic equipment. While medicinals & pharmaceuticals had the fourth highest weighted-mean R&D-sales ratio of 8.7 percent in 1980, office machines & computers had an R & D intensity of 17.5 percent. By contrast, the export share of the EC increased between the two periods in petroleum products, cork & wood, apparel, and footwear. All of these industries are classified by the OECD as being low in R&D intensity, with R&D-sales ratios of less than 0.6 percent. Thus, there has been a marked tendency for the EC to increase its export share in relatively low R&D-intensive industries.

Japan has had a small share of the exports throughout the entire period in industries in the food, beverages & tobacco, petroleum products, chemicals, animal & vegetable oils, and medicinals & pharmaceuticals sectors. By contrast, Japan's mean export share has been persistently high in the electrical machinery, metal products, and iron & steel sectors. Between the two periods, Japan has experienced a decrease in mean export share only in low R&D industries such as leather, cork & wood, textiles, stone, clay & pottery, apparel, and footwear. Some of the sectors in which Japan gained export share, such as electrical machinery, office machines & computers, and photographic equipment are among the highest in R&D intensity. The rest, including rubber, iron & steel, non-electrical machinery, and transportation equipment are classified by the OECD as having a medium R&D intensity. Thus, Japan, in contrast to the EC, has tended to gain export share in high R&D-intensive industries and lose export share in low R&D-intensive industries.

The U.S. has exhibited a persistently high mean export share throughout the time period in industries comprising the food, beverage & tobacco, crude materials, animal & vegetable oils, chemicals, medicinals & pharmaceuticals, paper, and office machines & computer sectors. In the footwear sector, however, the mean U.S. export share was less than 4 percent in both the early and recent periods. Of the two sectors in which the export share of the U.S. significantly increased, food, beverages & tobacco is among the lowest in R&D intensity, while medicinal & pharmaceuticals is among the most R&D-intensive. There was a substantial decrease in the mean export share in the iron & steel and non-electrical machinery sectors, both of which are classified as having a medium R&D intensity, and in the office machines & computer industry, which is the second greatest R&D-intensive industry. Thus, the trends in export share and R&D intensity are apparently more ambiguous for the U.S. than for either the EC or Japan.

The 20 industries with the greatest export share in the EC, Japan, and U.S. are shown in Table 2 for both the 1962-1974 and the 1975-1984 periods. There are three important observations regarding the leading export share industries. First, while there has been remarkable stability among the high export shares in both periods for the EC, the same was true for 11 industries for Japan and 12 for the U.S. However, this stability did not prevent "cross-overs" of an industry from one region in the early period to a different region in the more recent period. For example, the mean export share of the EC for passenger automobiles was 75.20 percent in the earlier period. In the more recent period, its mean export share fell to 29.05 percent, but that of Japan rose to 66.66 percent from 19.95 percent in the earlier period.

The general stability of the leading export share industries over time may reflect differences in factor endowments. Most of the leading export share industries for the U.S. were in the food, beverages & tobacco sector, where the U.S. clearly has a relative abundance of land and Japan an obvious scarcity. By contrast, a number of the leading export share industries for Japan were in either the transportation equipment sector or else the electrical machinery sector, where natural resources play only a minimal role.

Although not listed in Table 2, there is a tendency for the variance in a regions's export share over time for any given industry to be relatively low when the export share is also relatively small. For example, in the industries which are relatively high in natural resources, such as food, beverages & tobacco, petroleum products, and vegetable oils, not only do the EC and U.S. tend to dominate the export market, but the variance in export share over time is relatively high in these two areas, while it is considerably less in Japan. Similarly, Japan accounts for a small share of the exports in industries in the chemicals sector, and the variance of the Japanese export share over time is relatively low in the inorganic chemicals, dyeing, tanning & coloring, drugs, and fertilizer industries, while the relatively high variance in these industries for the EC and U.S. corresponds to their dominance in the export market. This same pattern emerges in the aircraft industry, where the Japanese firms play only a minor role in exports.

Industries in which a relatively high variance in exports share over time is observed for the EC and Japan but not for the U.S. tend to be markets where the U.S. has a small export share compared to that of the EC and Japan. This pattern is observed in the rubber products, ships, apparel, footware, iron & steel, metal products, and precision instrument industries. Finally, a high variance in the export share over time is observed for the U.S. and Japan and a low variance for the EC in the fish, animal oils,

TABLE 2 : The Industries with the Greatest Export Share in the EC, Japan and U.S. for 1962-1974 and for 1975-1984 (industry SITC classification in parentheses)

EC 1962 - 1974		EC 1975 - 1984	
Cheese	(024)	Cheese	(024)
Road motor vehicles	(783)	Prepared or preserved meat	(014)
Vegetable textile fibers	(265)	Alcoholic beverages	(112)
Prepared or preserved meat	(014)	Vegetable textile fibers	(265)
Alcoholic beverages	(112)	Footwear	(851)
Dyeing & tanning extracts	(532)	Dyeing & tanning extracts	(532)
Lime & cement	(661)	Non-alcoholic beverage	(111)
Railway construction materials	(676)	Flour, starch & cereal preps.	(048)
Confectionary	(062)	Lime & cement	(661)
Non-alcoholic beverages	(111)	Woven textile fabrics	(654)
Automobiles	(781)	Travel goods & handbags	(831)
Flour, starch & cereal preps.	(048)	Glassware	(665)
Art & antiques	(896)	Jewelry	(897)
Starches & glues	(592)	Furniture & parts	(821)
Organo-inorganic compounds	(515)	Milk & cream	(22)
Perfumes, cosmetics & toiletries	(553)	Cork products	(633)
Sugar & honey	(061)	Butter	(23)
Dyestuffs	(531)	Perfumes, cosmetics & toiletries	(553)
Footwear	(851)	Road motor vehicles	(783)
Glassware	(665)	Sugar & honey	(61)

TABLE 2 (cont.) : The Industries with the Greatest Export Share in the EC, Japan and U.S. for 1962-1974 and for 1975-1984 (industry SITC classification in parentheses)

Japan 1962 - 1974		Japan 1975 - 1984	
TV receivers	(761)	Radio receivers	(762)
Radio receivers	(762)	TV receivers	(761)
Gramophones & recording machines	(763)	Gramophones & recording machines	(763)
Preserved or prepared fish	(037)	Motorcycles & bicycles	(785)
Motorcycles & bicycles	(785)	Transportation motor vehicles	(782)
Pottery	(666)	Nails, screws, nuts & bolts	(694)
Fresh or frozen fish	(034)	Preserved or prepared fish	(037)
Optical instruments	(871)	Trailers & transport containers	(786)
Clay construction materials	(662)	Watches & clocks	(885)
Nails, screws, nuts & bolts	(694)	Photographic equipment	(881)
Textile clothing accessories	(847)	Office machines	(751)
Medical & radiological equipment	(674)	Pottery	(666)
Tubes, pipes & fittings	(678)	Ships & boots	(793)
Veneers & plywood	(634)	Telecommunications equipment	(764)
Cutlery	(696)	Tubes, pipes & fittings	(678)
Sporting goods, toys & games	(894)	Cutlery	(696)
Man-made woven fabrics	(653)	Optical instruments	(871)
Explosives	(572)	Automobiles	(781)
Textile outergarments - females	(843)	Optical goods	(884)
Photographic equipment	(881)	Household equipment	(775)

TABLE 2 (cont.) : The Industries with the Greatest Export Share in the EC, Japan and U.S. for 1962-1974 and for 1975-1984 (industry SITC classification in parentheses)

U.S. 1962 - 1974		U.S. 1975 - 1984	
Corn	(044)	Cereals	(045)
Cereals	(045)	Corn	(044)
Wheat	(041)	Wheat	(041)
Cotton	(263)	Rice	(042)
Rice	(042)	Barley	(043)
Wheat, flour & meal	(046)	Cotton	(263)
Animal feed	(081)	Animal feed	(081)
Fruits & nuts	(057)	Fruits & nuts	(057)
Office machines	(759)	Dried or smoked fish	(035)
Alcohols & phenols	(512)	Tobacco	(122)
Paper & paperboard	(641)	Cereals meals & flours	(047)
Tobacco	(122)	Eggs	(025)
Organic chemicals	(516)	Margerine & shortening	(091)
Aircraft equipment	(792)	Preserved meat	(012)
Boilers	(711)	Processed oils, fats & waxes	(431)
Animal oils & fats	(411)	Aircraft equipment	(792)
Processed oils, fats & waxes	(431)	Man-made fibers	(267)
Barley	(043)	Fresh or frozen meat	(011)
Margerine & shortening	(091)	Fixed vegetable oils	(424)
Cellulose	(584)	Disinfectants, insecticides & poisons	(591)

explosives, cork & wood products, non-electrical machinery (including metalworking machinery and general industrial machinery), television, radio & telephone equipment, and electrical machinery industries. While the EC tends to have a relatively low export share in these markets, that of the U.S. and Japan tends to be high. Thus, there is a pronounced pattern of a low variance in the export share over time to be observed in markets for which a region claims only small share of exports.[4]

2. THE TIME SERIES PATTERN OF EXPORT SHARES IN THE EC, JAPAN AND THE U.S.

In the previous section, we identified some striking patterns of export shares over time for the EC, Japan, and the U.S., which vary across industries and suggest an underlying dynamic behavior of export shares. In this section, we further examine the time-series movement of export share and ask the following two questions :

(1) Do the export shares for the EC, Japan, and the U.S. in a given industry move systematically over time ?
(2) If that is the case, how does the adjustment process of export shares over time among the three regions take place ?

In order to analyze systematic trend behaviour in export market share dynamics without imposing too much structure, we performed a (non-parametric) rank-correlation test. The rank correlations between market shares and time trend were computed for the pre-oil crisis period (1963-1974) and the post-oil crisis period (1975-1985). Each sector was classified as systematically gaining, losing, or showing no trend in its share of exports accounted for by all three regions based on the rank correlation coefficient between the export market share and the time trend. A 10 percent significance level was used to classify each industry. The first bar in Figure 1 depicts the percentage of EC trade experiencing systematic market share gains for six major sectors. The second bar shows the percentage of EC trade experiencing systematic market share losses for these sectors. The export market systematic gains or losses for the disaggregated industries are listed in Appendix B.

FIGURE 1 : Export market share gain/loss for EC, U.S. and Japan, 1963-74

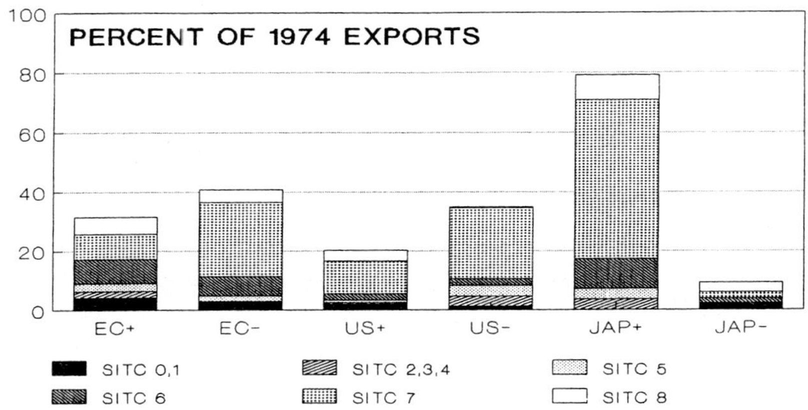

Not surprisingly, almost eighty percent of Japanese trade in this period was characterized by a trend in gaining market share. The U.S. and the EC, especially, had been systematically losing market share in many trade sectors, so that in 1974 trade in export-share losing sectors outweighed trade in export-share gaining sectors. This is not different for the period 1975-85 (see figure 2). Most of these trends occured in sectors 7 and 8 which mainly comprise the machinery, electric apparatus and transportation equipment industries (see appendix A).

As to the question of who loses at whose expense, figure 3 and 4 show the importance of exports from the gainers point of view. Hence, the first two bars in figure 3 show the 1974 percentage of trade accounted for by sectors for which both the EC had been gaining export share and either the US (first bar) or Japan (second bar) had been systematically losing export share over the period 1963-74. The next two bars apply to the US, while Japan's position is represented by the last two bars. Figure 4 repeats this for the period 1975-85. As can be seen in figures 3 and 4 trade sectors where both the US and the EC had been systematically losing, while Japan had been gaining export share accounted for over 50 percent of Japan's total trade in 1974 and over 60 per cent in 1985. The EC had been systematically losing market share

FIGURE 2 : Export market share gain/loss, for EC, U.S., and Japan 1975-85

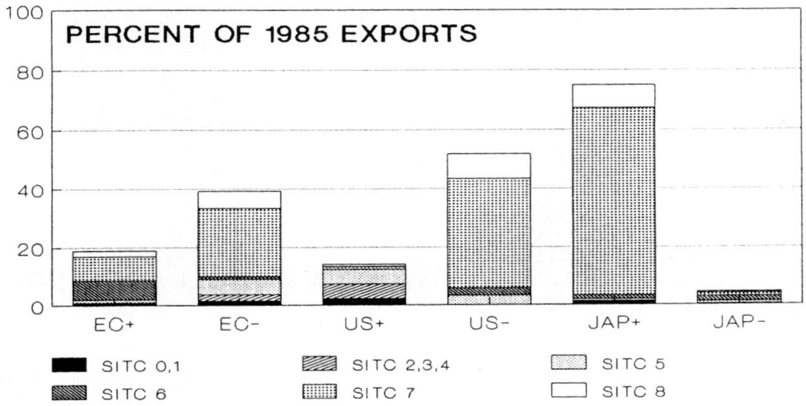

FIGURE 3 : Sources of gain in exports for EC, U.S. and Japan, 1963-74

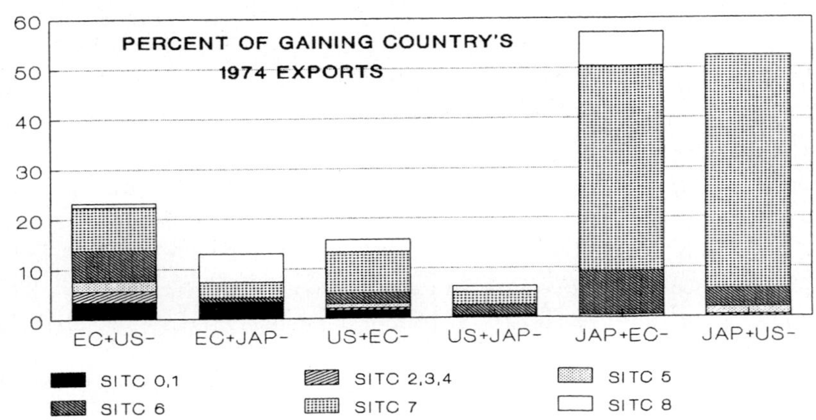

FIGURE 4 : Sources of gain in exports for EC, U.S. and Japan, 1975-85

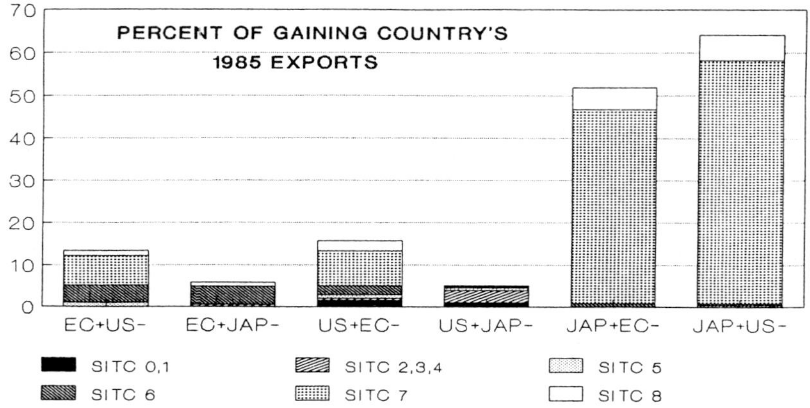

while Japan had been gaining market share for about 58 per cent of Japan's trade in 1974. In 1985 this percentage was reduced to 52 per cent. The EC trade for which the EC systematically gained export share in world markets while the US lost export market share decreased by about 10 percent in importance in 1985 compared to 1974.

The sources of gain in exports for the disaggregated industries within the machinery, electrical equipment, and transportation equipment sectors are identified for the 1963-1974 period in Table 3-A and for the 1975-1985 period in Table 3-B. Most striking is that the gains in American and European export shares were at the expense of Japan in only two industries in the first period and three industries in the second period. By contrast, U.S. firms were apparently significantly displaced in most of the markets in which European firms systematically gained market share, and in over half of the markets in which Japanese firms systematically gained market share.

The most significant finding in this section is that Japan has been gaining market shares in many industries in the machinery, electrical machinery, and transportation equipment sectors. Because of the importance of these sectors in trade among these regions 80 percent of the total Japanese exports showed systematic positive trends over the observation period. In the most recent period the gain in market shares by Japanese firms was achieved particularly at the expense of market shares of their U.S. firms.

TABLE 3-A : Sources of gain in exports for EC, U.S. and Japan for the machinery, electrical equipment and transportation equipment sectors, 1963-1974.

EC+ US-	EC+ JPN-
Vapour power units	Textile and leather machinery
Rotating electric plant	
Agricultural machinery	
Tractors	
Civil engineering plant	
Textile and leather machinery	
Paper manufacturing machinery	
Machine-tools for working metal	
Pumps for liquids	
Air pumps, compressors	
EDP-office machines	
Electrical switches, relays etc.	
Trailers	
US+ EC-	**US+ JPN-**
Aircraft	El.tubes, semiconductors
JPN+ US-	**JPN+ EC-**
Vapour power engines	Non EDP-office machines
Combustion engines	Off.mach.: parts & access.
Rotating electric plant	Radio receivers
Agricultural machinery	Telecommunications equipment
Tractors	Passenger motor cars
Civil engineering plant	Transport. motor vehicles
Paper manufacturing machinery	Motorcycles
Printing machinery	
Machine-tools for working metal	
Metal working machinery	
Heating & cooling equipment	
Pumps for liquids	
Non EDP-office machines	
Off.mach.: parts & access.	
Radio receivers	
Gramophones, sound recorders, etc.	
Telecommunications equipment	
Electrical switches, relays etc.	
Electrical household equipment	
Passenger motor cars	
Trailers	
Parts & access. of motor vehicles	

TABLE 3-B : Sources of gain in exports for EC, U.S. and Japan for the machinery, electrical equipment and transportation equipment sectors, 1975-1985.

EC+ US-	EC+ JPN-
Reaction engines	TV-receivers
Metal working machinery	
Mechanical handling equipment	
Off.mach.:parts & access.	
Electrical switches, relays etc.	
Aircraft	
US+ EC-	**US+ JPN-**
Boilers	Boilers
Vapour power units	TV-receivers
Motorcycles	
JPN+ US-	**JPN+ EC-**
Combustion engines	Agricultural machinery
Rotating electric plant	Machine-tools for working metal
Tractors	Non EDP-off.machines
Printing machinery	EDP-office machines
Machine-tools for working metal	Gramophones, sound rec., etc.
Metal working machinery	Passenger motor cars
Heating & cooling equipment	Parts & access. of motor vehicles
Pumps for liquids	Motorcycles
Air pumps, compressors	
Mechanical handling equipment	
EDP-office machines	
Off.mach.: parts & access.	
Gramophones, sound rec., etc.	
Electric power machinery	
Electical switches, relays etc.	
Electrical household equipment	
El.tubes, semiconductors	
Passenger motor cars	
Trailers	
Parts & access. of motor vehicles	
Aircraft	

3. VECTOR AUTOREGRESSIVE MODELS

The analysis of this section considers possible interrelations with the policy variables and asks whether unanticipated policy disturbances affect the behavior of other variables. We are particularly interested in examining the effects of R&D intensity and exchange rates on export shares. Since we do not have an explicit model based on a priori theory, it is convenient to use a vector autoregessive system (VAR) which summarizes the empirical regularities without imposing restrictions on the interrelations among the variables. In the vector autoregressive system, each variable is regressed both on lagged values of itself and the other variables, and the variables are treated as potentially endogenous.[5]

Using the Japanese and U.S. data, we estimated the vector autoregressive systems for 10 3-digit SITC industries where R&D activity is important to moderately important. Out of the 10 industries the 6 highly R&D-intensive are industrial organic chemicals, telecommunication equipment, electrical circuits, semiconductors & transistors, optical instruments, and medical instruments. The remaining moderately R&D-intensive industries are machine tools, metalworking machinery, passenger motor cars, and measuring & controlling instruments.

There are two systems. The first is a system that examines the Japanese export share to the U.S. market (XSJAUS), and the U.S. export share to the Japanese market (XSUSJA). The second is a system that examines the Japanese export share to the EC market (XSJAEC), and the U.S. export share to the EC market (XSUSEC). The R&D variables used in the two systems are identical and defined for Japan and the U.S. The variable definitions are as follows :

XSJAUS : Japanese exports to the U.S. divided by total exports in the EC, Japan, and the U.S.

XSUSJA : U.S. exports to Japan divided by total exports in the EC, Japan, and the U.S.

XSJAEC : Japanese exports to the EC divided by total exports in the EC, Japan, and the U.S.

XSUSEC : U.S. exports to the EC divided by total exports in the EC, Japan, and the U.S.

RDJA : R&D expenditures divided by total sales in Japan

RDUS : R&D expenditures divided by total sales in the U.S.

EXC : Average U.S.-dollar price of Japanese yen

Thus, each system consists of 5 variables and therefore 5 equations. The variables on the right-hand side of each equation are the same for each system, and the length of lags is set at two years to conserve degrees of freedom. The systems are estimated for the 1967-82 period.

3.1. Variance Decompositions

Since our primary concern here is to define what proportion of the variance in each of the variables in the vector autoregressive system is accounted for by itself and other variables, we calculated variance decompositions for each variable in the sytem. Table 4 shows variance decompositions which were calculated from the equations estimated for the 1967-82 period. The table presents variance decompositions for one and two years ahead which are expressed as the percentage of variance of the dependent variable explained by what has been termed as innovations of itself and the explanatory variables.[6] For a given variable, the variance is measured from the level towards which it would otherwise tend to move. In other words, the variance decompositions show the percentage of forecast error variance that is accounted for by unexpected disturbances in the variables in the system. Thus, a variable that is optimally forecast from its own lagged values will have all its forecast error variance accounted for by its own disturbances.[7] Otherwise, the variable's forecast error variance will be explained by unexpected disturbances in the other variables.

Since we are interested in whether there are unexpected disturbances or changes in R&D activities in Japan and the U.S., and in the exchange rate which move the export shares away from their expected levels, we present in Table 4 only the variance decompositions for the 4 dependent variables, namely XSJAUS, XSUSJA, XSJAEC, and XSUSEC. Table 4-A shows the variance decompositions for XSJAUS and XSUSJA for each of the 10 industries. The first 6 industries are more R&D-intensive than the last 4 industries. The typical pattern on XSJAUS that emerges from Table 4-A is that the one-year-ahead forecast error is the result mainly of its own innovations except for medical instruments and machine tools. However, innovations in other variables tend to play a larger role by period 2 in explaining the movement of XSJAUS away from the level to which it would otherwise tend to move. In fact, the role of innovations in RDJA increases significantly by period 2 in all the R&D-intensive industries except for medical instruments where the role of the R&D innovations remains high over the two periods. The percentage of variance of XSJAUS explained by the RDJA innovations in two year ahead is 27 percent for inorganic chemicals, 41 percent for telecommunications equipment, 19 percent for electrical circuits, 16 percent for semiconductors, 21 percent for optical instruments, and 19 percent for medical instruments. On the other hand, the role of innovations in RDJA in the less R&D-intensive industries remains smaller even by period 2, thus accounting for 10 percent of the variation for measuring & controlling instruments, 4 percent for machine tools, 2 percent for metalworking machinery, and 0.3 percent for passenger cars. This result implies that in the high R&D-intensive industries the variation of the Japanese export share in the U.S. market is more significantly accounted for by its own R&D activity than in the less R&D-intensive industries.[8] For the less R&D-intensive industries, the roles of own innovations and the exchange rate innovations instead tend to be important in explaining the forecast error variance of XSJAUS.

By contrast, the forecast error variance for XSUSJA does not show any clear pattern comparable to the one observed for XSJAUS. The role of the RDUS innovations is important in explaining the deviation of XSUSJA from the trend level for inorganic chemicals, semiconductors, and machine tools.

Table 4-B shows the variance decompositions for XSJAEC and XSUSEC for the 10 industries. Scanning the percentages of variance in XSJAEC explained by innovations in RDJA and EXC in Table 4-B, a pattern emerges which is different form the one for XSJAUS in Table 4-A. The role of the exchange rate in explaining

TABLE 4-A : Variance Decompositions, Vector Autoregressive Systems, 1967-1982

Dependent Variable		Innovation Variables XSJAUS	XSUSJA	RDUS	RDJA	EXC
Inorganic Chemical Elements (522)						
XSJAUS	1	60.8	6.2	4.0	10.2	18.8
	2	42.0	8.1	10.4	27.0	12.5
XSUSJA	1	10.1	78.1	0.0	0.1	11.7
	2	12.6	58.6	15.5	5.6	7.7
Telecommunications Equipment (764)						
XSJAUS	1	67.8	7.0	2.5	12.4	10.2
	2	45.0	5.3	2.9	40.5	6.3
XSUSJA	1	15.3	57.8	5.1	12.6	9.3
	2	42.7	33.0	6.9	7.2	10.2
Electrical Circuits (772)						
XSJAUS	1	81.9	0.0	12.8	3.0	2.3
	2	47.7	1.3	29.7	18.8	2.5
XSUSJA	1	12.5	64.2	0.0	18.8	4.4
	2	10.1	47.4	2.8	36.4	3.2
Semiconductors, transistors (776)						
XSJAUS	1	93.0	1.2	0.1	4.8	1.0
	2	78.8	2.3	0.7	16.4	1.8
XSUSJA	1	41.1	28.9	0.3	5.4	24.3
	2	28.3	13.2	32.7	3.3	22.5
Optical Instruments (871)						
XSJAUS	1	56.8	27.8	6.0	10.4	0.0
	2	52.2	21.0	5.7	21.4	0.1
XSUSJA	1	1.0	89.0	4.8	2.0	3.2
	2	1.5	67.9	5.2	18.4	6.9
Medical Instruments (872)						
XSJAUS	1	17.0	32.9	7.6	19.9	22.6
	2	20.7	31.1	7.9	19.1	21.3
XSUSJA	1	2.3	30.2	10.0	0.4	57.0
	2	14.8	13.4	9.1	8.2	54.4

TABLE 4-A (cont.): Variance Decompositions, Vector Autoregressive Systems, 1967-1982

Dependent Variable		Innovation Variables: XSJAUS	XSUSJA	RDUS	RDJA	EXC
Measuring and controlling Instruments (874)						
XSJAUS	1	84.4	1.5	3.5	5.1	5.6
	2	75.2	3.1	5.1	10.4	6.3
XSUSJA	1	6.4	41.0	4.7	7.5	40.3
	2	33.9	28.1	4.7	6.4	26.9
Machine Tools (736)						
XSJAUS	1	52.5	16.3	0.8	0.8	29.5
	2	65.0	9.9	3.9	4.4	16.8
XSUSJA	1	31.2	53.8	0.3	0.1	14.6
	2	25.6	37.2	14.7	6.9	15.6
Metalworking Machinery (737)						
XSJAUS	1	71.2	0.3	13.7	0.3	14.6
	2	55.9	0.5	4.6	1.6	37.4
XSUSJA	1	30.9	60.4	3.3	4.3	1.1
	2	36.9	41.2	2.9	8.2	10.7
Passenger Motor Cars (781)						
XSJAUS	1	78.5	13.1	8.3	0.2	0.0
	2	74.0	18.0	7.6	0.3	0.2
XSUSJA	1	21.9	70.1	0.0	5.5	2.5
	2	38.4	48.3	1.3	5.5	6.5

Note : Entries show the percentage of variance of the dependent variable, one and two years ahead, that is account for by innovations in the explanatory variables.

the variation of export share tends to be more important for XSJAEC than for XSJAUS, particularly in organic chemicals, electrical circuits, semiconductors, optical instruments, medical instruments, and passenger motor cars. Furthermore, the role of the RDJA innovations becomes much stronger for XSJAEC in machine tools, metalworking machinery, and passenger cars where the RDJA innovations do not have major roles in explaining the forecast error for XSJAUS.

TABLE 4-B : Variance Decompositions, Vector Autoregressive Systems, 1967-1982

Dependent Variable		Innovation Variables				
		XSJAEC	XSUSEC	RDUS	RDJA	EXC
Inorganic Chemical Elements (522)						
XSJAEC	1	42.1	13.7	7.3	0.1	36.7
	2	38.6	19.1	6.6	1.8	33.9
XSUSEC	1	15.4	62.6	19.4	0.2	2.5
	2	25.0	35.4	11.8	22.9	4.9
Telecommunications Equipment (764)						
XSJAEC	1	84.1	1.3	2.5	10.9	1.1
	2	47.0	1.2	2.8	48.2	0.9
XSUSEC	1	17.1	23.9	0.6	53.0	5.5
	2	33.1	11.8	18.4	26.5	10.3
Electrical Circuits (772)						
XSJAEC	1	60.7	0.6	15.5	6.6	16.6
	2	44.2	1.3	9.3	31.4	14.0
XSUSEC	1	45.1	14.0	6.4	27.7	6.9
	2	19.7	6.7	12.0	53.7	8.5
Semiconductors, transistors (776)						
XSJAEC	1	57.7	8.6	2.9	21.4	9.3
	2	54.0	7.5	3.3	25.8	9.4
XSUSEC	1	3.2	74.4	1.2	6.6	14.6
	2	14.2	75.5	3.4	7.8	9.2
Optical Instruments (871)						
XSJAEC	1	74.9	1.8	23.1	0.0	0.1
	2	40.1	16.8	10.8	7.3	25.1
XSUSEC	1	11.3	80.0	6.0	0.8	1.9
	2	8.9	57.3	10.6	7.8	15.3
Medical Instruments (872)						
XSJAEC	1	12.6	12.3	5.9	0.0	69.3
	2	25.2	45.2	3.4	1.4	24.8
XSUSEC	1	0.3	25.4	14.1	17.3	42.9
	2	11.0	51.4	10.7	8.4	18.5

TABLE 4-B (cont.) : Variance Decompositions, Vector Autoregressive Systems, 1967-1982

Dependent Variable		Innovation Variables				
		XSJAEC	XSUSEC	RDUS	RDJA	EXC
Measuring and Controlling Instruments (874)						
XSJAEC	1	91.5	2.1	0.1	4.2	2.1
	2	81.6	3.3	3.1	4.8	7.1
XSUSEC	1	44.6	41.2	2.3	10.4	1.6
	2	19.9	18.7	6.7	44.4	10.4
Machine Tools (736)						
XSJAEC	1	87.9	0.5	1.7	0.3	9.6
	2	47.0	6.2	1.9	31.7	13.1
XSUSEC	1	10.9	70.6	5.1	12.1	1.3
	2	12.1	50.0	7.9	27.5	2.7
Metalworking Machinery (737)						
XSJAEC	1	38.8	0.1	9.8	45.0	6.3
	2	27.9	0.1	10.2	54.3	7.4
XSUSEC	1	7.1	20.2	32.4	35.7	4.6
	2	18.3	12.1	7.2	61.4	1.1
Passenger Motor Cars (781)						
XSJAEC	1	68.4	0.9	6.4	0.0	24.4
	2	34.1	0.8	5.2	44.1	15.8
XSUSEC	1	0.8	40.1	2.1	54.0	3.0
	2	1.6	16.1	0.8	59.8	21.6

Note : Entries show the precentage of variance of the dependent variable, one and two years ahead, that is account for by innovations in the explanatory variables.

We do not have any clear explanation for these patterns of the importance of the roles of innovations in RDJA and EXC which vary between XSJAUS and XSJAEC.[9] However, a major point which is made from Tables 4-A and 4-B is that R&D intensity and the exchange rate influences together account for a non-trivial part of the observed variation of the Japanese export shares to the U.S. and EC markets.

One very interesting pattern of the forecast error variance for XSUSEC is that the role of innovations in RDJA is significantly larger than for XSUSJA. Thus, the percentage of variance of XSUSEC in period 2, explained by innovations in RDJA, reaches 60 percent for passenger cars, 54 percent for electrical circuits and metalworking machinery, 44 percent for telecommunications equipment, semi-conductors, and machine tools. This result clearly suggests that the observed variations of the U.S. market shares in the EC market are accounted for by the variability of R&D activity in Japan. This further implies that the U.S. market shares in the EC in these industries are highly dependent on its rival's R&D activity.

4. CONCLUSIONS

In this paper we have identified four distinct patterns of the behavior of export shares for the EC, Japan and the U.S.. In particular Japanese export shares were found to move with the trend, showing a systematic gain in market shares in the machinery, electrical machinery and transportation equipment sectors. This has contributed to the positive trend in export shares in over 80 percent of the total Japanese exports. This gain in export share has come predominantly at the expense of both EC and U.S. firms, although during the most recent period U.S. firms have experienced a greater loss in export shares. Based on a vector autoregressive model, there is at least some evidence that R&D intensity may explain some of the variation in export shares. We find that a country's export share is associated not only with its own R&D expenditures but with the R&D expenditures of its trading partners. This suggests that, in fact, competitive interaction in R&D behaviour plays an important role in explaining trade patterns within these three major regions. Thus, an important direction of future research is to consider in more detail the nature of this competitive process in the export market.

APPENDIX A

Industries Included in Sample

SITC No.	Industry Description
011	Meat and edible meat offals, fresh, chilled or frozen
012	Meat and edible meat offals (except poultry liver), salted in brine, dried or smoked
014	Meat and edible meat offals, prepared or preserved, n.e.s.; fish extracts
022	Milk and cream
023	Butter
024	Cheese and curd
025	Eggs, birds', and egg yolks, fresh, dried or otherwise preserve, sweetened or not
034	Fish, fresh (live or dead), chilled or frozen
035	Fish, dried, salted or in brine; smoked fish
036	Crustaceans and molluscs, fresh (live or dead), chilled, frozen, salted, in brine or dried
037	Fish, crustaceans and molluscs, prepared or preserved, n.e.s.
041	Wheat (including spelt) and meslin, unmilled
042	Rice
043	Barley, unmilled
044	Maize (corn), unmilled
045	Cereals, unmilled (other than wheat, rice barley and maize)
046	Meal and flour of wheat and flour of meslin
047	Other cereals meals and flours
048	Cereals preparations and preparations of flour or starch of fruits or vegetables
054	Vegetables, fresh, chilled, frozen or simply preserved; tube and other edible vegetable products
056	Vegetables, roots and tubers, prepared or preserved, n.e.s.
057	Fruits and nuts (not including oil nuts), fresh or dried
058	Fruits, preserved, and fruit preparations
061	Sugar and honey
062	Sugar confectionery (except chocolate confectionery) and other sugar preparations
071	Coffee and coffee substitutes
072	Cocoa
073	Chocolate and other food preparations containing cocoa, n.e.s.
074	Tea and maté
075	Spieces
081	Feeding stuff for animals (not including unmilled cereals)
091	Margarine and shortening
111	Non-alcoholic beverages, n.e.s.
112	Alcoholic beverages
121	Tobacco, unmanufactured; tobacco refuse
122	Tobacco, manufactured
233	Synthetic rubber latex; synthetic rubber and reclaimed rubber; waste and scraps of unhardened rubber
261	Silk
263	Cotton
264	Jute and other textile bast fibres, n.e.s., raw of processed but not spun; tow and waste thereof
265	Vegetable textile fibres (other than cotton and jute), and waste of such fibres
266	Synthetic fibres suitable for spinning

267 Other man-made fibressuitable for spinning, and waste of man-made fibres
334 Petroleum products, refined
411 Animal oils and fats
423 Fixed vegatables oils, "soft", crude, refined or purified
424 Other fixed vegetable oils, fluid or solid, crude, refined or purified
431 Animal and vegetable oils and fats, processed, and waxes of animal or vegetable origin
511 Hydrocarbons, n.e.s., and their halogenated, sulphonated, nitrated or nitrosated derivatives
512 Alcohols, phenols, phenol-alcohols, and their halogenated, sulphonated, nitrated or nitrosated derivatives
513 Carboxylic acids, and their anhydrides, halides, peroxides and peracids, and their halogenated, sulphonated, nitrated or nitrosated derivatives
514 Nitrogen-function compounds
515 Organo-inorganic and hetrocyclic compounds
516 Other organic chemicals
522 Inorganic chemical elements, oxides and halogen salts
523 Other inorganic chemicals; organic and inorganic compounds of precious metals
524 Radio-active and associated materials
531 Synthetic organic dyestuffs, etc., natural indigo and colour lacks
532 Dyeing and tannin extracts, and synthetic tanning materials
533 Pigments, paint, varnishes and related materials
541 Medicinal a pharmaceutical products
551 Essential oils, perfume and flavour materials
553 Perfumery, cosmetics and toilet preparations (excluding soaps)
554 Soap, cleansing and polishing preparations
562 Fertilizers, manufactured
572 Explosives and pyrotechnic products
582 Condensation, polycondensation and polyaddition products, whether modified or not
583 Polymerization and copolymerization products
584 Regenerated cellulose; cellulose nitrate, cellulose acetate and other cellulo esters, cellulose ethers
591 Disinfectants, insecticides, fungicide, weed killers, anti-sprouting products, rat poisons and similar products
592 Starches, inulin and wheat glute; albumioidal substances; glues
611 Leather
612 Manufactures of leather or of composition leather, n.e.s.
613 Furskins, tanned or dressed
621 Materials of rubber (e.g., pastes, plates, sheets, rods, thread, tubes, of rubber
625 Rubber tyres, tyre cases, interchangeable tyre treads, inner tubes and tyre flaps, for wheels of all kinds
633 Cork manufactures
634 Veneers, plywood, "improved" or reconstituted wood, and other wood, worked, n.e.s.
641 Paper and paperboard
642 Paper and paperboard, cut to size or shape and articles of paper or paperboard
651 Textile yarn
652 Cotton fabrics, woven (not including narrow or special fabrics)
653 Fabrics, woven, of man-made fibres (not including narrow or special fabrics)

654	Textile fabrics, woven, other than of cotton or man-made fibres
655	Knitted of crocheted fabrics (including tubular knit fabrics, pile fabrics and open-work fabrics)
656	Tulle, lace, embroidery, ribbons, trimmings and other small wares
661	Lime, cement, and fabricated construction materials (except glass and clay materials)
662	Clay construction materials and refractory construction materials
664	Glass
665	Glassware
666	Pottery
671	Pig iron, spiegeleisen, sponge iron, iron or steel powders and shot, and ferro-alloys
672	Ingots and other primary forms of iron or steel
673	Iron and steel bars, rods, angles, shapes and sections (including sheet piling)
674	Universals, plates and sheets of iron or steel
675	Hoop and strip, of iron or steel, hot-rolled or cold-rolled
676	Rails and railway track construction material, of iron or steel
677	Iron or steel wire (excluding wire rod), whether coated or not
678	Tubes, pipes and fittings, or iron or steel
679	Iron and steel casting, forgings and stampings, in the rough state, n.e.s.
691	Structures and parts of structures, n.e.s., of iron, steel or aluminium
692	Metal containers for storage and transport
693	Wire products (excluding electrical wiring) and fencing grills
694	Nails, screws, nuts, bolts, rivets and the like, or iron, steel or copper
695	Tools for use in the hand or in machines
696	Cutlery
711	Steam and other vapour generating boilers, supper-heated water boilers, and auxiliary plant for use therewith; and parts thereof, n.e.s.
712	Steam and other vapour power units, not incorporating boilers; steam engines (including mobile engines), and parts thereof, n.e.s.
713	Internal combustion piston engines, and parts thereof, n.e.s.
716	Rotating electric plant and parts thereof, n.e.s.
721	Agricultural machinery (excluding tractors) and parts thereof, n.e.s.
722	Tractors, whether or not fitted with power take-offs, winches or pulley
723	Civil engineering and contactors' plant and equipment and parts thereof, n.e.s.
724	Textile and leather machinery, and parts thereof, n.e.s.
725	Paper mill and pulp mill machinery, paper cutting machines and other machinery for the manufacture of paper articles; and parts thereof, n.e.s.
726	Printing and bookbinding machinery, and parts thereof, n.e.s.
727	Food-processing machines (excluding domestic), and parts thereof, n.e.s.
736	Machine-tools for working metal or metal carbides, and parts and accessories thereof, n.e.s.
737	Metalworking machinery (other than machine tools), and parts thereof, n.e.s.

741 Heating and cooling equipment, and parts thereof, n.e.s.
742 Pumps (including motor and turbo pumps) for liquids, whether fitted with measuring devices or not
743 Pumps (other than pumps for liquids) and compressors; fans and blowers; centrifuges
744 Mechanical handling equipment, and parts thereof, n.e.s.
751 Office machines
752 Automatic data processing machines and units thereof; magnetic or optical readers, machines for transcribing data into media in coded form and machines for processing such data, n.e.s.
759 Parts, n.e.s. of an accessories (other than covers, carrying cases and the like) suitable for use solely or principally with machines of a kind falling within heading 751 or 752
761 Television receivers (including receivers incorporating radio-broadcast receivers or sound recorders or reproducers)
763 Gramophones, dictating machines and other sound recorders and reproducers; television image and sound recorders and reproducers, magnetic
764 Telecommunications equipment, n.e.s.; and parts, n.e.s. of and accessories for the apparatus and equipment falling within devision 76
771 Electric power machiners (other than the rotating electric plant of heading 716), and parts thereof, n.e.s.
772 Electrical apparatus for making and breaking electrical circuits, for the protection of electrical circuits, or for making connections to or in electrical circuits; resistors, fixed or variable (including potentiometers); printed circuits; switchboards and control panels, n.e.s.; parts, n.e.s.
773 Equipment for distributing electricity
774 Electric apparatus for medical purposes and radiological apparatus
775 Household type, electrical and non-electrical equipment, n.e.s.
776 Thermionic, cold cathode and photo-cathode valves and tubes (including vapour or gas filled valves and tubes, cathode-ray tubes, television camera tubes and mercury are rectifying valves and tubes); photocells; mounted piezo-electric crystals; diodes, transistors and similar semiconducor devices; electronic microcircuits; and parts thereof, n.e.s.
781 Passenger motor cars (other than public-service-type-vehicles), including vehicles designed for the transport of both passengers and goods
782 Motor vehicles for the transport of goods or materials and special purpose motor vehicles
783 Road motor vehicles, n.e.s.
784 Parts and accessories, n.e.s. of the motor vehicles falling within heading 722, 781, 782 or 783
785 Motorcycles, motor scooters and other cycles, motorized and non-motorized; invalid carriages
786 Trailers and other vehicles, not motorized, n.e.s. and specially designed and equipped transport containers
791 Railway vehicles (including hovertrains) and associated equipment
792 Aircraft and associated equipment, and parts thereof, n.e.s.
793 Ships, boats (including hovercraft) and floating structures
821 Furniture and parts thereof
831 Travel goods, handbags and similar containers
842 Outer garments, men's and boy's, of textile fabrics (other than knitted or crocheted goods)

843	Outer garments, women's, girls' and infants', of textile fabrics (other than knitted or crocheted goods)
844	Under garments, of textile fabrics (other than knitted or crocheted goods)
845	Outer garments and other articles, knitted or crocheted, not elastic nor rubberized
846	Under garments, knitted or crocheted
847	Clothing accessories, of textile fabrics, n.e.s.
848	Articles of apparel and clothing accessories for other than textile fabrics; headgear of all materials
851	Footwear
871	Optical instruments and apparatus
872	Medical instruments and appliances, n.e.s.
873	Meters and counters
874	Measuring, checking, analysing and controlling instruments and apparatus, n.e.s.; parts and accessories, n.e.s. of groups 873 and 874
881	Photographic apparatus and equipment, n.e.s.
882	Photographic and cinematrographic supplies
883	Cinematographic film, exposed and developed, whether or not incorporating sound track or consisting only of sound track, negative or positive
884	Optical goods, n.e.s.
885	Watches and clocks
892	Printed matter
894	Baby carriages, toys, games and sporting goods
895	Office and stationery supplies, n.e.s.
896	Works of art, collectors' pieces and antiques
897	Jewellery or semi-precious materials, n.e.s.
898	Musical instruments and parts and accessories thereof (including phonograph records and the like)

APPENDIX B : Export Market Share Gains (+) and Losses (-) for EC, US and Japan for 1963-1974 (I) and 1975-1985 (II)

Period I 1963-1974 Period II 1975-1985

	EC		US		JPN	
SITC	I	II	I	II	I	II
011					-	-
012	-	-		+	+	
014	+	-	-	+	-	-
022	+		-			+
023	+		-		NA	
024		-		+	+	
025	+		-			-
034	+		+	+	-	-
035	-		+		-	
036						
037	+				-	
041					NA	NA
042					+	-
043					NA	
044					NA	
045						+
046	+		-	-		+
047		-		+	+	
048		+	-		+	
054						+
056			-		+	
057	-		+		+	
058	+	+	-			-
061	+		-		+	
062			-		+	
081	+				-	
091	-	+	+	-		
111					+	+
112	-		+	-	+	
122	+	-	-	+	+	+
233	+	+	-		+	-
261	+				-	
263			-	+	+	-
264	+			-	-	
265	-		+			
266		+				-
267	-	-	+	+		-
334	+	-	-	+		
411		-				
423					+	+
424	-		+	+		-
431		+		-		
511		-		-	+	-
512		-	+		+	-
513		-	+	+	+	-
514	+	-	+		+	-
515	-		-	-	+	
516				-	+	-
522	+		-		+	

Period I 1963-1974 Period II 1975-1985

	EC		US		JPN	
SITC	I	II	I	II	I	II
523	-		+		+	-
524						
531	+		-	-	+	+
532	-			-	+	+
533		+	-	-	+	+
541		-		+		
551		-		+		
553	-				+	+
554	+					+
562	-	-	+	+		
572			+		-	
582	+	+	-	-	+	+
583			-		+	
584	+		-			+
591			-		+	
592	-		+		+	
611	+		-		+	
612		+		+		-
613					-	
621				-		+
625		-	-		+	+
633	-	+		-	+	-
634	-	+	+	-	-	
641				-		
642	-	+			+	
651	+		-			
652	-	+	+	-	-	+
653	+		-	-		
654	+	+	+		-	-
655		-	-		+	
656	-					
661		+	+	-		
662	+	+		-	-	-
664	-		+		+	+
665	+	+		-		
666			+	+		
671	-	+				-
672	+	+				-
673	-				+	
674	+		-			
675	-			-	+	
676				-	+	
677	-				+	
678	-	+	-	-	+	
679	+		-		+	
691		+			+	
692	+		-	-	+	+
693	-				+	
694	-			+	+	
695	-	+	-	-	+	
696	-	-			+	
711		-		+	+	-
712	+	-	-	+	+	

Period I 1963-1974 Period II 1975-1985

	EC		US		JPN	
SITC	I	II	I	II	I	II
713			−	−	+	+
714		+		−	+	
716	+		−	−	+	+
721	+	−	−		+	+
722	+		−	−	+	+
723	+		−		+	
724	+		−		−	
725	+		−		+	+
726			−	−	+	+
727					+	+
736	+	−	−	−	+	+
737		+	−	−	+	+
741			−	−	+	+
742	+		−	−	+	+
743	+		−	−		+
744		+	−	−	+	+
751	−	−	−		+	+
752	+	−	−	−		+
759	−	+	−	−	+	+
761	−	+	−	+	+	−
762	−		−		+	
763		−	−	−	+	+
764	−		−	−	+	
771	NA		NA	−	NA	+
772	+	+	−	−	+	+
773				+	+	
774					+	+
775			−	−	+	+
776			+	−	−	+
781	−	−	−	−	+	+
782	−		−	−	+	+
783				+		
784		−	−	−	+	+
785	−	−		+	+	+
786	+		−		+	
791					+	
792	−	+	+	−		+
793		+				
821			−			−
831		+		−		−
842		+			−	
843	+	−		−	−	+
844	+		+		−	
845			+			−
846	−	−	+		+	
847	+	+	−			−
848	−				+	−
851	+	−		+	−	−
871			+			
872	−			−	+	+
873	−	−		+	+	+
874				−	+	+

Period I 1963-1974 Period II 1975-1985

	EC		US		JPN	
SITC	I	II	I	II	I	II
881	-	+		-	+	
882	-		+	-	+	+
883	+				-	
884	-	-			+	+
885	-	-		-	+	+
892		-		+	+	+
894	+	-	+		-	+
895		-	-	-	+	+
896	-		+			-
897	+		-	-	-	+
898	-	-	+	-	+	+

NOTES

1 The export data are from the annual reports of the Organization for Economic Co-Operation and Development (OECD), Trade by Commodities (Market Summaries) : Exports, Paris.

2 Since the EC constitutes a region and not a country, we adapt the standard of referring to the EC, Japan and U.S. as regions.

3 The original EC countries included are Belgium, France, Germany, Italy, Luxembourg, and the Netherlands.

4 In several industries a high variance in the export share over time emerged for just one of the three regions. For example, in the leather and road vehicle industries there was a high variance only for Japan, while a similar pattern emerged for the EC in industries in the clay, stone & pottery sector. A relatively high variance in the export share over time was observed only for the U.S. in the cereals, synthetic rubber, plastic materials and power generating machinery industries. A similar variance in export shares for all three regions was found only in the textile fibers and textiles industries.

5 Vector autoregressive systems and their rational are discussed in Sims (1980 and 1982). For an application, see Fischer (1981).

6 See Sims (1980) and Fischer (1981). Such innovations may be called shocks or unexpected disturbances.

7 Sims (1982), pp. 131-137.

8 Caves and Porter (1978) found in a different context that product R&D increases the variation of market share and acts as a disturbance.

9 One possible explanation would be that the Japanese R&D-intensive industries regard the U.S. market as the major market and try to maintain their target long-run market shares, while they adjust their market shares in the EC market to adapt to the effect of unexpected short-run disturbances. Yamawaki (1987) shows that Japanese exporters tend to keep their export prices constant by reducing margins over production costs when the Japanese yen appreciates against the U.S.-dollar.

REFERENCES

CAVES, Richard E., and Michael E. PORTER (1978), "Market Structure, Oligopoly, and Stability of Market Shares", Journal of Industrial Economics, vol. 26, pp. 289-308.

DEARDORFF, Alan (1984), "Testing Trade Theories and Predicting Trade Flows", in Jones, R., and P. Kenen (eds.), Handbook of International Economics, Vol. 1, Amsterdam : North-Holland.

FISHER, Stanley (1981), "Relative Shocks, Relative Price Variability, and Inflation", Brookings Papers on Economic Activity, 2, pp. 381-441.

SIMS, Christopher A. (1980), "Macroeconomics and Reality", Econometrica, vol. 48, pp. 1-48.

SIMS, Christopher A. (1982), "Policy Analysis with Econometric Models", Brookings Papers on Economic Activity, A, pp. 107-152.

YAMAWAKI, Hideki (1988), "Export Pricing Behavior and Market Structure", mimeo, International Insitute of Management, Berlin.

YAMAWAKI, Hideki and David B. AUDRETSCH (1988), "Import Share Under International Oligopoly with Differentiated Products ; Japanese Imports in U.S. Manufacturing", Review of Economics and Statistics, vol. 70, november 1988.

IV

INNOVATION AND TRADE

The Convergence of International and Domestic Markets
D.B. Audretsch, L. Sleuwaegen, and H. Yamawaki (Editors)

9. NATIONAL POLICY RESPONSES TO INNOVATIVE MULTINATIONALS : A CLUB THEORETIC APPROACH, WITH AN APPLICATION TO THE PHARMACEUTICAL INDUSTRY *

Patrick J. VAN CAYSEELE
Centrum voor Economische Studiën, Catholic University Leuven, Belgium and M.E.R.I.T., University of Limburg, The Netherlands.

O. INTRODUCTION

Several contributions have been made regarding the optimal use of domestic policies (price controls, export taxes, ...) when a monopolistic export industry operates in a particular country (see Auquier and Caves, 1979). In this paper the use of government policies like price controls (or import taxes or royalty ceilings) are studied from the point of view of an importing country facing a monopolistic exporter.

Of course, also this problem has already been studied. Although an extensive survey of the literature in this area isn't the purpose of this contribution, it is useful to highlight some important developments, if only to contrast these with the approach followed here. This is done in the next section.

Then the discussion is narrowed down to price controls. Host countries often argue that they use these controls to limit their contribution toward overhead R&D-expenditures to a "fair" share.

* I wish to thank R. De Bondt for his suggestions as well as M. Neumann for his constructive remarks. This paper is based on Chapter five of my Ph.D. dissertation: "Regulation and International Innovative Activities in the Pharmaceutical Industry". The financial support by I.C.M. Brussels which allowed me to investigate these problems in the conducive environment of Northwestern University is equally appreciated.

But equally often it is heard that these controls merely serve to free ride on those countries that allow to extract "appropriate" contributions to the R&D-expenditures. Hence it is important to agree what a fair contribution amounts to, and some proposals regarding this issue conclude the second section.

The third section discusses international innovative activities in an European environment before 1992. The analogy between innovative multinationals and clubs providing local public goods is indicated.

The fourth section then shows why the "fair" prices aimed at by price regulators often do not exist, the main point of the present contribution. It is shown how the non-existence of such prices is related to the non-existence of an internal European market. Club theory then is used to explain national policy responses such as price controls (or royalty ceilings) as a form of disloyalty towards the international patent agreements.

In section five a detailed case study of international innovative activity in the pharmaceutical industry is presented. It is shown that the divergent safety regulations characterising the introduction of new drugs do not allow for the fair prices that are aimed at by price regulation and hence a critical analysis of the effectiveness of price regulation in the European Community is given. In a concluding section the general consequences for innovation in the mixed open economy then are discussed, especially in view of the plausible regulatory dynamics of price controls.

1. NATIONAL POLICY RESPONSES TO MULTINATIONALS

There is a large variety in recipient country government policies vis-à-vis multinational enterprises. Price controls, percentage ceilings on royalties paid, taxes, registries, joint venture requirements, exchange rate controls a.s.o., all try to get a hold on the MNE. Especially in respect to the inflow of technology, host countries interfere with the multinational, see Contractor and Sagafi-Nejad, 1981.

The theories explaining government behaviour regarding multinational enterprises are less abundant (the discussion presented here draws upon the excellent survey in Caves, 1982). In view of the widespread use of these policies by both developed and less developed countries, it is remarkable that only a few explanations for these government policies have been offered.

The traditional approach to explain government policy is that of welfare economics. Government then tries to maximise "social welfare". This approach is discussed further below, in the perspective of price controls. Alternative explanations for government interventions vis-à-vis multinationals have relied more on positive theory. Elected government seeking to remain in office can redistribute income from non-voters (the MNE's) to voters (e.g. the consumers of the MNE's products) by imposing low prices. Of course, several constraints such as the threat to cut back on activities by the MNE, may keep host governments from going too far in this respect.

The "sovereignity-at-bay" school has regarded the latter constraints as a sufficient reason on their own to explain detailed policy action toward multinationals. If multinationals are in a better position to evade the policies implemented by a government, the greater mismatch between goals and outcomes that will result in the presence of MNE's is likely to invite more detailed government interference.

The present contribution is in the same spirit : the market allocation achieved by the multinational regarding the contributions toward R&D-overheads is not at the taste of governments. In their view the multinational exploits the protection offered by the international patent system beyond what they consider reasonable. As a reaction, price controls or royalty ceilings are established, and therefore, as already argued above, government policies emerge as a form of disloyalty to the patent convention.

There is however one important difference with the theories that explain government interference as a reaction to the less compliant behaviour of multinationals. Usually the better alternatives (shift operations toward other countries) available to the multinational are used to evade or block government policies. Here, the cause of the mismatch between the market outcome realised by the multinational on the one hand and public goals on the other hand, is not the result of a power struggle between MNE and government. The mismatch is simply due to technological conditions inherent to international innovative activity. Therefore, the goals aimed at by governments using price controls often can not be realised. These price controls are investigated next.

2. FAIR CONTRIBUTIONS TO INTERNATIONAL DEVELOPMENT COSTS, SUBSIDY-FREE PRICES AND PRICE CONTROLS

Different goals can motivate price controls, for a detailed survey see Faulhaber, 1983. Clearly, from the viewpoint of static efficiency, price controls can be justified to enforce marginal cost pricing. Indeed, if the product concerned is new and the innovator has some legal monopoly power, marginal cost pricing is unlikely to be the market outcome. At the introduction date, the R&D-expenditures for the new product are largely sunk. Hence countries can use price controls to enforce marginal cost pricing without jeopardising the development of the current new product, but almost certainly future innovative activity will be harmed and a price will be paid in terms of dynamic efficiency.

As a matter of fact, evidence (see Van Cayseele, 1987b) indicates that price controls allow for a contribution to sunk R&D-expenditures. Most of the time this moreover is consistent with the goals of price controls, since it is often stated that the purpose is to limit a countries' contribution toward R&D-expenditures to a "fair" share, not to enforce a static welfare maximising policy like p = mc (von Grebmer, 1981 and Schellhaas & Stumpf, 1983)

Often it is argued that these controls merely serve to free-ride on the countries that make "appropriate" payments for R&D-expenditures. Hence it is important (but also difficult) to agree what a fair contribution amounts to, for invariantly regulators in open economies claim that they guard their country against paying a more than fair share in international development costs.

The problem then of course becomes to determine what constitutes a "fair share". Some hold the view that all countries should pay an equal amount of total development costs. Others have argued that each country should share in overheads according to the amount they consume (prices then will be fixed according to a fully distributed cost practice, Breautigam, 1980). And still others argue that equality should prevail between consumers which is comensurate with prices alligned to the level abroad. These different views on what constitutes a fair share illustrate that different regulated prices are comensurate with one goal: fairness between consumers.

Here none of the above "views" on fairness between consumers, all of which are concerned with fixing prices given the costs that have been made, is retained. Instead the more fundamental question "what constitutes a fair cost figure for the development costs necessary to introduce a new product in a particular country" will be tackled. Solving this question is tantamount to allocate common R&D-costs over the different countries that receive the new product. Singling out portions of common costs and assigning them to particular groups of users is a difficult economic problem arising in a variety of environments. Many suggestions to solve this problem have been put forward, all different according to the criteria that are used to determine the appropriate (fair, just) amount of costs to be charged to a user, see Brown and Sibley, 1986, in the context of public utilities.

The only criterion required from a fair solution here will be that it is individually rational. Fair then merely means that consumers in one country should not pay for the development costs to serve other consumers, or they should not cross-subsidise others. To formulate the criterion in still another way: consumers in one country are supposed to pay an amount of money to the multinational innovator that equals at most what they would pay if they developed the new product for their own account. That is what it would cost them if they contracted with a laboratory to develop the new product for their country, independently of the multinational innovator.

In the remainder of this paper it is shown that a solution satisfying only this simple straightforward principle does not always exist. But what will happen if there exists no allocation of costs for which nobody pays more than he would pay on his own ? In order to see clear in these issues, something more needs to be said on the environment of multinational innovation.

3. APPROACHING INNOVATIVE MULTINATIONALS AS CLUBS

An innovator who introduces a new product in several countries will have to adopt this product to local tastes, standards a.s.o. (It is assumed that all R&D is done in one lab.) In most of the recent analyses of innovative activities, it has been assumed that time compression diseconomies underly the development process (see Kamien and Schwartz, 1982), it essentially means that increasing the R&D-effort during a particular time interval will increase more than proportionally the outlays). As introducing the new product in another country implies that more R&D-effort is done to adapt the innovation to local tastes or standards, time compression diseconomies will induce congestion on the lab. Countries thus crowd on the knowledge creation facilities of the multinational.

On the other hand, if one lab. undertakes the development of a new product, knowledge obtained to introduce in one country becomes available for the introduction in another. That is to say that the researchers working on the adaption of the new product to the tastes or standards in one country learn something valuable for introducing it in another country. This amounts to the assumption of spillovers between research projects, embodied in the lab. (see Van Cayseele, 1986 for a further discussion of spillovers between research projects completed by one innovator instead of the better documented spillovers between innovators e.g. Spence, 1982). Countries under this assumption then share knowledge or there is a commonality.

The analytical foundation to analyse situations in which agents share some facility that can get crowded is to be found in the economic theory of clubs (Buchanan, 1965). A further discussion of the other aspects of the club at hand is deferred to later sections. Approaching multinational innovators from a club perspective allows to shed light on the question who (which members) pays for international drug development.

4. WHO PAYS FOR INTERNATIONAL PRODUCT DEVELOPMENT?

In this section an attempt is given to answer the question: who pays for international new product development? What constitutes a fair share in development expenditures has already been explained: every country is required to contribute only up to what it would cost if the new product was developed for that country alone, or the stand-alone cost. Consumers in one country thus are not supposed to cross-subsidise the introduction of the new product in other countries, or the prices that can be charged should be subsidy-free.

In order to investigate if regulators can implement such prices it pays to make some simplifying assumptions. In order to avoid the difficulties associated with comparing new products being available at different times when discussing fairness (is it fair that people in France cannot use the improved technology while it is already available in Germany?) the discussion is limited to multicountry introduction without lags, that is if there are n countries and T_i is the introduction date in country i,

$$(1) \qquad T_1 = T_2 = \ldots = T_i = \ldots = T_n$$

A further assumption is related to the amount of spillovers that becomes available each time that a country is served, or conversely to the additional effort that is necessary for adapting the new product to the tastes or standards prevalent in another country. Again for the sake of simplicity it is assumed that each time the innovator wants an additional introduction of the new product, he needs the same amount of effort, regardless the number of countries the new product was already introduced in. The first introduction requires an amount of R&D-effort equal to A, while each additional country that is served needs effort up to a level B. This could be explained by standards which differ between countries regarding the same item in the development process while all other items are compatible and result immediately from the initial market approval procedure.

If in addition to these assumptions, the relation between manhours of R&D (y) and money (m) can be written as $m = (1/2)y^2$, the innovator faces an optimal control problem: minimise the discounted expenditures (m) over the horizon T while enough manhours of R&D (y) are accumulated to obtain introduction in all the countries that are envisioned. The solution to this problem is derived elsewhere, see Van Cayseele, 1987a. In fact, the following lemma can be proven:

Lemma 1.
The costs for developing the new drug by time T for the subset of countries S is:

$$C(T,S) = \frac{1}{2} \frac{(A+(s-1)B)^2 r}{(e^{rT} - 1)} \tag{2}$$

where s is the number of countries in S.

Discussion:

As stated above, for a formal proof the reader is refered to Van Cayseele, 1987a. There the optimal control problem that the innovator faces when he decides to introduce a new product in several countries and with spillovers between the development processes is discussed at large. Here it is sufficient to note the following characteristics of the solution:

- if the length of the development period decreases, the development costs increase, and at an increasing rate. Equation (2) thus defines a time-cost trade-off of the type extensively discussed in Scherer, 1980 ;
- if the effort to introduce increases either because the initial effort A to introduce in one country, or the additional effort B to introduce in the other countries or the number of additional countries in which the new product is introduced, s increases, the development costs of course also increase.

Since a relation of the type $m = (1/2)y^2$ has been used extensively in the literature, see for example Lucas, 197 ; Kamien and Schwartz, 1972; Vislie, 1982 (the particular form is Reinganum, 1982), it is possible to obtain previous results as special cases. If the new product is only developed for one country, this amounts to setting s=1 in (2) to get the well-known single project cost function by Kamien and Schwartz, 1982. For the "gran coalition" including all countries the costs then are:

$$(3) \qquad C(N,T) = \frac{1}{2} \frac{(A + (n-1)B)^2 r}{(e^{rT} - 1)}$$

where n of course is the total number of countries.

These tools can be used now to answer the question whether fair prices exist in this simplified environment. It was the merit of Faulhaber (1975) to show that in order to determine the existence of subsidy-free prices, it has to be established that the set of undominated imputations or the core of the game which has the cost function as characteristic function is non-empty.

More formally, the core is the set of imputations I_i which jointly satisfy the restrictions:

$$(4) \qquad \sum_{i \in N} I_i \geq C(N,T)$$

$$(5) \qquad \sum_{j \in S} I_j < C(S,T)$$

where (5) has to hold for all possible subsets S, and C(S;T) now stands for the costs of developing the new product for the subset of countries S by time T. These expressions respectively mean that the innovator has to break even when he introduces the new product in all countries, while all conceivable (both in size and composition) subgroups of countries cannot pay more than the costs they would face when developing the new product on their own. In the terminology of clubs introduced earlier, if a core exists, clubs to which everyone would like to belong exist . For a further analysis of the link between clubs and cores, see Pauly (1967). To put it still another way, obtaining the new product from the innovative multinational is for every country the preferable alternative.

It then can be shown that with n countries the inequalities (4) and (5) impose (n-1) restrictions on the development technology, of the type:

$$(6) \qquad (A + (n-1)B)^2 < \frac{n}{j} (A + (j-1)B)^2$$

where j is the size (= number of countries) of the subgroups considered.

For a proof of this result in general, see Ponssard, 1981, theorem 2 on page 147. A sketch of the proof for the specific game dealt with, is given here. For three countries we have that going alone has to be more expensive than to belong to the "gran coalition", or the imputation from country i, I_i to the innovator has to be such that:

$$(7) \qquad I_i \leq \frac{1}{2} \frac{A^2 r}{(e^{rT} - 1)} \quad \text{for all } i$$

which implies that

$$(8) \qquad I_1 + I_2 + I_3 \leq \frac{3}{2} \frac{A^2 r}{(e^{rT} - 1)}$$

Together with (4), the condition stating that the innovator has to break even or

$$(9) \qquad I_1 + I_2 + I_3 \geq \frac{1}{2} \frac{(A + 2B)^2 r}{(e^{rT} - 1)},$$

this implies

$$(10) \qquad (A + 2B)^2 \leq 3 A^2$$

which is the first of two constraints induced by imputations in the core of the development technology.

But the possibility of two countries going together needs to be considered also. Again then the imputation the multinational receives from a group of two countries together may not exceed what it costs for these two countries to develop the new product on their own. Moreover this must hold for all conceivable combinations of countries or:

$$(11) \qquad I_1 + I_2 \leq \frac{1}{2} \frac{(A+B)^2 r}{(e^{rT} - 1)}$$

$$(12) \qquad I_1 + I_3 \leq \frac{1}{2} \frac{(A+B)^2 r}{(e^{rT} - 1)}$$

$$(13) \qquad I_2 + I_3 \leq \frac{1}{2} \frac{(A+B)^2 r}{(e^{rT} - 1)}$$

which implies

$$(14) \qquad 2\,(I_1 + I_2 + I_3) \leq \frac{3}{2} \frac{(A+B)^2 r}{(e^{rT} - 1)}$$

Again, using the break-even requirement:

$$(9)\ \text{rep.} \qquad I_1 + I_2 + I_3 \geq \frac{1}{2} \frac{(A + 2B)^2 r}{(e^{rT} - 1)}$$

it has to be true that:

$$(15) \qquad \frac{(A+2B)^2 r}{e^{rT} - 1} < \frac{3}{2} \frac{(A+B)^2 r}{e^{rT} - 1}$$

or:

$$(16) \qquad (A+2B)^2 < \frac{3}{2} (A+B)^2$$

Now (10) and (16) are of the type (6) as can be seen by filling in n = 3 and resp. j = 1, j = 2 in (6). Thus there are indeed (n-1) restrictions imposed on the development-technology, by requiring that imputations lie in the core.

Clearly, these restrictions impose constraints on the relative sizes of efforts A and B. A calculation reveals that the range of values that allows for a core is very restrictive. For four countries we need B < 0.05A, or less than 5 % of the total amount of R&D-effort needed to introduce the new product in the first country should be sufficient to adapt the innovation to meet the tastes or standards in another country. And as compression diseconomies increase (a becomes bigger than 2), the necessary spillovers increase to even more critical levels. This becomes clear from the following table in which the entries are the ratio B/A, for different values of the compression diseconomies parameter and a different number of countries to be served.

TABLE 1 : Ratio of additional tests over tests for the first introduction required for a non-empty core, given different magnitudes of compression diseconomies and number of countries.

No. of countries	Compression diseconomies parameter	
	2	4
3	.11	.05
4	.05	.02
5	.02	.01

Source: computations based on (6).

What if the development technology does not satisfy the restrictions imposed by the imputations lying in the core? Then there exist no imputations which simultaneously satisfy individual rationality and allow the innovator to break even. The set of these imputations, the core then is empty. <u>Prices which are subsidy free then cannot be found!</u>

The <u>intuitive reason for the non-existence of a core</u> is that although effort is saved when the same innovator decides to introduce in an additional country, the countries which were already sure to get the new product now will have to pay more for its development due to the compression diseconomies triggered by the additional effort needed to get market approval in this additional country. Although first of all effort is saved, and second developing the new product for all countries together might be a cheaper solution than developing it for different subgroups (economies of scope exist), from the perspective of a single country the "gran coalition" might subsidise introduction in other countries.

If that is the case, what is likely to happen? In answering this question, approaching multinational innovation by means of club theory is extremely useful. In order to exploit fully the analogy, some additional characteristics of the club at hand need to be clear. First, since all countries provide patent protection for the innovator, no country can exit the club to go on his own in developing the drug after that it has been discovered (as long as the innovator has deposited a patent). Membership is compulsatory in this club (Cornes and Sandler, 1986).

A second feature of the club on hand also is related to the aspect of membership: since nearly all countries in the world offer patent protection, the innovator can group the entire world, or there is a single club in which all relevant economic agents are represented. Calculating the costs for completing the necessary R&D for introduction in a country thus merely is the matter of a thought experiment to find out if the country is cross-subsidising the others. If it turns out that this is the case and the multinational innovator has deposited a patent, any " lonesome wolf " developing the same blueprint into the new product would infringe on patent law. The only way to stop cross-subsidisation then is by (stronger) price controls or royalty ceilings.

These actions in turn can be interpreted in terms of club theory. It is well-known that members of a club who disagree can undertake different actions, among them exit and disloyalty (see Mueller, 1979). In the present case exit is ruled out as it is impossible to develop the new product independently from the multinational or to step out of the club of countries that he serves, since this would imply patent infringement (the multinational intends to introduce the new product in that country and hence it is not a "sleeping" patent). The alternative left thus is, as already said, to enforce price controls. This in turn can be interpreted as a form of disloyalty of some members of the club, since in principle a patent awards the innovator a monopoly position enabling him to extract the full potential of the market. Price controls limit this ability and in the extreme case where regulators fix the price at the level of marginal costs, awarding patent protection doesn't make sense for there is nothing to protect. The property rights designed to stimulate innovative activity are infringed by other governement interventions.

5. THE CASE OF PHARMACEUTICAL DRUG DEVELOPMENT

The pharmaceutical industry provides an excellent application to illustrate the above ideas. Nearly all countries have safety regulations which the innovator must pass before he obtains the authorisation to sell the drug. Often these regulations are very divergent. For each country the innovator thus needs additional R&D effort to introduce the new drug. On the other hand, the lab. that has done the tests for introducing the drug in one country can transfer part of these results (the part that is accepted by the regulator in another country) by means of testimonials. This accounts for the spillovers between research projects. Finally, near all countries of the European Community (exceptions are Germany and to some extent the Netherlands) have adopted price controls. The main reason of course being the reduction of the deficits that arise when society shares in the financial risks associated with illness. Since the market shares held by the domestic firms in most countries remain below 50%, the reason is clearly to prevent that funds raised by domestic taxes excessively contribute to international R&D. Price regulators thus try to limit the contribution of their country to a "fair" share in international R&D.

Since the restrictiveness of the conditions necessary to have a non-empty core and hence subsidy-free prices is impressive, it is justified to ask whether the goal of fairness is attainable at all in this world. Therefore, for some countries, the <u>actual</u> ratio of additional tests to the tests needed to introduce a drug in

Germany is estimated. On the average, this ratio is far above what is allowed for according to Table 1, as can be seen from Table 2.

In computing this table difficulties have been encountered to disentangle the reasons that underly the non-acceptance of tests. On the one hand some countries (like France,Italy and the U.S.A.) do not accept particular types of tests that have been carried out abroad (unless done by experts they acknowledge). This indicates that tests are the same but need to be done locally (or with an acknowledged expert), that is in a different laboratory. On the other hand often tests can be carried over by testimonials , but the market approval procedure dictates that different tests need to be done (at least regarding some topics of safety). Then the same laboratory will be used to do different tests and it is precisely this situation that the present study has in mind.

The substantial differences in market approval procedures have far reaching implications for price regulation in the pharmaceutical industry. Given divergent safety regulations and the reasonable condition of time compression diseconomies in testing, the core of the development game is empty, or subsidy-free prices do not exist. Cross-subsidisation is unavoidable. Fairness between consumers in different countries as expressed by the requirement that nobody pays more than what it costs to serve him cannot be met. The effectiveness of price regulation in the pursuit of this goal then simply is nil because the target cannot be realised ab initio.

If price regulators refuse to realise that in these circumstances they cannot prevent that their country contributes to the development costs incurred on behalf of introduction in other countries, they probably will interfere with the development process in a conspicious way.

Meanwhile it seems justified to stress that the unexistence result regarding subsidy free prices depends on simultaneous introduction. In the case where drug lags exist as in reality, the fact that more time becomes available offsets the congestion effects. The countries which receive the drug later also pay less to the innovator. Under these circumstances subsidy free prices

TABLE 2 : Actual ratios of additional test for several E.E.C. countries and the U.S.A. Initial tests are done in Germany.

Research and Development Activities	(1) Share in the total of R&D costs	(2) Country Fr.	U.S.A.[a]	It.	U.K.	Belg.	Switz.
Synthesis and Isolation of Substance	19 %	A	A	A	A	A	A
Biological Active Ingredient search	12 %	A	A	A	A	A	A
Animal Activity Testing	12 %	NA	NA	NA	A	A	A
Toxicology	10 %	NA	NA	NA	A	A	A
Metabolism & Pharmacokinetics	7 %	NA	NA	NA	A	A	A
Analyses Research	5 %	NA	NA	A	NA	NA	A
Action and Tolerance in Man	16 %	NA	NA	A	NA	NA	A
Galenic Processing	7 %	A	A	A	A	A	A
Proces Technology	12 %	A	A	A	A	A	A
	Ratio B/A	.50	.50	.29	.21	.21	0

Legend: NA: not accepted
A : accepted
a : prior to 1975 the F.D.A. did not accept any clinical testing

Sources: 1. Thesing J.; 1977, Drug Research in the Pharmaceutical Industry: Requisites and Potential, in Bedrijfsraad Scheikunde; 1982, De Geneesmiddelenindustrie in België, Brussel, p. 45.
2. - Heiduk G.; 1981, p. 11
- Hanssen R.; 1982, p. 37
- Koninklijk Besluit i.v.m. de Geneesmiddelenregistratie (Royal Decree on the Registration of Drugs), 1976.

may become possible. But then "economic fairness" is paid with "medical unfairness", or as it was stated at the beginning: why should a French patient wait several years before he can be treated with a new therapy which is currently available to Germans?

TABLE 3 : Number of Requests for Market Authorisation to Different Countries using the Common Market Procedure in 1978-1982

COUNTRY						
B.	G.	F.	U.K.	I.	Lux.	N.
23	17	12	13	21	26	25

Source: Labo-Pharma, Probl. Tech, 31 n° 327, p.31

A final remark is related to the differences in the market authorisation procedure that equally account for the impossibility of subsidy-free prices. There seems to be a trend within the European Community to bring into harmony the different registration procedures. Some time ago a common market authorisation procedure has been installed. The procedure allows to obtain authorisation in a country when authorisation in another country is already obtained and directives by the European Community have been followed in obtaining authorisation. There exists however a trend by national authorities to require more evidence than available in the files that served the E.C.-procedure (Labo-Pharma, Probl.-Tech. (1983), p.31). The harmonisation thus seems yet unaccomplished in practice. From 1978 until 1982 only 28 requests have been registered. From the following table it seems that the procedure serves mostly to introduce in the smaller countries. Bunching together these countries which usually are open to foreign evidence presumably saves separate paper work.

6. THE REGULATORY DYNAMICS OF PRICE CONTROLS: SOME CONCLUDING REMARKS ON INNOVATION IN THE MIXED ECONOMY

Suppose price regulators in the European Community pursue the goal of fairness between consumers, that is they want to limit the contribution of their country to a fair share of international R&D-costs. Suppose furthermore that the development technology does not allow for a non-empty core due to too divergent safety regulations, as documented in table 2 for the pharmaceutical industry. Then at least some countries will experience that they are subsidising the introduction of the drug in other countries. Hence they will conclude that the innovative multinational doesn't realise their goal.

What is the probable reaction to such a situation? Since it is felt that the country pays for the development costs of others, price controls will result. This implies that the revenues to be realised on new products of which introduction was planned will go downward. Accordingly the innovator will develop his lately discovered molecules into new drugs at a slower pace. But then the development cost will be lower and again cross-subsidisation will take place. Future revisions then will adjust prices downward, which in turn again will reduce the speed of development. The limit probably is a world characterised by no new drugs because prices do not cover R&D-expenditures.

Of course, the above scenario is just one out of many possible. It however illustrates how the pursuit of "fairness between different consumers", the main but often unattainable goal of price regulation, might have disastrous effects on innovation. Policy proposals to realise a true common market (see European Commission, 1988) therefore need to be approved for they eliminate a <u>double</u> "cost of non-Europe". First of all, these divergent market authorisation procedures <u>induce</u> additional R&D-<u>costs</u>, a fact well known. But in addition, they account for the unexistence of subsidy-free prices which might trigger price controls by unpleased governments. This <u>reduces</u> the <u>revenues</u> of introducing new products, and likely harms innovative activity as well.

REFERENCES

AUQUIR, A. and R. CAVES (1979), "Monopolistic export industries, trade taxes and optimal competition policy", The Economic Journal, vol. 89, pp. 559-89.

BRAEUTIGAM, R. (1980), "An analyses of fully distributed cost pricing in regulated industries", Bell Journal of Economics, vol. 11, pp. 182-96.

BROWN, S. and D. SIBLEY (1986), The theory of public utility pricing, Cambridge U. Press, Cambridge.

BUCHANAN, J. (1965), "An economic theory of clubs", Economica, vol.32, pp. 1-14.

CAVES, R. (1982), Multinational Enterprise and Economic Analysis, Camebridge University Press, Camebridge.

COMMISSION OF THE EUROPEAN COMMUNITIES (1988), "The Economics of 1992", European Economy, no. 35.

CONTRACTOR, F. and T. SAGAFI-NEJAD (1981), "International Technology Transfer : Major Issues and Policy Responses", Journal of International Business Studies, pp. 113-135.

CORNES, R. and T. SANDLER (1986), The theory of externalities, public goods and club goods, Cambridge U. Press, Cambridge.

FAULHABER, G. (1983), "A public enterprise pricing primer", in FINSINGER, J. (ed.), Public Sector Economics, St. Martin's Press, New York.

FAULHABER, G. (1975), "Cross subsidisation: pricing in public enterprise", American Economic Review, vol. 65, pp. 966-977.

HANSSEN, R. (1982), Regulation, patents and innovation in the pharmaceutical industry, Center for research in government policy and business working paper, University of Rochester.

HEIDUK, G. (1982), "Multinationalisation in the pharmaceutical industry as a response to national health policies", Managerial and Decision Economics, vol. 3, No. 4, pp. 194-204.

KONINKLIJK BESLUIT I.V.M. DE REGISTRATIE VAN GENEESMIDDELEN (1976), Belgisch Staatsblad, Brussel.

KAMIEN, M. and N. SCHWARTZ (1972), "Timing of innovations under rivalry", Econometrica, vol. 40, pp. 43-60.

KAMIEN, M. and N. SCHWARTZ (1982), Market structure and innovation, Cambridge U. Press, Cambridge.

LUCAS, R.E. (1971), "Optimal management of a research and development project", Management Science, vol. 17, No. 11, pp. 679-97.

MUELLER, D. (1979), Public Choice, Cambridge University Press, 297p.

PAULY, M. (1967), "Clubs, Commonality, and the Core: An Integration of Game Theory and the Theory of Public Goods", Economica, august, pp. 314-324.

PONSSARD, J.P. (1981), Competitive Strategies, North-Holland, Amsterdam.

REEKIE, D. (1984), Drug prices in the U.K., U.S.A., Europe and Australia, Australian Economic Papers, June.

REINGANUM, J. (1982), "A dynamic game of R.&D.: patent protection and competitive behavior", Econometrica, vol. 50, pp. 671-688.

SCHELLHAASS, H.-M. and U. STUMPF (1983), "Price regulation in the European pharmaceutical industry, benefits and costs", in FINSINGER, J. (ed.), Economic analyses of regulated markets, Croom-Helm, London.

SCHERER, F. (1967)," Research and Development ressource allocation under Rivalry", The Quarterly Journal of Economics, vol. 81, pp. 367-91.

SCHERER, F. (1980), Industrial Market Structure and Economic Performance, Rand Mc Nally, Chicago.

SPENCE, M. (1984), "Cost reduction, Competition, and industry performance", Econometrica, vol 54, no. 1, pp. 101-121.

VAN CAYSEELE, P. (1986), "Spillovers and the Cost of Multiproject R&D", Managerial and Decision Economics, vol. 7, pp. 133-139.

VAN CAYSEELE, P. (1987a), "Economies of scope in research and development", Journal of Economics (Zeitschrift für Nationalökonomie), vol. 47, no. 3, pp. 273-285.

VAN CAYSEELE, P. (1987b), Regulation an International Innovative Activities in the Pharmaceutical Industry, Unpublished Ph.D.- dissertation, 169 p.

VISLIE, J. (1982b), "A note on an intertemporal cost function for a class of dynamic problems", Economics Letters, vol. 8, No. 3, pp. 215-19.

von GREBMER, K. (1981), "International pharmaceutical supply prices: definitions-problems-policy implications", Managerial and Decision Economics, vol. 2, No. 2, pp. 74-81.

von GREBMER, K. (1983), "The international drug market", in Drugs made in Germany, pp. 47-54.

The Convergence of International and Domestic Markets
D.B. Audretsch, L. Sleuwaegen, and H. Yamawaki (Editors)

10. THE CHANGING DYNAMICS OF INTERNATIONAL TECHNOLOGICAL COMPETITION*

Kirsty S. Hughes
University of Manchester
Department of Economics

0. INTRODUCTION

In the last decade there have been major changes in the operation and organisation of research and development activities in the advanced industrial countries. In the USA, Western Europe and Japan, both corporations and governments are increasingly looking towards co-operation in research as a means to achieving technological success and international competitiveness. A wide variety of co-operative research relationships have come into existence, involving different participants, different structures and different aims. The potential effects of this trend towards co-operation are wide-ranging and raise a number of questions about the likely nature both of future global competition and of technological advance.

This paper considers the reasons for the changing nature of research and development activities, and assesses the implications of these co-operative developments. In particular, it addresses the possibility that there may be various adverse effects on innovation of increasing collaboration. It also argues that

---

* I would like to thank David Edgerton and Philip Gummett for comments on this paper and also participants at the EIASM conference and at seminars at Nottingham University and Southbank Polytechnic.

fundamental changes in the processes of international competition are occurring and that, if these trends towards co-operation continue, there will be yet more changes - in particular, technological competition may become <u>less</u> important.

The paper first looks at some of the various forms of co-operation in R & D within and between countries. It then considers why co-operative research occurs, why it has increased in recent years and the implications of this for innovation. The paper then goes on to consider likely future patterns of global competition and the relationship between these potential patterns and innovation.

1. NATIONAL AND INTERNATIONAL R&D COLLABORATION

Collaboration and co-operation in R & D takes many different forms, in terms of participants, of organisational structure and of aims and extent of the co-operation. Firms may collaborate in a joint R & D project, they may set up and subscribe to a separate research corporation. They may have national or foreign partners or both. There may be collaboration between firms and a university, or between many firms and universities. Government institutions may also be involved in collaboration, either directly through public research institutes or indirectly through organisation and/or funding of the collaboration. Collaboration may only involve R & D, or it may continue through to production and marketing. Equally joint ventures - expecially in high technology industries - concerned with production and marketing may result in important levels of technology transfer between participating firms. It is not the intention here to describe or list these projects in detail but to give a brief indication of their scope and a guide to some sources of detailed information.

Looking at the three blocs - Japan, the US and West Europe - there has been a large increase in co-operative R & D in recent years. Japan through MITI, has, for a long time, encouraged co-operative R & D efforts. This co-operation increased in the 1970s (Freeman 1987). Co-operative R & D projects have occured in many areas such as the fifth generation computer systems' project, the VLSI project, bictechnology and so forth. Similarly, in West

Europe there have been a number of developments in European collaborative projects in recent years. These cover many areas, such as information technology (ESPRIT), biotechnology, telecommunications (RACE) and energy (for a recent summary see Eurotec Nr S5-87). In the US, there have been a number of developments, such as the establishment of MCC - the Microelectronics and Computer Technology Corporation - and other joint research projects in areas such as biotechnology, chemicals, robotics, and a large increase in co-operative research between firms and universities (Government-University-Industry Roundtable report 1986; Fusfeld and Haklisch 1985). In the US, there has been less government involvement in co-operative research - with the major exception of defence-related projects.

In addition to these co-operative ventures within the three blocs, there has also been increasing collaboration between firms in different parts of the Triad. Again this takes a variety of forms and occurs in a number of areas. Many of these joint ventures are not directly with respect to R & D, but they are in high technology industries and so are likely to allow significant learning opportunities. There have been some joint ventures between US and Japanese firms in automobiles, computers/microchips, robotics, machine tools, pharmaceuticals and plastics (for more detailed lists and examples see Ohmae 1985, Reich and Mankin 1986, Fusfeld and Haklisch 1985). Similarly, there are/have been a number of Japanese/European collaborative ventures, for example in electronic components, carbon fibres, robotics and biotechnology (Ohmae 1985). There are also various European/US ventures, such as the Philips/AT & T link-up (Hill 1983), including the participation of US firms in some of the European collaborative projects, such as RACE and ESPRIT (Taylor 1986, Braggar 1984).

Thus, the trend towards co-operation is observed both within the three Triad regions and across the regions. Ohmae (1985) claims that there is, if anything, stronger pressure towards collaboration across the regions :

> "instead of geographically close competitors joining forces, the current trend is for distant competitors to merge and share functions such as R & D and production."

2. REASONS FOR CO-OPERATIVE RESEARCH AND DEVELOPMENT

As co-operation in R & D takes many different forms, it is not to be expected that the motivation for joint research is the same in all cases. Nevertheless, it is possible to consider the likely motivations for co-operative research, and to identify the likely major causes of its rapid increase in recent years.

Two frequently quoted reasons for co-operative R & D are that it can reduce both the risks and the costs of R & D. The uncertainty and risks associated with innovation arise for three reasons - demand uncertainty, technolocical uncertainty and uncertainty about behaviour and likely success of competitors. Not only does joint research spread these riks across firms, it will also reduce the third type of uncertainty. Through co-operation, the risks and the costs of a particular research project or strategy can be borne jointly by the participants. Furthermore, to the extent that firms were previously duplicating research, a joint programme will reduce costs to all participants. Alternatively, it will allow firms to broaden their range of activities and so increase their chances of success in innovation. This might even involve seperate research establishments. Grossman and Shapiro (1987) argue that

> "given the assumption of decreasing returns to devoting more resources to a fixed supply of ideas and techniques, it may be more efficient for the firms to forego the (fixed) cost savings associated with a unified operation, and to use the joint venture only as a means to set the research outlays at their separate facilities collusively."

Dasgupta and Maskin (1987) suggest that market forces may result in research that is too risky and done too fast, and may produce too much parallel research resulting in an insufficiently diversified portfolio of research projects. Whether co-operative research can reduce or eliminate these market failures may, however, depend crucially on whether the co-operative venture includes all competing firms (see, for example, Ordover and Willing 1985, Katz 1986). In addition, as will be discussed further below, there may be many reasons why joint research will not result in a sufficient diversity of projects.

The difficulty of appropriating R & D output is another cause of R & D co-operation. Through joint R & D, spillovers from firms' R & D can be internalized (Katz 1986). However, as Katz points out, if co-operative R & D reduces the production costs of one firm this is likely to reduce competitors' profits and so there may be an incentive to restrict R & D. Vickers (1985) also suggests research joint ventures may reduce the incentive to innovate by reducing the competitive stimulus between firms. Joint research does not, anyway, solve all the appropriability problems associated with innovation - even though cost-sharing and internalisation will help. While co-operation may avoid profit dissipation through R & D rivalry, a research joint venture may increase direct rivalry in the market and so reduce profits (Grossman and Shapiro 1987).

A wider range of reasons for co-operation in R & D become apparent once we allow for differences between firms. These differences may be asymmetric in that one firm has superior technological knowledge to another but may still benefit from access to the weaker firm's markets, productive capacity, scientific and technical skills and so forth. Alternatively, firms may benefit from a mutual exchange of technological knowledge and joint use of skilled staff and other firm-specific factors. Many of the reasons for research joint ventures (RJVs) can then be seen to relate to the market failures associated with trade in knowledge and in this sense are similar to explanations of reasons for multinational firms. Thus, R & D co-operation may be preferable to licensing or cross-licensing due to problems of moral hazard, opportunism and due to the tacit, uncodified nature of parts of technological know-how and the difficulties of separating this know-how from the rest of a firm, when it may be closely dependent on particular staff and particular organisational structures (see, for example, Teece 1981). Furthermore, costs of transferring technology can be very high (Teece 1977, Rosenberg and Frischtak 1985). However, the ability of RJVs to resolve all these problems are not clear-cut. In particular, while transfer of tacit knowledge may be easier in a RJV than through the market and easier to control (Mowery 1986), it is still likely to encounter difficulties, and the transfer can be expected to be far from costless. In addition, if the RJV does not also entail joint production, then its output - new knowledge

- at some stage must be transferred back to participating firms. This will not be costless. These costs can be expected to vary, depending on a number of factors such as the precise structure of the RJV or co-operative R & D organisation and the nature of the new technological knowledge and its relation to the firm's existing technology and to its independent R & D activity.

Overall, then, firms with different technological knowledge can benefit in various ways from R & D co-operation. They may get a better balance and range of skills and of projects through joint research, (though this may in part be a simple scale economies benefit). To the extent that organisations develop rigidities in their patterns of information accumulation, co-operative research may break these down and create new synergies (Imai and Itami 1984). Firms can broaden and deepen their technological knowledge and obtain access to a much wider range of ideas and experience; they may extend their product range, or diversify into related areas. Where co-operation extends into production this may give access to new and larger markets and to marketing and distribution networks (see, for example, Ohmae 1985). Many cases of mutual benefit from co-operation arise when a large firm wants access to innovations of a small firm, while the small firm may want access to the larger firm's capital, markets and distribution system (see, for example, Klein 1986, Posner 1985, Rothwell 1983).

While the discussion so far has been in terms of RJVs between firms, many of the motivating factors will apply to co-operative research between firms (both public and private) and universities. Thus, firms may benefit from joint research with universities - even if this may make appropriability more difficult - due to the greater ease of technology transfer via co-operative research and due to the accumulated skills and availability of other inputs. The more basic the research is, the more, of course, there is an incentive for co-operation and in particular for co-operation with universities. Again, though, it should be emphasized that transfer of knowledge back to firms is not costless.

It is clear from the discussion so far that the pressures towards collaboration in R & D arise not only in order to spread and reduce risk in a probablistic sense. Uncertainty, unavoidably associated with innovations, also reinforces or results in such pressures. The path of development of a technology will depend, in an uncertain manner, on the following : existing knowledge and the form in which it is held (codified or tacit, restricted access, limits to storage and processing abilities); the procedures and hierarchies involved in the attempt to increase technological knowledge; the areas in which competitors and suppliers and users are working; any underlying, though unknown, 'real' constraints; changes in firms' or the industry's environment; and chance. Collaboration cannot remove all these uncertainties but it can reduce or alleviate some. Firstly, as discussed above, collaboration may lead to sharing of information and of information processing abilities. Secondly, uncertainty about activities of other firms can be reduced through collaboration. One factor that a firm knows will influence the future pattern of technological developments are activities of other firms. Their efforts and their interdependencies will affect the nature and path of technology. Uncertainty can, therefore, be reduced both by finding out about their activities <u>and</u> by carrying out similar research. Thus, both competitive and technological uncertainties can be reduced by competitive firms (and user and supplier firms) carrying out R & D in the same technological area. (These arguments are developed in more detail in Hargreaves-Heap and Hughes 1986.) Through collaboration, not only does each firm have more knowledge about its competitors, but it can also benefit from spillovers and is more likely to be working in the area where technological developments are going to occur in the uncertain future.

There is, therefore, a wide range of reasons why firms may engage in co-operative R & D. This co-operation can take various forms and may be more or less successful. It is not possible here to analyse in depth what factors promote co-operative success. Nelkin and Nelson (1986) stress that, in the US at least, many of these joint research organisations are experimental and cannot all be expected to succeed. Ohmae (1985) and Mowery (1987) both provide interesting discussions of causes of success and failure in joint ventures of various sorts (not restricted to R & D). Generalisation is difficult, but the importance of effective communication comes out strongly - Ohmae talks about the need for two corporations to speak the same 'language' or to work to develop a common language. It appears important that management and organisational structures should be clearly developed and laid out taking into account the particular needs and features of the specific situation. Nevertheless, such ventures could prove in many cases to be lacking in stability since as the research develops it may benefit one partner more than another or the participants may want the research to go in different directions. This would result in a buy-out by one partner or in break-up of the RJV.

Mowery stresses one cause of failure as linked to the extent to which co-operating firms are competitors elsewhere. Similarly, Jacquemin (1987) argues that valuable RJVs may be discouraged unless collaboration can continue through to the product market. However, the static anti-trust implications of such collaboration would then be of concern. More importantly, the competitive dynamic encouraging innovation in the future may be seriously impeded. The potential adverse effects of collaboration on innovations are discussed in Section Three. In Section Four the implications for technological competition are considered.

3. EXPLANATION OF THE INCREASING TREND IN CO-OPERATIVE R&D

A number of reasons have been proposed as to why there has been an increase in co-operative R & D in the last decade or so. These reasons are mostly clearly linked to, and reflect an intensification of, the causes of joint research discussed in the previous section.

A frequent argument is that co-operation in R & D has increased due to an increased intensity of global competition (see, for example, Fusfeld and Haklisch 1985, Ohmae 1985, Rosenberg 1981, Shepherd et al. 1983). Technological competence and innovative ability are seen as crucial ingredients in global competitiveness. International technological competition is seen to have intensified firstly because medium or high technology industries are the main areas where the advanced industrial economies can expect or hope to have a competitive advantage, given the pressures of competition from the newly industrialising countries in less technology intensive products. Secondly, the advanced countries are tending to become more similar in their technological abilities and knowledge and in their markets and consumers. Opportunities for growth no longer exist simply by virtue of catching up with the US, and the broad technological hegemony of the US in the 1950s and 1960s has faded. As countries and firms become more similar technologically, competition has intensified.

Japan's success in catching up with - and in some areas overtaking - the US is well documented (for a recent discussion, see Freeman 1987). Meeting the challenge from Japan is frequently cited as a reason for R & D co-operation in the US and catching up with both the US and Japan as a reason for European R & D co-operation (see, for example, Shepherd et al. 1985, Geroski and Jacquemin 1985, Kolodziej 1987). However, as Patel and Pavitt (1987) stress, generalisations about the relative technological positions of the US, Japan and West Europe are liable to be misleading. Furthermore, they argue, Japan and the US also perceive themselves as facing difficulties with respect to the level of, and trends in, their technological activities. West Europe is not alone in this respect.

Various reasons for R & D co-operation emerge from this stress on intensified global competition. Firstly, a greater degree of competition leads both to pressure for speed in innovation - which increases costs - and to an increase in the risks of innovation. Product life cycles are becoming shorter (Rosenberg 1981, Snyder and Blevins 1986). Secondly, to the extent firms and countries perceive themselves as lagging behind technologically, then joint R & D can reduce the costs and time of eliminating or reducing the technology gap. Thus, Grosch (1985) argues that IBM's dominance has been the stimulus to co-operative research in many countries, including the US. Thirdly, if other firms or countries - notably Japan - are seen to be investing heavily in co-operative R & D in areas thought to be of future significance, then imitation of this strategy through joint research may again be seen as necessary to try to prevent future pre-emption in these areas.

Costs of innovation have also increased for other reasons. Costs of both the development and commercialization of new technologies have and are increasing due in part to : an increased complexity of technology; increasing interaction between science and technology; and the increasingly multi-disciplinary, cross-industry nature of both science and technology (see, for example, Ohmae 1985, Fusfeld and Haklisch 1985, Rosenberg 1981). In addition, capital and skill intensity of product and process research is perceived to be rising (Edge 1985). Increasing complexity and interdependence of technology not only increases costs but also implies that any one firm is unlikely to have the abilities and knowledge necessary for R & D and product and process development. Thus, as Fusfeld and Haklisch (1985) argue, the evolution of the international technological structure is such that corporations need to draw upon a growing range of technical areas. Firms are, thus, increasingly less self-sufficient and are more dependent on external links. New scientific and technological knowledge is also tending to be relevant to a wider range of industries. Furthermore, if the importance of the science/technology interface increases, basic research increases in importance, resulting in a further impetus to co-operation between firms and with universities (Government-University-Indusry-Research Roundtable 1986).

The legal environment is important in allowing, encouraging or discouraging co-operation. Such barriers have been relatively unimportant in Japan. As pressures for co-operative research have increased, changes have been made in US and EC legislation to establish a more permissive environment for such ventures (Kolodziej 1987, Hunnings 1986). Legal prohibitions may also encourage international co-operation where this is considered less harmful to competition than domestic co-operation.

Joint ventures and other forms of inter-firm links can and do extend beyond research, into production, marketing and distribution (see, for example, Reich and Mankin 1986). In technology based industries, such joint ventures can also serve as an important basis for transmission and sharing of knowledge, although such technology transfer may be less than participants expect (Mowery 1987). The increasing scale of R & D and the need for co-operative R & D may not only result in international R & D links between firms, but may require such links to be extended to production and marketing in order to gain access to global markets to recover the high costs of R & D. This argument is developed by Ohmae (1985). He argues that competitive success requires corporations to be able to penetrate all of the Triad markets of Japan, US and West Europe swiftly and effectively. He further considers that the main channel to achieve this penetration is through international joint ventures, and gives examples of many international links between Triad companies that have already adopted this approach. He argues that these markets are becoming increasingly similar, and that industrial and economy boundaries are changing. Understanding of these markets, and marketing and distribution skills, are then of central importance. International joint ventures can provide these skills and, Ohmae believes, will not undermine competition since competition will come from domestic competitors and other international joint ventures.

4. IMPLICATIONS FOR INNOVATION

This section considers the potential effects of current trends in innovative activities.

As discussed above, not only are there currently many pressures leading to co-operative R & D but much of this co-operation is international in nature. Various people have argued that we can expect to see increasing links between firms as technologies become more complex, and as costs rise. The search for complementarities and synergies in the research process need not, and has not, stopped at national boundaries. Furthermore, there are strong pressures encouraging international links in areas other than research. Global co-ordination across the Triad becomes a crucial aspect of competitiveness (Porter 1986).

One possible outcome of this combination of (1) increased internationalisation of firms' operations and of their links with each other, and (2) increased research co-operation, is that there may be less diversity and more uniformity of technological knowledge and skills across firms and countries. As discussed above, uncertainty about technological developments may encourage firms to focus their R & D on similar areas. This tendency towards uniformity may be encouraged by co-operation. However, it could be argued that co-operation resolves this particular uncertainty and so a collaborative structure could allow for diversity. While this is theoretically possible, it seems unlikely for a nunber of reasons.

If firms are collaborating in R & D, this may involve particular institutional structures, hierarchies and decision-making procedures. This lack of structural diversity may encourage inflexibility and consensus decision-making. Change in structures or in participants may be difficult. Furthermore, one major stimulus to co-operation is to economize on costs and to benefit from scale economies. A different, more costly, project may be undertaken through collaboration, but there will not be diversity across firms. Some of the models, discussed above, imply that the free market will involve duplication and lack of diversity. However, not only may some duplication be a necessary, desirable part of the innovation process, but firms can also only consciously duplicate or copy each other's activities if they have the relevant information. Through collaboration, firms will be much more aware of each other's technological knowledge, and will come to share the same knowledge base. If there is a limit to the amount of information that firms can store and use, then collaboration is again liable to lead to uniformity, and firm-specificity of technological knowledge will decrease in importance.

There is a limit to which collaboration can reduce uncertainty about R & D efforts and their effect on future technological developments since collaborative ventures are unlikely to include all competitors. The pressure still remains for an RJV, therefore, to reduce uncertainty further by attempting to work in similar areas to competitors. The pressure to uniformity are likely to be reinforced by attempts to imitate and copy Japan's institutional structures and modes of promoting research co-operation. The Japanese system has frequently been praised for managing to combine co-operation and competition. By achieving consensus, Japanese firms reduce the risks facing them individually, as they develop and invest in certain technologies and industries. However, it has been argued that while Japan may be good at incremental innovation, it may not have such strengths with respect to radical innovation (Imai and Itami 1984). If other countries increasingly attempt to follow paths similar to Japan, then the potential problems Japan may face - precisely due to its consensus features - may be reduced. In other words, if Japan establishes a consensus, and other countries follow this, there will be less diversity and so less chance that there will be major technological developments in areas which Japan is unfamiliar with. Thus, as Yamamura (1986) suggests, there may be both high risks but possible advantages to delay in copying Japan's strategy with respect to co-operation in high technology, and possibly in adopting a different approach, such as greater reliance on the market. A strategy of diversity may be highly risky for any one country but it could be socially as well as privately rewarding.

To express this point somewhat differently, while the notion of a given natural trajectory may be misleading for a number of reasons, firms may be concerned to act as if such trajectories exist, in order to end up in a similar part of the technological spectrum as other firms. As Fusfeld and Haklisch (1985) say, in discussing US co-operative research,

> "the level of technical effort...is high enough to influence the direction of research in related fields."

Japanese policy may be interpreted as guiding firms towards a particular technological paradigm to reduce the uncertainty and risks that diversity would entail. The more there is consensus with respect to the area or nature of the likely development of technology, the more this is likely to be self-fulfilling. Given spillovers and interdependencies, progress is more likely if firms and other research organisations are all working in a given area. Suppliers and users will then be working on connected problems and areas; university scientists may start thinking with respect to those particular problems and so on. Once such interdependencies develop, the returns to one innovation or area may appear considerably greater than to another area that would require very different interdependencies and have different implications than those with which the current consensus is familiar. The pressures towards conformity may then be strong. This may be undesirable in that options may be ignored or left behind that would, in fact, have been preferable (Arthur 1987). While there will be benefits to the interdependencies described, which means we must accept some irreversibility, there are difficult and unresolved questions here about the nature and extent of the trade-offs between flexibility and diversity versus interdependencies and commitment. While the individual firm may increase its flexibility by co-operation with other firms, overall - at industry or economy level - flexibility is likely to be reduced.

5. FUTURE PATTERNS OF GLOBAL COMPETITION

The increasing interdependence of firms and countries, and the increasing internationalisation of markets and of technologies is resulting in many pressures for change in economic organizations and in the pattern of competition. Co-operative research is occuring both nationally and internationally as a response to these pressures. At the same time, the changing relationships between firms (and between firms and other institutions) affect the patterns of global competition and the nature of technological developments. The likely structure of corporations and the likely pattern of future global competition is not clear, but current trends and developments suggest various possibilities.

Two different scenarios of future competitions among the advanced industrial economies are frequently envisaged. The first is one where asymmetries between countries or at least between the three blocs - US, Japan and West Europe - are important and where Japan is increasingly dominant. The second is where there is some rough symmetry between the three blocs, with competition between and co-operation within the blocs. Neither of these scenarios, as commonly described, takes fully into account the implications of the increasing interdependence of firms and countries. We first briefly consider these scenarios and then turn to the implications for them of increasing interdependence. Finally, we consider the potential effects of increased uniformity of innovation and technological knowledge on international competition.

The first scenario envisages that the likely outcome of increasing internationalisation and intensified competition is an increasing asymmetry between countries with Japan as the technological leader. Japan's success in catching up with, and in some cases overtaking, the US and Western Europe is well documented. However, disagreement still exists about the role of government policy in this performance relative to Japan's entrepreneurial skills or relative to other economic characteristics of the Japanese economy, which would anyway, it is argued, have tended to lead to high growth. Similarly, there are also disagreements as to whether Japan is going to be equally successful in dominating technological developments now it too is at the frontier (for opposite views on this, see Yamamura 1986, Freeman 1987).

Freeman (1987) stresses the many advantages of what he calls Japan's national system of innovation. The role of MITI is seen as of considerable importance both in the past and for future activities. Freeman also argues that the balance between competition and co-ordination, between consensus and long-run planning and market forces, must be understood to comprehend the success of the Japanese system. He considers that this system is particularly well-suited to the adoption and diffusion of information technology. If other countries are to compete, then they, too, must adopt and develop some of the key features of the Japanese national technology system.

In contrast, Yamamura (1986) argues that Japan faces many more difficulties now it is a large, and technologically advanced, industrial power. He considers that Japan has lost much of its previous policy flexibility and the effectiveness of its administrative guidance has been diminished. Whether MITI is capable of orchestrating and directing high technology developments in the future, is , therefore, open to doubt. Furthermore, the consensus approach may not be the ideal means of tackling major technological development (Imai and Itami 1984).

To the extent that countries are increasingly interdependent, and the speed of technology transfer is increasing - and where a strategy of fast second may be more and more effective - the ability of Japan to pull ahead as a clear technological leader may seem in doubt. However, this depends not only on technological developments, but on performance in all other aspects of production and sales. Reich and Mankin (1986) argue with respect to the US that "joint ventures give away our future". From the analysis of a number of joint ventures between US and Japanese firms, they conclude that these have tended to involve transfer of knowledge and learning experience form the US to Japan. The US partners, they say, tend to assemble, sell and market Japanese products, but are often not involved in component design and production, experience of which is necessary to future innovative ability. However, as they point out, joint ventures need not take this form. Given the increasing number of research joint ventures and other forms of co-operation within the US, it might seem unlikely that US firms would only engage in international joint ventures that impeded their future innovative abilities.

It is common for arguments about the dominance of Japan to go on to suggest that, with appropriate policies and behaviour by governments and firms, the US or Western Europe could reduce the Japanese challenge and compete more equally - the second scenario. This is clear in Freeman's and in Reich and Mankin's argument. It is an implicit or explicit argument behind much recent joint research, EC-organised co-operative R & D programmes and other such activities. Having caught up with Japan, then the US, Japan and West Europe would compete on equal terms on the basis of a rough technological parity - at least in 'strategic' industries - and with offsetting specific competitive advantages in non-strategic industries. However, is this a likely outcome given current trends, and is it desirable ? Nelson (1984) states

> "in the nature of the case, five countries cannot all be first in the product cycle race, and the competition appears to have reduced the size of the prize and increased the costs of entry."

A common argument is that a key means of improving European competitiveness is to move swiftly to integrate the European market - thus, both providing European firms with a large domestic market comparable to the US and Japan, and ensuring a sufficient degree of competition (see, for example, Geroski and Jacquemin 1985). While this may be an important step - though there are arguments against it - it is not straightforward that this would directly help European firms more than US or Japanese firms and it is particularly unlikely that this would result in some sort of 'Europe Inc.' (Linton 1987) to compete with the US and Japan. Ideally, presumably, we would observe both co-operation and competition between European firms (supposedly the Japanese model) and then fierce competition with Japan and the US. However, in a world of increasing internationalisation and interdependence, it is not clear how 'Europe Inc.' is supposed to arise. Furthermore, these types of argument seem to presuppose that potentially we can all be Japans, that there is an attainable growth process whereby all of the three blocs benefit from ongoing technological competition and from roughly equal output and productivity growth. From previous historical experience this seems unlikely. If current trends towards internationalisation were reversed, then it is conceivable we might observe co-operation in R & D in Europe, in Japan and in the US, and competition between the three blocs. However, in this case the ability to promote the right mix of co-operation and competition within one's bloc may be crucial. If the three blocs did come out of this race technologically equal, then the severity of competition may result in little opportunity to appropriate any returns to innovation. Such a situation may not be very stable and a dominant area may again re-emerge. Who is first or second in the race may be crucial, though, again, it is not necessarily clear which is the desirable position.

Current trends are, however, towards the increasing internationalisation and interdependence of firms, markets and countries. This can be seen, in part, as a result of pressures of global competition and in part as stimulated by technological developments. The last two decades have seen a major expansion of multinational activities, with a larger number of countries being the home of MNEs, and with MNEs investing and expanding in old and new markets, in particular, in the advanced industrial countries. The Japanese market has been least susceptible to penetration by imports or by foreign direct investment, but this situation is changing. The size of the Japanese market and the base it provides for Japanese firms, means that US and European firms cannot afford to let this market go unchallenged. However, as we have already discussed, increasing international investment and international operations are not the only sources of internationalisation and interdependence across countries. International joint ventures and co-operation in research, production, marketing and distribution have also developed as a means to increase firms' competitiveness and to ensure their access to all the Triad markets (Ohmae 1985).

The increasing internationalisation of firms and national and international interdependence of firms has also been encouraged by technological developments. Firstly, as has frequently been discussed, rapid technological change in transport and communications has both made international operations more feasible - technically and economically - and tended to reinforce trends towards similarity in markets in terms of consumers' demands. Secondly technological trends, as well as competitive pressures, are leading firms to link up to exploit complementarities in their technological abilities. The scope for such links has increased as more and more countries have caught up with the US technologically (Rosenberg 1981). Rosenberg envisages a scenario where different firms and countries contribute different parts of a product, undermining the conventional notion of an industry and leading to the possibility of "entirely new patterns of specialization at the common technological frontier". Newly industrialising countries may also be able to fit into 'niches' in parts of high technology industries. In such a world, Rosenberg suggests, the concepts of technology gaps or technological leadership may not apply either to industries or to countries. This is a similar outlook to that implied by Ohmae (1985) where firms from different countries need to link up to gain a competitive position in the Triad markets of the US, Japan and Western Europe, thus undermining the concept of firm-specific or country leadership. Nelson (1984) also stressed that "increasingly, technological knowledge and capability are international rather than national". He argues that while the connectedness of complex technological systems means that

> "Companies do need broad-gauged competence to compete in complex, connected, fast-moving fields, companies in such fields are increasingly multinational. And joint ventures of a relatively broad and long-lived nature will become increasingly important, further blurring national lines."
>
> (Nelson 1984, p. 76)

In such a global, interconnected economy, the concept of the competitiveness of a particular economy or group of economies becomes increasingly complex. Competitiveness will still depend in part on which firms locate in an economy and what they produce. However, if global interdependencies predominate, then no economy may encompass the whole of one industry or even the whole of one product. Demand for output of firms in a given economy will then also depend on the competitiveness of firms in other economies that are producing other parts of the same product. In addition, firms' success will also depend on their global network, not on their performance in any single economy alone. The success of firms is then neither fully dependent on one economy nor, importantly, is it sufficient for, or a guarantee of, economic success to any one economy. Put simply, the overall health of the economy will depend, in part, on how good it is at producing its part of various products and on the value of those 'parts' relative to other parts. It will also depend on the international activities both of firms located in its economy and of firms not located in its economy. The concept of competitiveness does not completely disappear but it becomes more complex; in particular, any simplistic notions of competitiveness of an economy are undermined. Country-specific variables will still have some impact - income levels, natural resources, infrastructure, education, training, etc. - but these are only one part of a complex picture of global interrelationships :

> "governments act as if they did not see clearly the increasingly international nature of capabilities in high technology industries, or as if, like King Canute, they could preserve their own technological islands from the seas."
>
> (Nelson 1984)

How does the nature of the two scenarios and the nature of technological competition alter in such an interdependent world ? As we have argued, the notion of competitiveness of an economy becomes increasingly difficult to pin down. There may be no reason to expect that any one economy will be dominant in such a world. This does not imply equality between areas will be the most likely outcome. Rather, it implies that areas of economic success - and failure - will not necessarily be clearly economy-specific or even location-specific. However, we would still expect to observe some synergies and spillovers from firms locating in the same area. These synergies will depend partly on the benefits each firm gains from other firms locating there and partly on area and/or country characteristics. It is possible, therefore, that we may observe both intra- and inter-country synergies. This might allow for the possibility of Japan being dominant in an interdependent world. The more that Japan can dictate technological developments, the less that may be gained from inter-country synergies, and the more unequal these may be. It remains unlikely that rough parity among the advanced countries would be observed since this would require all countries to have, and to benefit to a similar extent from, intra-country synergies and inter-country synergies. Variety in technology is necessary for any chance of rough parity among countries - unless a country attempts to disengage completely from world markets. If technology becomes increasingly global, through the combination of increasing collaborative R & D and increasing interdependencies between firms, the ability to control or to determine the competitiveness of a single economy - or in the European case, group of economies - becomes increasingly weak.

Increasing interdependency, therefore, has major implications for future patterns of global competition and competitiveness. If this picture of increasing interdependence is valid, the system as a whole could be quite fragile, in that dislocation or crisis of any kind in one area would feed through fairly swiftly to other areas. If we add to this scenario the tendency of collaborative R & D to lead to uniformity in technological knowledge, then a situation can be envisaged where technological competition is of minor importance to global market structures and performance.

Current policies encourage collaborative R & D, yet the more important collaboration becomes, the more it is likely to undermine technological competition, and to undermine the ability to have any policy control with respect to an economy. If there is increasing uniformity in research aims and efforts, combined with internationalisation of research and other activities, this may have major implications for the nature of global competition. In the extreme, if firms have similar research aims, if imitation is quick and knowledge diffuses fast, then competition, within the advanced industrial countries at least, will no longer depend directly on innovation, and will come to depend increasingly on other aspects of the competitive process - particularly advertising, marketing and distribution. Thus, innovative competition may become relatively unimportant both within and between the blocs. In effect, we would be faced with a reversal of Schumpeter - no longer is innovation the key aspect of competition. This is not to say innovation is no longer necessary to firms, rather that it is not directly through innovation that they can expect to derive their competitive advantage. As we argued above, this is for two reasons. Firstly, co-operation in R & D may be likely to encourage uniformity among participating firms. Secondly, there will be pressures to reduce uncertainty further by focussing R & D on areas similar to other collaborative groups. If one group did produce a clearly superior innovation then the exent to which it would derive a competitive advantage from this will depend on the speed of imitation and the ease or difficulty of preventing spillovers. The existence of other co-operating groups may seriously impede appropriability, such that any competitive advantage based on the innovation alone will be short-lived and profitability of the innovation will be curtailed.

This lack of, or reduced, profitability does not remove the pressure to innovate, due to the existence of more than one co-operating group, but it does sharply reduce expected profitability of innovating. This may reinforce pressures towards co-operation and towards co-operating groups. It may also increase the importance to firms of keeping price competition at bay - through implicit collusion, advertising, exclusive marketing ties, etc. If there are perceived to be few advantages of being first in innovation, then this may slow the pace of innovation, as firms attempt to retain their ability to imitate swiftly, but do not push to be first, given the probable greater costs of being first (Mansfield et al. 1981).

In such a world of increased uniformity of technological knowledge, co-operative R & D, and competition through means other than innovation, the scope for oligopolistic collusion and dominance must be high. This is reinforced by firms' increasing tendency to build links with each other across global markets. To the extent that global organisation and the ability to penetrate all major Triad markets becomes a central part of competitiveness, then the potential for concerted activities and for market dominance grows.

The pressures resulting in increased co-operation may, of course, change. If we accept the argument that a major shift in technological paradigm is occuring based on information technology (Freeman 1987), then once this shift has occurred, costs and risks of innovation may fall. However, by that stage, major structural changes would have resulted due to firms' co-operation in R & D and other activities. It is possible that pressures for increased co-operation may reverse more quickly. Nelkin and Nelson (1986) argue that as the US deficit is reduced and the dollar falls there is likely to be a reduction in university-industry co-operation. However, this does not imply a reversal of all pressures and trends towards internationalisation and interdependence of firms.

6. CONCLUSION

This paper has considered some of the forces leading to increased co-operation and collaboration in R & D. These developments are occurring in the context of a changing world economy, where firms are becoming increasingly international and interdependent. Various implications of these developments have been analysed. It was argued, in particular, that increasing co-operative R & D may have adverse effects on innovation and future innovation possibilities. The possibility was raised that global competitiveness may come to depend less on innovative advantage and more on other aspects of firms' behaviour and performance. As economies, and firms, become more interdependent, the nature and structure of international competition and specialisation was considered likely to alter radically. The full implications of such developments are complex, but there are potentially serious issues and problems here with respect to innovation, with respect to the dominance and power of international firms and, more generally, with respect to the stability and fragility of the international economy.

REFERENCES

ARTHUR, B. (1987), "Competing technologies : An Overview", Mimeo.

BRAGGAR, H. (1984), "Major US Firms Announce Participation in ESPRIT", Computer world, Vol. 18, No. 46, p. 46.

DASGUPTA, P. and E. MASKIN (1987), "The Simple economics of Research Portfolios", Economic Journal, Vol. 97, pp. 581-95.

EDGE, G. (1985), "Using Outsiders to Develop Products and Processes", Accountancy, Vol. 96, No. 1102, pp. 127-8.

EUROTEC (1987), Number S5-87, "Technology in Europe", Commission of the European Communities.

FREEMAN, C. (1987), Technology Policy and Economic Performance, Pinter, London.

FUSFELD, H. and C. HAKLISCH (1985), "Co-operative R & D for Competitors", Harvard Business Review, November-December, pp. 60-76.

GEROSKI, P. and A. JACQUEMIN (1985), "Industrial Change, Barriers to Mobility and European Industrial Policy", Economic Policy, Vol. 1, pp. 170-218.

Government-University-Industry Research Roundtable (1986), New Alliances and Partnerships in American Science and engineering, National academy Press, Washington DC.

GROSCH, H. (1985), "Cheaper by the dozen : Joining Together in the computer Jungle", Management technology, Vol. 2, No. 12, pp. 52-6.

GROSSMAN, G. and C. SHAPIRO (1987), "Dynamic R & D Competition", Economic Journal, June, pp. 372-86.

HARGREAVES-HEAP, S. and K. HUGHES (1986), "Flexibility, Uncertainty and Success in R & D", Mimeo.

HILL, R. (1983), "The German Giant Struggles to Stay Light on Its Feet", International Management, Vol. 38, No. 10, pp. 40-7.

HLADIK, K. (1985), International Joint Ventures, D.C. Heath & Co., Lexington, Mass.

HUNNINGS, M. (1986), "Company Co-operation : A New Framework", European Trends, No. 2, pp. 44-8.

IMAI, K.I. and H. ITAMI (1984), "Interpenetration of Organisation and Market", International Journal of Industrial Organisation, Vol. 2, pp. 285-310.

JACQUEMIN, A. (1987), "Collusive Behaviour, R & D, and European Policy", Economic Papers, No. 61, Commission of the European Communities.

KATZ, M. (1986), "An Analysis of Co-operative Research and Development", Rand Journal of economics, Vol. 17, No. 4, pp. 527-43.

KLEIN, E. (1986), "Managing Assets : Synergy Strategy", D & B Reports, Vol. 34, No. 3, pp. 22-5.

KOLODZIEJ, S. (1987), "US R & D Consortia growing to Counter Foreign Threat", Computerworld, Vol. 21, No. 27A, p. 15.

LINTON, P. (1987), "Global Perspectives : Europe Inc.", Management Review, Vol. 76, No. 4, pp. 60-62.

MANSFIELD, E., SCHWARTZ, M. and S. WAGNER (1981), "Imitation Costs and Patents : An Empirical Study", Economic Journal, Vol. 91, December, pp. 907-18.

MOWERY, D. (1987), Alliance Politics and Economics, AEI/Ballinger.

NELKIN, D. and R. NELSON (1986), "commentary" in New Alliances and Partnership in American Science and Engineering, National Academy Press, Washington DC.

NELSON, R. (1982), "The Role of Knowledge in R & D Efficiency", Quarterly Journal of Economics, Vol. 97, No. 3, pp. 453-70.

NELSON, R. (1984), High Technology Policies - A Five Nation Comparison, AEI, Washington DC.

OHMAE, K. (1985), Triad Power, The Free Press, New York.

ORDOVER, J. and R. WILLIG (1985), "Anti-Trust for High Technology Industries", Journal of Law and Economics, Vol. 28, pp. 311-33.

PATEL, P. and K. PAVITT (1987), "Is Western Europe Losing the Technologic Race ?", Research Policy, Vol. 16, Nos. 2-4, pp. 59-86.

PORTER, M. (ed.) (1986), Competition in Global Industries, Harvard Business School Press.

POSNER, B. (1985), "Strategic Alliances", Inc., Vol. 7, No. 6, pp. 74-80.

REICH, R. and E. MANKIN (1986), "Joint Ventures with Japan Give Away Our Future", Harvard Business Review, March-April, pp. 78-86.

ROSENBERG, N. (1982), Inside the Black Box : Technology and Economics, Ch. 12, Cambridge University Press, Cambridge.

ROSENBERG, N. and C. FRISCHTAK (eds.) (1985), International Technology Transfer, Praeger, New York.

ROTHWELL, R. (1983), "Innovation and Firm Size : A Case for Dynamic Complementarity : Or is Small Really so Beautiful ?", Journal of General Management, Vol. 8, No. 3, pp. 5-25.

SHEPHERD, G., DUCHENE, F. and C. SAUNDERS (eds.) (1983), Europe's Industries, Frances Pinter, London.

SNYDER, D. and D. BLEVINS (1986), "Business and University Technical Research Co-operation : Some Important Issues", Journal of Product Innovation Management, Vol. 3, No. 2, pp. 136-44.

TAYLOR, R. (1986), "US Firms Benefit From EC Programs", Europe, No. 27, pp. 24-5.

TEECE, D. (1977), 'Technology Transfer by Multinational Firms : The Resource Cost of Transferring Technological Know-How", Economic Journal, Vol. 87, pp. 242-61.

TEECE, D. (1981), "The Market For Know-How and the Efficient International Transfer of Technology", Annals, No. 458, pp. 81-96.

VICKERS, J. (1985), "Pre-emptive Patenting, Joint Ventures and the Persistence of Oligopoly", International Journal of Industrial Organisation, Vol. 3, No. 3, pp. 261-73.

YAMAMURA, K. (1986), "Caveat Emptor : The Industrial Policy of Japan", in Krugman, P. (ed.), Strategic Trade Policy and the New International Economics, MIT Press, Cambridge, Mass.

The Convergence of International and Domestic Markets
D.B. Audretsch, L. Sleuwaegen, and H. Yamawaki (Editors)

11. MARKET SIZE, MONOPOLY POWER AND INNOVATIONS UNDER UNCERTAINTY

Manfred Neumann
University of Erlangen-Nürnberg

0. INTRODUCTION

This paper aims at developing a unified theoretical framework encompassing a variety of factors usually invoked ad hoc to explaining technological change emerging from research and development. The point of vantage is a firm maximizing expected present value of the future cash flow by selecting the level of employment of labor and investment in both physical capital and research and development. The single firm acts as Cournot oligopolist both with respect to output and to R&D effort. The outcome is subject to uncertainty which can arise in two different ways. First, the "innovation production function" may be stochastic. Second, demand may be governed by a random process.

The method employed is stochastic optimal control. I can build on prior work of Pindyck (1982) who, in treating a similar problem, disregarded technological change, however. He was furthermore unable to find unequivocal results because the third derivative of the adjustment cost function could not be signed unambiguously. By replacing the cost function by a dual production function to account for adjustment costs unambiguous results can be obtained. Pindyck used a stochastic analogue of the calculus of variations. I shall instead employ the more transparent Stochastic Maximum Principle.

Optimal R&D effort will be shown to depend on the size of the market, monopoly power, and uncertainty. The rest of the paper is organized as follows. The model is set up in section 1. Section 2 provides the solution to the stochastic optimization problem. In sections 3 and 4 the deterministic case and the stochastic one are compared to show how monopoly power, the size of the market and uncertainty affect the solution. In section 5 diversification is considered. Section 6 offers some additional interpretation, and the final section 7 contains a summary and some conclusions regarding the consequences of completing the internal market in Europe.

1. THE MODEL

The production technology of the firm under consideration is described by assumption

<u>A1</u> : Production $q = F(K,AL)$ depends on capital K and labor L where A is an efficiency parameter. F is linearly homogenous and strictly quasi concave.

The firm's capital stock evolves deterministically according to

$$(1) \quad dK = (h(I) - \delta K)dt$$

where δ is a constant rate of depreciation. That implies perfect malleability of capital. As a matter of simplification it is thus assumed that any change in technology can be incorporated in the existing stock of capital.

Since installing of a new piece of equipment involves adjustment costs the stock of physical capital is raised by $h(I)$, which is a fraction of gross investment, I. The function $h(I)$ is subject to assumption

<u>A2</u> : $h(0) = 0$, $h'(I) > 0$ and $h''(I) < 0$ for all $I > 0$, and $h'''(I)$ does not change sign.

That implies $h'''(I) > 0$. To prove this lemma assume the opposite $h'''(I) \le 0$. In this case $h'(I)$ will become negative at some finite I > 0 which contradicts <u>A2</u>. An illustration is provided in Figure 1.

FIGURE 1

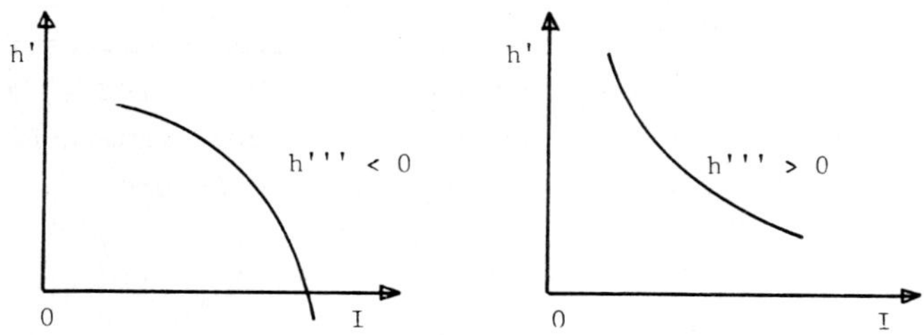

To justify the crucial assumption that $h'''(I)$ must not change sign consider Figure 2, where h''' changes sign once.

Figure 2

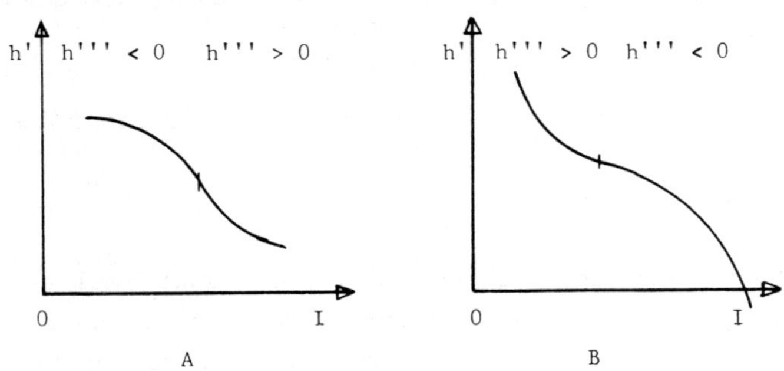

Obviously $h'' < 0$ is predicated on the assumption that investment draws on some fixed resource.

In Panel A h''' changes in such a way that the force of the law of diminishing returns becomes less severe as the level of investment increases in a particular period. That is counter-intuitive since diminishing returns are due to an increasing scarcity of some hidden resource. Economic intuition suggests that scarcity becomes more severe upon an increase in investment. Hence the case depicted in Panel A can be discarded. The alternative case illustrated in Panel B cannot be accepted either because $h'(I)$ becomes negative at some finite $I > 0$. Cases where h''' changes sign more than once can be discarded by a similar reasoning.[1]

The technology changes according to the stochastic differential equation

$$(2) \quad dA = a(r)Adt + \sigma_A A dz_A$$

where $z_A(t)$ is a Wiener process, and $(\sigma_A A)^2$ is the variance of $A(t)$.

The drift term, $a(r)$, can be affected by R&D effort, where $r := R/AL$ is R&D expenditure R per efficiency unit of labor. The results of R&D are assumed to be appropriable under a patent system.

Output net of R&D expenditure is given by $F(K,AL) - rAL$. Obviously net output is linearly homogeneous in K and L, provided r is constant. It will be shown in due course that a steady state with a constant r exists. That implies that in the long run constant returns to scale apply. Thus competition is viable.

The impact of R&D effort on the drift term is summarized by assumption

<u>A3</u> : Let $a'(r) > 0$, $a''(r) < 0$ for all $r > 0$, and $a'''(r)$ does not change sign.

That implies $a'''(r) > 0$. The proof can be omitted since it is analogous to the one provided for the lemma implied by <u>A2</u>.

The variance of $A(t)$ reflects uncertainties associated with research and development and the use of the results. Given appropriability by obtaining a patent a rival may be faster and may pre-empt the opportunity to obtain a property right in a particular invention for the firm under consideration. Thus increasing rivalness in R&D may augment the uncertainty.

Firm k faces a demand function characterized by assumption

<u>A4</u> : The inverse demand function $p(Q,\theta)$ with $Q = \Sigma_k q_k$ obeys $\partial p/\partial Q < 0$, $\partial p/\partial \theta > 0$ where $\theta(t)$ is stochastic according to the differential equation

$$(3) \quad d\theta = g\theta dt + \sigma_\theta \theta dz_\theta$$

where $z_\theta(t)$ is a Wiener process, and $(\sigma_\theta \theta)^2$ is the variance of $\theta(t)$.[2] It reflects unpredictable changes in demand in a case of a downward sloping curve and of the price in the case of perfect competition. An unforeseen imposition of a tariff, the introduction of non-tariff-barriers or other government interventions, and exchange rate volatility are important examples.

To simplify the index k will be dropped if a misunderstanding can be ruled out. Hence q refers to production of the individual firm under consideration.

It will further be assumed that

<u>A5</u> : The processes $z_A(t)$ and $z_\theta(t)$ are stochastically independent.

The firm attempts to maximize cash flow, discounted at the prevailing rate of interest, i, which is assumed to be constant,

$$(4) \quad E\int_0^\infty \pi(t)e^{-it}\,dt$$

by choosing employment L(t), the level of investment I(t), and R&D expenditures per efficiency unit of labor, r(t).

The firm's instantaneous profit is given by

$$(5) \quad \pi(t) = p(Q,\theta)q - wL - vI - rAL$$

where w is the wage rate and v is the constant purchase price of a unit of gross investment, and $q = F(K,AL)$ according to <u>A1</u>.

Finally, regarding the domain of the various variables, let

A6 : $K(t), L(t), A(t), I(t), r(t) \geq 0$.

2. THE SOLUTION

The optimal value function of the present problem is given by

$$J(K,A,\theta,t_0) = \max_{(L,I,r)} E \int_0^{\infty} \pi(t)e^{-it}\, dt$$

which, upon using the multiplication rules implied by Ito's Lemma[3], gives rise to the fundamental Hamilton-Jacobi-Bellman equation of stochastic control theory (cf. Malliaris and Brock 1982, p. 114),

$$-J_t(K,A,\theta,t) = \max_{(L,I,r)} \{\pi(t)e^{-it} + J_K(h(I) - \delta K) + J_A a(r)A$$

$$+ J_\theta g\theta + \frac{1}{2} J_{AA} (\sigma_A A)^2 + \frac{1}{2} J_{\theta\theta} (\sigma_\theta \theta)^2\}.$$

Now define $\psi_1 := J_K$, $\psi_2 := J_A$, $\psi_3 := J_\theta$, and $\psi_j := e^{-it}y_j$, $(j = 1,2,3,)$, where y_j are current value adjoint variables. Then $d\psi_j = (dy_j - iy_j dt)e^{-it}$.

Furthermore define the current value Hamiltonian,

$$H := \pi(t) + y_1(h(I) - \delta K) + y_2 a(r)A + y_3 g\theta$$

$$+ \frac{1}{2} \frac{\partial y_2}{\partial A} (\sigma_A A)^2 + \frac{1}{2} \frac{\partial y_3}{\partial \theta} (\sigma_\theta \theta)^2.$$

The Stochastic Maximum Principle, as applied to the present case, requires that H be maximized with respect to L, I, and r. That yields $H^\circ = \max_{(L,I,r)} H$.

It is furthermore required (see Appendix), that

(6a) $(1/dt)\, E\, dy_1 = (iy_1 - \partial H^\circ/\partial K)$

$$(6b) \quad (1/dt)\, E\, dy_2 = (iy_2 - \partial H^{\circ}/\partial A) \,.$$

Maximization of H implies

$$(7) \quad \partial H/\partial L = MR.F_L - w - rA = 0$$

$$(8) \quad \partial H/\partial I = -v + y_1 h'(I) = 0$$

$$(9) \quad \partial H/\partial r = (-L + y_2 a'(r))A = 0$$

where MR := p(1-m) is marginal revenue, and $m = s(1+\lambda)/\epsilon$ is the Lerner-Index of monopolistic market power, as determined by market share, s, conjectural variation, λ, and the price elasticity of demand (cf. Cowling and Waterson 1976). Second order conditions are satisfied by A1, A2, A3, and A4.

Partial derivatives of H with respect to K and A are

$$\frac{\partial H}{\partial K} = MR.F_K - \delta y_1$$

$$\frac{\partial H}{\partial A} = MR.F_L \frac{L}{A} - rL + y_2 a + \frac{\partial y_2}{\partial A} \sigma_A^2 A.$$

Inserting into equations (6a) and (6b) yields

$$(10a) \quad (1/dt)\, E\, dy_1 = (i + \delta)y_1 - MR.F_K$$

$$(10b) \quad (1/dt)\, E\, dy_2 = (i - a)y_2 + rL - MR.F_L \frac{L}{A} - \frac{\partial y_2}{\partial A} \sigma_A^2 A$$

which depicts the expected development of the adjoint variables y_1 and y_2.

In order to obtain differential equations for the controls I(t) and r(t) we use equations (8) and (9) to eliminate y_1 and y_2. We get

$$dy_1 = -\, v d[h'(I)]/[h'(I)]^2$$

$$dy_2 = [dL/L - d(a'(r))/a'(r)]\, L/a'(r).$$

Note that I(t) and r(t) are stochastic since along an optimal path $I^* = r(K,A,\theta)$ and $r^* = r(K,A,\theta)$, where A(t) and θ(t) are stochastic.

Then

$$d(h'(I)) = h''(I)dI + \frac{1}{2} h'''(I) (dI)^2$$

$$d(a'(r)) = a''(r)dr + \frac{1}{2} a'''(r) (dr)^2.$$

Using the multiplication rules implied by Ito's Lemma, yields

$$(dI)^2 = [(I_A \sigma_A A)^2 + (I_\theta \sigma_\theta \theta)^2] dt$$

$$(dr)^2 = [(r_A \sigma_A A)^2 + (r_\theta \sigma_\theta \theta)^2] dt$$

where I_A, r_A, I_θ and r_θ denote partial derivatives.

Both terms in square brackets are clearly positive. After collecting terms one arrives at

$$\text{(11a)} \quad (1/dt)\, E\, dI = -\frac{(h')^2}{vh''} \{(i + \delta) \frac{v}{h'} - MR.F_K + \frac{1}{2} \frac{vh'''(I)}{(h')^2} [(I_A \sigma_A A)^2 + (I_\theta \sigma_\theta \theta)^2]\}$$

$$\text{(11b)} \quad (1/dt)\, E\, dr = -\frac{a'(r)}{a''(r)} \{[i - a(r) - \frac{(1/dt)E\, dL}{L}] + ra'(r) - MR.\frac{F_L}{A} a'(r) - \frac{A\, \partial y_2}{y_2 \partial A} \sigma_A^2 + \frac{1}{2} \frac{a'''(r)}{a'(r)} [(r_A \sigma_A A)^2 + (r_\theta \sigma_\theta \theta)^2]\}$$

which in conjuction with equation (7) describes the expected development of the controls. The optimal path is influenced by both kinds of uncertainty, as reflected in the variance of demand, $(\sigma_\theta \theta)^2$, and of the succes of R&D effort, $(\sigma_A A)^2$.

3. THE DETERMINISTIC CASE

To evaluate the impact of uncertainty and to identify the influence of market size and monopolistic market power it is most convenient to firstly look at the special case of a deterministic solution, i.e., the case where all terms in (11a) and (11b) associated with σ_θ and σ_A disappear. It shall furthermore be assumed that adjustment costs do not arise. Hence $h(I) \equiv I$. In that case equations (11a) and (11b) boil down to

$$(12a) \quad (i + \delta)v - MR.f'(x) = 0$$

$$(12b) \quad dr/dt = (-a'^2/a'') \{(i-a-n)/a' + r - MR. [f(x) - xf'(x)]\}$$

where $x := K/AL$ and $n := (1/L)dL/dt$.

A steady state solution is depicted in Figure 3.

FIGURE 3

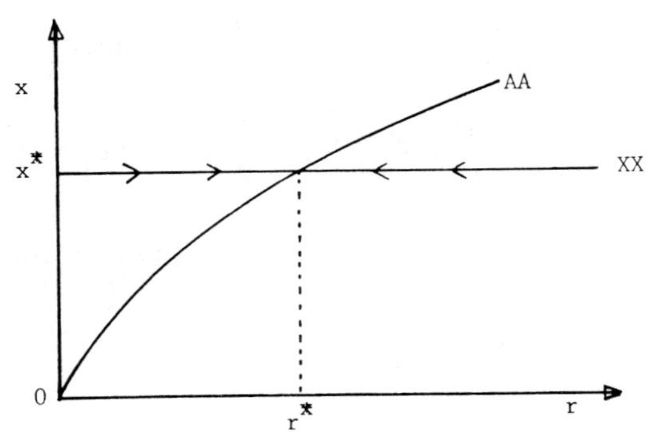

Equation (12a) is graphically given by the schedule XX which, at a given user cost of capital, $(i+\delta)v$, uniquely determines x^*. Since adjustment is not costly x^* will be attained all the time.

Equation (12b) is depicted by the schedule AA. Since

$$\frac{\partial x}{\partial r} = \frac{(i-a-n)(a''/a'^2)}{MR.xf''}$$

it is sloping upward if i-a-n > 0, which is necessary to ensure finiteness of the present value of cash flow at a steady state. As pF(K,AL) - wL - vI - rAL = [pf(x) - w/A - v(K/K + δ)x - r]AL, and the term in square brackets is constant at a steady state, cash flow grows at the rate $a(r^*) + n^*$.

As can be seen from Figure 3 an equilibrium exists at the point of intersection of schedules XX and AA.[4]

Raising the rate of interest entails a lower x^*. Thus the XX schedule shifts down and the AA schedule shifts upwards because from [i-a-n] (1/a) + r - MR.(f-xf') = 0, at a given r, $\partial x/\partial i = -1/a'.MR.xf'' > 0$. Consequently the optimal rate of R&D per efficiency unit of labor decreases and the rate of productivity is reduced as shown in Figure 4.

FIGURE 4

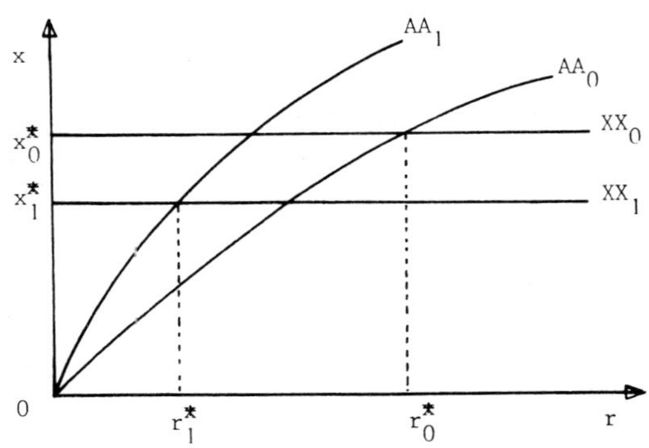

Hence we have

<u>Proposition 1</u> : In the absence of uncertainty and adjustment costs raising the user cost of capital engenders a decline in R&D effort and technological progress.

The impact of both a change in monopoly power and of the size of the market can be appraised by using the total differential of equations (12a) and (12b), as evaluated at a steady state. Both variables affect marginal revenue. We can thus consider the effect of a change of MR, the rest of the exogenous variables being held constant.

$$\begin{bmatrix} MR.f'' & 0 \\ MR.xf'' & -(i-a-n)a''/a'^2 \end{bmatrix} \begin{bmatrix} dx \\ dr \end{bmatrix} = \begin{bmatrix} -f'dMR \\ (f-xf')dMR \end{bmatrix}$$

one obtains

$$\frac{\partial x}{\partial MR} = \frac{f'}{-\ MR.f''} > 0$$

$$\frac{\partial r}{\partial MR} = \frac{f}{-\ (i-a-n)a''/a'^2} > 0$$

Since marginal revenue is an increasing function of θ we have

$$\frac{\partial r}{\partial \theta} = \frac{\partial r}{\partial MR} \cdot \frac{\partial MR}{\partial \theta} > 0.$$

That yields

<u>Proposition 2</u> : An exogeneous expansion of demand engenders an increase in R&D effort and an augmented rate of technological progress.

Hence, expanding demand, i.e., $g > 0$, can be expected to give rise to increased innovative activity while in declining markets ($g < 0$) innovative activity will slow down.

If, upon an enlargement of the market, entry of new competitors occurs the individual demand curve shifts back to the left. In particular, in the case of perfect competition with completely free entry the market price falls back to equal average cost. Therefore, the acceleration of innovative activity engendered by an enlargement of the market turns out to be only a transitory one once entry occurs.

Marginal revenue declines upon an increase in monopoly power, as measured by the Lerner index m. Hence $\partial MR/\partial m < 0$ and consequently

$$\frac{\partial r}{\partial m} = \frac{\partial r}{\partial MR} \cdot \frac{\partial MR}{\partial m} < 0.$$

We thus obtain

Proposition 3 : Monopoly power exerts an adverse influence on R&D effort and innovations.

4. UNCERTAINTY

The impact of uncertainty can be appraised by checking whether the terms reflecting uncertainty have the same sign as the user cost of capital.

In equation (11a), since $h'''(I) > 0$, uncertainty works into the same direction as the user cost of capital. The XX schedule therefore is shifted down in consequence of uncertainty, as illustrated in Figure 4. The AA schedule is shifting upwards upon an increase in uncertainty since $\partial y_2/\partial A = e^{-it}J_{AA} < 0$ by concavity of the optimal value function and $a'''(r) > 0$ by A2. As shown in Figure 4 the optimal r^* declines upon increased uncertainty. That yields

Proposition 3 : Uncertainty reduces R&D effort and the rate of technological progress.

Notice that a depressing effect on innovative activities is engendered by both kinds of uncertainty.

5. DIVERSIFICATION

Diversification by selling into different markets can affect the magnitude of uncertainty and thus influence investment behaviour and innovative activity.

Let the firm face inverse functions $p_j(Q_j, \theta_j)$, $j = 1,2$ where $\theta_j(t)$ develops according to

$$d\theta_j = g_j \theta_j dt + \sigma_{\theta_j} \theta_j dz_j$$

The Wiener processes $z_j(t)$ may be stochastically interdependent with a coefficient of correlation $\rho_{12} \gtreqless 0$.

In this case, in the Hamilton-Jacobi-Bellman equation, the term πe^{-it} must be replace by $[\pi + \mu(F(K,AL) - q_1 - q_2)]e^{-it}$ where μ is a Lagrangian multiplier, and $\frac{1}{2} J_{\theta\theta}(\sigma_\theta \theta)^2$ must be replaced by

$$\frac{1}{2} J_{\theta_1\theta_1} (\sigma_{\theta_1} \theta_1)^2 + J_{\theta_1\theta_2} \sigma_{\theta_1} \sigma_{\theta_2} \rho_{12} \theta_1 \theta_2 + \frac{1}{2} J_{\theta_2\theta_2} (\sigma_{\theta_2} \theta_2)^2 .$$

Furthermore

$$(ds)^2 = [(s_{\theta_1} \sigma_{\theta_1} \theta_1)^2 + 2\, s_{\theta_1} s_{\theta_2} \sigma_{\theta_1} \sigma_{\theta_2} \rho_{12} \theta_1 \theta_2 + (s_{\theta_2} \sigma_{\theta_2} \theta_2)^2]$$

where $s := (I,r)$.

Since $s_{\theta 1}$ and $s_{\theta 2}$ are of equal sign the magnitude of $(ds)^2$ depends inter alia, on ρ_{12}.

If ρ_{12} is negative $(ds)^2$ is reduced and uncertainty is less harmful to innovative activity. In particular, if the case of exchange rate volatility the correlation coefficient is negative for a firm selling into both the domestic and foreign markets and those firms which maintain subsidiaries in various countries. Such a firm is thus less affected by exchange rate fluctuations than a firm selling only into a domestic market which is open to import competition.

6. INTERPRETATION

The model provides a new interpretation of a result which has usually been attributed to learning by doing. The learning curve suggested by that approach implies that average cost of production of firm k,

$$c_k = G\left(\int_{-\infty}^{t} q_k(\tau)d\tau\right), \qquad G'(.) < 0,$$

is a declining function of cumulative production of the past and

$$(13) \quad dc_k/dt = G'(.)q_k(t) < 0.$$

The same result is implied by the model of the present paper.

Recall that, according to Proposition 2, $\partial r/\partial\theta > 0$, which implies $\partial r/\partial\theta = r'(a)\partial a/\partial\theta > 0$. Hence,

$$(14) \quad a = \emptyset(\theta),\ \emptyset'(\theta) > 0$$

is an increasing function of θ.

Furthermore, from $p = p(Q,\theta)$, one obtains

$$(15) \quad \theta = b(p,Q),\ \partial b/\partial p > 0,\ \partial b/\partial Q > 0, \quad \text{and } Q = \Sigma_k q_k.$$

The cost function $C_k = c_k(i,w,A)q_k$ implies $\partial c_k/\partial A < 0$. Therefore, at some initial $t = t_0 = 0$, $dc_k/dt = (\partial c_k/\partial A)dA/dt$ and thus

$$(16) \quad dc_k/dt = (\partial c_k/\partial A)Aa \quad .$$

Collecting terms yields

$$dc_k/dt = (\partial c_k/\partial A)A\emptyset(b(p,\Sigma_k q_k))$$

or

$$dc_k/dt = (\partial c_k/\partial A)A\psi(q_k(t))$$

which bears a close resemblance to (13).

So the model of the present paper encompasses a result which previously had to be rationalized ad hoc by invoking learning by doing. It thus appears that not all phenomena which look like learning by doing have to be attributed to a learning curve.

The impact of monopoly power and rivalry on innovations has been surrounded by controversies starting from Schumpeter's claim that monopoly position held by large firms would foster innovations. The present model gives a differentiated answer. Monopoly power at the level of production is clearly inimical to innovations, confirming the finding of Arrow (1962). On the other hand, rivalry in R&D may raise uncertainty and thus inhibit innovations.[5] The probability of such a case depends on the possibility of obtaining a pre-emptive patent. The probability appears to be small for applied research since in that case usually a large variety of opportunities is availabe. It appears to be more probable in the case of basic research. That suggests that results of basic research should not be eligible for patenting. It should be done cooperatively or supported by the government as a public good.

The finding that monopoly power is harmful to innovations must not be confused with the claim that higher concentration depresses innovative activity. Concentration is not always equivalent to monopoly power. It should be kept in mind that in the long run R&D expenditures do not preclude constant returns to scale. Insofar as constant returns to scale apply the size of the individual firm is indeterminate. The size distribution is determined by Bibrat's law. The skewness and thus the degree of concentration is increasing with the variance of the rate of growth which depends crucially on the variance of the success of R&D effort. That variance, in turn, exerts and adverse influence on innovative activity. Thus, a high variance engenders both high concentration and a low rate of innovative activity. This coincidence must not be misinterpreted as a causal one. Still, high concentration may facilitate collusion and thus decrease innovations by giving rise to enlarged monopoly power.

7. CONCLUSION

By using a model of stochastic control, as applied to a firm in a partial equilibrium framework, it has been shown that the size of the market enhances innovative activity. Monopoly power, ceteris paribus, is inimical to technological change. Uncertainty of R&D effort inhibits innovations. The model thus encompasses both demand pull effects on innovations, as suggested by Schmookler (1966), and technology push effects which give rise to an improvement of opportunities for research and development.

In the light of the present model completing the internal market of the European Community holds the promise of accelerating economic growth. The results regarding the impact of monopoly power suggest that a vigorous antitrust policy at the European level is a prerequisite to ensure the full benefits of an enlarged market area to be brought home. Since floating exchange rates and divergent monetary and fiscal policies of the member countries entail uncertainty which exerts an adverse influence on innovations creating a monetary union and coordination fiscal policy can be expected to enhance economic growth.

APPENDIX

Consider the problem $\max_u E \int_0^\infty f(t,x,u)dt$ s.t.

$$dx = g(t,x,u)dt + \sigma(x)dz.$$

The Hamilton-Jacobi-Bellman equation is

$$\text{(i)} \quad -J_t(t,x) = \max_u [f(t,x,u) + J_x(t,x)g + (1/2)J_{xx}(t,x)\sigma^2]$$

Let $f = Fe^{-it}$,

$$\text{(ii)} \quad \psi := J_x(t,x) \text{ and } \psi := e^{-it}y,$$

where y denotes the current value of the adjoint variable.

Then

$$\text{(iii)} \quad d\psi = (dy - iydt)e^{-it}.$$

Define the current value Hamiltonian

$$H = F + yg + (1/2)\sigma^2\partial y/\partial x.$$

From (i) one obtains

$$\text{(iv)} \quad -e^{it}J_t = \max_u [F + yg + (1/2)\sigma^2\partial y/\partial x] = \max_u H =: H^\circ.$$

Partial differentiation yields

$$\text{(v)} \quad -e^{it}J_{tx} = \frac{\partial H^\circ}{\partial x} + \frac{\partial H^\circ}{\partial y}\frac{\partial y}{\partial x} + \frac{\partial H^\circ}{\partial y_x}\frac{\partial^2 y}{\partial x^2}$$

$$= \frac{\partial H^\circ}{\partial x} + g\frac{\partial y}{\partial x} + (1/2)\sigma^2\frac{\partial^2 y}{\partial x^2}.$$

Then, using a Taylor expansion of (ii) yields

$$d\psi = J_{xt}dt + J_{xx}dx + (1/2)J_{xxx}(dx)^2.$$

By applying Ito's Lemma one obtains

$$d\psi = (J_{xt} + J_{xx}g + (1/2)J_{xxx}\sigma^2)dt + J_{xx}\sigma dz.$$

Multiply by e^{it} and use (iii) to arrive at

$$dy - iydt = (J_{xt}e^{it} + g\partial y/\partial x + (1/2)\sigma^2\partial^2 y/\partial x^2)dt$$
$$+ (\partial y/\partial x)\sigma dz.$$

Since $J_{xt} = J_{tx}$ inserting from (v) gives

$$dy = (iy - \partial H^{\circ}/\partial x)dt + (\partial y/\partial x)\sigma dz.$$

Take expectations of both sides to obtain

$$(1/dt)E\ dy = iy - \partial H^{\circ}/\partial x.$$

A generalization to the case where x, u, and y are vectors is obvious (see Malliaris and Brock 1982, p. 115).

NOTES

1 An example where $h'''(I)$ does not sign is given by the case where the underlying "production function" $h(I) = z(I,B)$, B being some fixed factor, is of the Cobb-Douglas type. Let $z(I,B)=I^{\alpha}B^{1-\alpha}$, then $h'''(I)=\partial^3 z/\partial I^3 = \alpha(\alpha-1)(\alpha-2)z/I^3 > 0$. In the more general case of a CES function, $z(I,B) = (I^{-\beta} + B^{-\beta})^{-1/\beta}$ where $\beta: = (1-b)/b$, one obtains

$$h'''(I) = \frac{\partial^3 z}{\partial I^3} = \frac{1}{b}\alpha(\alpha-1)(\alpha-2)\frac{z}{I^3}\left(1 + \frac{1-b}{b}\ \frac{2\alpha-1}{\alpha - 2}\right)$$

where $\alpha: = Iz_I/z < 1$.
It can be shown that $b > 0.5$ ensures $h'''(I)$ to be positive everywhere. Obviously, the validity of any assumption cannot be established by its intuitive plausibility but only by empirical testing.

2 In a more general approach g might be assumed to reflect changes of demand engendered by product innovations which in turn depend on R&D effort.

3 The multiplication rules are summarized by the following Table

	dt	dz_1	dz_2	...
dt	0	0	0	....
dz_1	0	dt	$\rho_{12}dt$	....
dz_2	0	$\rho_{12}dt$	dt	....
.	.	.	.	....

Note that $\rho_{12} = 0$ by <u>A4</u>

4 It might also be noticed that a steady state implies a dual cost function which exhibits constant marginal and average cost. For example, let $q = F(K,AL) = K^{\alpha}(AL)^{1-\alpha}$, $v = 1$ and $\delta = 0$. Then the necessary conditions (7) and (12a) for a maximum imply $\alpha w'AL = (1-\alpha)iK$ where $w':=w/a + r$ which is constant at a steady state. The cost function is given by $C = cq$ where $c:=\alpha^{-\alpha}(1-\alpha)^{-(1-\alpha)}i^{\alpha}(w')^{(1-\alpha)}$.

5 This aspect has been treated extensively in the recent literature dealing with games theoretic models of R&D rivalry. See Reinganum 1984, 1985.

REFERENCES

AITCHISON, J. and J.A.C. BROWN (1957), The Lognormal Distribution with special references to its uses in economics, Cambridge : Cambridge U.P.

ARROW, K. (1962), "Economic Welfare and the Allocation of Resources for Invention", in Natural Bureau of Economic Research (ed.), The Rate and Dipection of Inventive Activity, New York.

COWLING, K. and M. WATERSON (1976), "Price-Cost Margins and Market Structure", Economica, May, Vol. 43, pp. 267-74.

GOULD, J.P. (1968), "Adjustment Costs in the Theory of Investment of the Firm", Review of Economic Studies, January, vol. 35, pp. 47-55.

MALLIARIS, A.G. and W.A. BROCK (1982), Stochastic Methods in Economics and Finance, Amsterdam : North Holland Publishers.

NEUMANN, M. (1987), "Redistributive Income Taxation, Labour Force Growth and the Productivity Slowdown", mimeo, Nürnberg, August.

NICKELL, S.J. (1978), The Investment Decisions of Firms, Cambridge : Cambridge U.P.

PINDYCK, R.S. (1982), "Adjustment Costs, Uncertainty and the Behavior of the Firm", American Economic Review, June, vol. 72, pp. 415-27.

REINGANUM, J. (1985), "Practical Implications of Game Theoretical Models of R&D", American Economic Review, May, vol. 74, pp. 61-6.

REINGANUM, J. (1985), "Innovation and Industry Evolution", Quarterly Journal of Economics, February, vol. 100, pp. 81-99.

SCHMOOKLER, J. (1966), Invention and Economic Growth, Cambridge, Mass. : Harvard U.P.

INDEX